LEARNING IN THE INFORMATION AGE

AMJAD ALI

Ess Ess Publications

4837/24, Ansari Road, Darya Ganj,
New Delhi-110002
☏ : 23260807
Fax : 23274173
E-mail: info@essessreference.com
url:http://www.essessreference.com

First Published 2004

ISBN : 81-7000-393-8

Price : Rs. 650/-

Published by :

Ess Ess Publications

4837/24. Ansari Road, Darya Ganj,
New Delhi - 110 002
Phone : 23260807
Fax : 23274173
E-mail: info@essessreference.com
url:http://www.essessreference.com

Laser Typesetting:

Mukesh Graphics

L-2/8, DDA Market,
Mangolpuri, New Delhi
Ph. : 27924405

Printed at :

Print Line

Dedicated to

My Son AMAAN

Preface

The rise of information and communication technologies is observable both in quantitative and qualitative developments. During the last one decade, methodologies for instruction have undergone serious changes. The conventional correspondence education paved the way for the present day e-learning, which in turn triggered the growth and development of self-learning.

A large body of information grew in electronic form during the last few years. In the first lot, much of the information was textual rather than research based. It was unavailable in multimedia format. Most of the learning materials have been contributed by scholars from all over the world specifically USA, UK, Australia and New Zealand. India too is making a rapid stride with its unparallel IT workforce. The development of multilingual software and availability of Internet services in Indian languages tell the story of its success.

Now, the electronic media, mainly, the online information services are available internationally without any barriers of space and time. It has really democratized the means for anyone who wants to seek knowledge, as a lot of literature is available online free of cost.

This book is an effort to bring together a selected set of future oriented technologies, which are making inroads into the present day educational system. The intension is to make aware of the opportunities that can be grabbed for educational developments since the gap between the information rich and poor has almost been eliminated with the advent of the new information and communication technologies.

My thanks are due to all the individuals and organizations who contributed their ideas and works to the World Wide Web, which I referred to bring out this volume. I am equally indebted to my family members who took all the pains and gave me a free hand to complete this book in a very short time. My thanks are also due to the publisher of this book.

Dr. Amjad Ali
E-mail: Amjad_alig@yahoo.co.in

Contents

1
Introduction

We live in the age of information. It started with the advancements in computer during the last 60 years. The 1990s heralded an era of dramatic and rapid improvement in information and communication technology accompanied by price falls, which made the technology accessible to an ever-increasing audience. The proliferation of the Internet and World Wide Web gave an unprecedented access to vast quantities of information, as well as enabling communication and the formation of alliances unhindered by physical distance or national borders.

The recent technological advancements will have an impact upon society as great as that seen by the industrial revolution of two centuries previously which saw the emphasis shift from agriculture to manufacturing. This new era has been variously termed the information age, new economy, information society, knowledge economy etc. The reality of the concept is witnessed by Google [*http://www.google.com*] searches returning 770,000, 880,000, 643,000 and 173,000 hits on these four phrases respectively. Google is having the largest information resources which were about 4.2 billions of web pages by the end of 2003.

The methodologies which were successful in the industrial age are no longer applicable due to the inherent unpredictability of rapidly changing technology. It is not just that there are new rules or that some of the rules have changed. The new rules which apply in the digital world of communications and e-commerce are sometimes the exact opposite of the proven and accepted dogmas which apply in the conventional world.

Change in the industrial age tended to be planned and predictable. This is no longer the case. Intel founder G. E. Moore observed in 1965 that computing power was growing exponentially, doubling around every eighteen months (specifically Moore's observation concerned the number of transistors per square inch, but it has been shown to be valid for processor power and data density). Moore's observation continues to hold and has become known as Moore's law.

The industrial age remained dominated by large corporations. Their size meant they could benefit from economies of scale and provided high entry barriers to would be competitors. Big corporations are generally organized as militaristic style hierarchies with a chief executive officer delegating control through numerous layers of management to operational personnel at "the bottom". Operational staff were usually employed on rigid contracts with fixed job descriptions and much of their role could be described as algorithmic (eg a worker might be trained to pull lever B whenever light C comes on).

IBM was a classic example of he large industrial age corporation. Its fall from grace as the world's leading computer manufacturer has been attributed to its inability to respond fast enough to the changing market. Whittle [1997] writes "nimbler competitors offered change, ready or not, to the market before IBM could because of its rigidly hierarchical structure that devalued individual initiative."

The rapidity and unpredictability of change inherent in the information age will demand increased responsiveness and flexibility from the businesses and organizations of tomorrow. Top-down hierarchies will be replaced by more egalitarian ad-hoc teams and partnerships in which all members are valued and rewarded for their individual ability to contribute to the whole. The job description will be consigned to the wastepaper basket as roles change continually to take advantage of ever-evolving opportunities.

One of the perversities of the industrial age was that it would spend several years and a lot of money on training individuals to do particular jobs. As soon as they had mastered their chosen field they would be encouraged to aspire to promotion to management, at which point they would cease to carry out the role they had been so expensively prepared for.

The exalted status of management found in traditional hierarchies is likely to diminish as self-managed teams increasingly become the standard organizational model. Companies that have experimented with self-managed teams have found impressive results.

In an article for Wired magazine, Kelly [1999] predicted the number of enterprises in the U.S. would double by 2020 and that the number of workers per enterprise would halve to just three. It further predicted that many workers would be engaged in more than one enterprise, a phenomenon it terms "polyemployment". This suggests society is moving from the division between managers and managed to a situation where everyone manages, or owns, their own career.

The information age has the potential to empower individuals, economically and otherwise. In addition to raising the status of the humble employee, we now have access to greater information than ever before allowing us to make more informed decisions as consumers and citizens. We have greater choice in how we spend our hard-earned money, and have a greater range of businesses and service providers from around the globe competing for our custom.

It is often said that knowledge is power. Traditionally knowledge has been jealously guarded by those in authority, either in government or boardrooms. In the information age knowledge, and thus power, will be diffused.

Traditionally the mass media has been few-to-many in nature. A relatively small number of publishers and broadcasters have been able to transmit their message for passive absorption by the masses. The Internet and World Wide Web offer a many-to-many communication medium. Every individual with 'net access can speak to the world through the numerous discussion forums such as USENET or the many proprietary bulletin boards, or by publishing on the Web.

The shift in the role of the citizen from that of industrial age "factory fodder" to empowered individual brings unprecedented potential and opportunity, but it also bestows greater responsibility. It is said that a little knowledge is a dangerous thing, but now we all have access to considerably more than a little. This suggests the need for appropriate learning opportunities to be accessible to all.

For many the case of having access to insufficient information has been replaced by the new problem of having access to an overwhelming amount of information, so much so that it can be almost impossible to find what we need from the morass of irrelevance clogging the metaphorical superhighway. This has been termed "information overload". The ease with which anyone from college professor to disturbed adolescent may publish "information" demands a high degree of discernment on the part of the seeker.

In technologically sophisticated countries it is now reasonable to assume that the vast majority of the population will have some form of access to information and communication technology. However, it is sobering to reflect that some 90% of the world's population does not have Internet access, based upon figures by Global Reach [*http://www.glreach.com*], September 2002. These tend to be the people of the world's least developed countries. For them, far from being a liberating and empowering force, technology threatens to exacerbate their disadvantage by further excluding them from the information-centred world.

The information age has replaced the relative predictability of the industrial age with an increased degree of uncertainty that will require greater levels of flexibility and adaptability in order to survive and thrive.

Workers will be more involved in the planning and decision-making processes. Individuals will need to develop the discernment required to make sense of the mass of facts, figures claims and counter-claims that surround them.

Education will need to change from being a process of conditioning to one of empowerment. Learning will need to change from being a homogeneous commodity to a customized experience tailored to the needs and characteristics of the individual. Learning will no longer end in the teens or early-twenties. Instead it will continue throughout life as individuals need to continually update knowledge and skills to keep pace with ever-changing technical and social conditions.

In order to meet the learning requirements of the information age learning opportunity providers should adopt a more constructivist approach to learning, creating conditions in which learners may learn by actively engaging with realistic scenarios and exchanging views and experiences with peers and mentors.

Students are now able to obtain information from a variety of sources. The World Wide Web provides access to, for example, academic libraries, multi- media databases and discussion groups from which individuals can obtain a range of up to date information for use in their course work assignments. However, instruction in methods of carrying out effective information searches is important if students are going to move away from using just their lecture notes or perhaps only one course book as their main sources of reference. LT materials which provide outlines of efficient ways of carrying out literature searches such as the TILT software can be used more effectively if used in conjunction with face to face sessions involving the subject based librarians and at an appropriate stage of the course. This helps not only to identify the relevant person from whom a student might seek assistance in the future, but also helps students to relate the information to their own particular institutional environment.

Some other ideas to encourage students to make use of computer based information retrieval systems might be:

* Students can be directed to the World Wide Web as a source of information. Ask the students to recommend useful URLs and use these to build up a departmental Resource base for future students' reference.
* Setting a collaborate project where a group has to give a presentation to the rest of the class about a topical subject but each group member researches only one specified part of the topic. The group work is then dependant on each of the student's contributions.
* Ask first year student groups to retrieve information from the library about a topic and to present their finding on a poster which could then be assessed by the rest of the class
* Students could be asked to prepare an assignment which uses only the World Wide Web as a source of information and has to cite the URLs used in their reference list.

One of the major underlying messages of the institutionalized learning system in our society is that learning comes in a specific pre-packed form, delivered in a predetermined place bearing public recognition, dispensed by people certified as capable of doing so. On the positive side, this has undoubtedly made it possible to extend teaching way beyond the chosen few. Yet one of the disadvantages of mass pre-packed education is that it embodies the idea that satisfactory, accredited learning can only take place in specific institutions. It shifts the emphasis from learning to teaching and subsequently disembowels the would-be learner. Learning, however, is most efficient when it is anchored in the context of the learner's life, whereas institutionalized learning de-conceptualizes it and removes the foundations on which learning can meaningfully take place.

In modern society the relative importance of stabilized, formal knowledge - on which institutionalized education is based - is decreasing. The decline of hard and fast values, the rise of such scientific paradigms as indeterminacy, relativity, fuzziness and chaos theory and last but not least the impact of extensive distributed multimedia networking are indicative of and contribute to such a shift. What's more, in the field of professional know-how, the need to constantly change and adapt in a cut-throat competitive world puts a premium on other types of knowledge than those that take years to materialize.

This state of things is so taken for granted that it becomes extremely difficult to use the word "learning" to mean anything other than a measurable commodity. Much of the talk about education in the Information Society - in particular with Open and Distant Learning (ODL) - is based on such an assumption. Are not such expressions as "virtual classroom" significant of the way "home education" is seen: learning that takes place in a controlled, limited environment. Yet learning can and does take place in the most unexpected circumstances. Moreover, much of the most significant knowledge in relation to the use of telematics is in the hands of the users themselves and is developed both individually and via informal peer exchange.

In considering learning in the Information Society, considerable emphasis is put on "delivering" the goods, but there is no guarantee that providing affordable access and teaching everybody basic operational skills will avoid discrimination. Once again the metaphor here is that of supplying the pre-packed commodity rather than creating the meaningful learning experience on a personal or collective basis. Despite lip service paid to "learner-centred" education, it is no easier to achieve in the current institutional context than is the client-centred approach in a traditional product-centred industry.

Technology is taken as being a pre-requisite to learning in the Information Society. Clearly the shift to a society based on massively mediated communication must take steps to minimize the undesirable social repercussions, in particular exclusion due to lack of access and basic know-how in the use of the tools. This is why a strong case is made by some education providers and by advocates of technology in general for having access to improved equipment and communications infrastructures.

Technology alone, however, is no solution. Migration to the Information Society is seen as a way to stimulate growth, to combat unemployment, to enhance social cohesion and to generally improve the quality of life. The promoters of this change in Europe tacitly recognize that its success depends very heavily on human factors. Education and training are seen as major factors in dealing with the human aspects of migration to the Information Society.

Confronted with the acceleration of changes in products and standards, the task of "keeping up" becomes ever more costly and time consuming, if not impossible. The current institutionalized system of education may well not be the best model for keeping abreast. As products, in particular information products, take on an unfinished nature (being constantly up-dated and improved) and their use becomes experimental (users discover and employ as yet unused aspects of complex products on a trial and error basis) and educational (learning about use is incorporated into the product itself) the model of formal syllabus-based education becomes less and less appropriate. In many cases solutions learnt yesterday can become tomorrow's obstacles. Some educational institutions have attempted to shift the emphasis to meta-level skills like learning how to learn. However they have difficulties providing satisfactory answers to the dilemma of dealing with change, in particular when it is fast and often unpredictable. Their very structure makes it impossible for them to deal with the problem for themselves let alone for their students. Moving to the Information Society aggravates these difficulties, yet at the same time the tools of the Information Society provide a possible answer so long as the nature of the learning process is understood and so long as we are prepared to seek and implement other less formalized ways of encouraging and enabling this learning process.

Migration to the Information Society could be an excellent opportunity to set aside preconceived ideas and to take a fresh look at what learning is, what needs to be learnt and how. This is unfortunately no easy task. Institutionalized learning plays an all-pervasive role in our society and it is difficult to avoid being led astray by certain deep-seated assumptions that are an integral part of the words we use to talk about the problem. Whether or not the opportunity of the advent of Information Society is taken advantage of also depends very much on our ability to convince those groups of society with a vested interest in keeping learning methods and structures as they are, that considering a change would be worthwhile for everybody including themselves.

2
IT in India

/c

India remained a centre of great civilizations of the world. It's contribution to mathematics, medical sciences, astronomy and political science is unparallel. Mathematics being the 'mother of all sciences' was one of the most potential disciplines for technical knowledge to grow. The natural resources of the country, specially its high yielding land always remained a source for prosperity.

India is still an agriculture-based country where 60% of the population is engaged in farming. About 25% of its workers are engaged in service sector. The country is rapidly transforming to information society and the millions of its information workers lead lifestyle similar to information workers in the advanced countries. Their number is escalating day by day bringing a sea change in its culture specially the urban elite. Although the percentage of information workers in the Indian society is very low still their collective strength is more that the information workers in Japan and about the same number in the United States.

The overall roads and highways scenario in India has also witnessed major improvements over the last few years. Most cities and fist and second tier towns are connected and interlinked to each other. Major investments have gone into the development of highways, both on the side of the central and state Governments. Clearly, the Indian Government has understood the importance of infrastructure to industries such as IT and created a conducive environment for its development and expansion.

The communication technologies including its various applications in telecommunication such as radio, television, cable, satellites, Internet etc are driving the social shift toward the information society. These technologies are converging today in order to form new ones and making their separate identity difficult. Computer has affected them the most with its application in almost all the areas of information collection, storage and dissemination.

Credit for India's rapid growth in the IT sector goes to the availability of a robust infrastructure, telecom, power and Roads in the country. Relevant telecom facilities are an important prerequisite for the success of the software industry and over the years, the Government has taken steps to ensure that telecom remains a priority area.

Similarly, regular, reliable, uninterrupted power, a major necessity for running IT software and services businesses, has also received substantial attention from the Government. Recent steps to privatize the distribution of power and bring in greater efficiencies and customer centricity in the market, have been welcomed by the ICT industry.

Computer is undoubtedly the key technology in an information society. The United States has led the way in computer era but the other countries are equally making headways in it. The first computer of the world ENIAC was developed in the year 1945. Funds were made available by the U. S. Department of Defence and it was used for military purposes. ENIAC cost millions of dollars to build, took up a lot of space and was initially used for number-crunching tasks. The worlds' first main frame computer used vacuum tubes for its millions of switches.

The first computer in India was acquired by the Indian Statistical Institute, Calcutta in 1955. Additional computers in the country were purchased from IBM. By 1972, there were 172 computers and three-fourth of them were made by IBM. Microcomputer was developed as a result of miniaturization of the computer in the early 1970s using semiconductors. Microcomputer was later converted into personal computer.

The advent of PC witnessed a boom in India during the decade of 1980s. Many large institutions including the Air Lines, Railways, banks, hospitals introduced computer for managing their in house functions. It proved to be very effective and also user-friendly with the passage of time. Then came the turn of medium and small entrepreneurs since its cost became affordable for them also. By the turn of the 1990s, millions of Indian began to use computers in their workplaces and homes for varied purposes. Sale of PCs crossed the mark of one million by 1999. In 2000, the installed based of computers in the country was about five millions, translating into about five computers for every 1,000 people which has now gone to10 computers per thousand.

Many factors influenced the decision of buying computers by a middle class family but the main reason was the ever-falling cost during the last few years. The availability of the assembled system

India's information revolution took a boost in early 1980s. Still India's present status as an information society comparing with the United States, Japan, and Western European nations cannot be equated. But it is clear that India is off to a start. India's information revolution encouraged by the declining cost of microelectronics technology worldwide, and the increased encouraged by many factors, particularly the availability of high-quality microelectronics products in the country.

Many institutions besides government efforts are actively venturing into the field of education and are offering professional and technological courses by using communication technologies, prominent among these in India are NIIT, APTECH and Zee Education. They are using television, computer communication, e-mail and Internet for reaching their students. Their enrolment is rising, and the geographical area covered by them is also increasing day by day. Indira Gandhi National Open University (IGNOU) is engaged in task of developing a network of Open Universities in the country called OPENET-Open Education

Network a market of competition where a full spectrum of channels is available to them

By the turn of the century, the cable and satellite distribution reached out to 18 million homes with a penetration of 35 percent and India will be the world's largest cable and satellite network with a connectivity of over 40 million homes comprising óf 200 million cable viewers. Already Star TV and other media giants are working on projects to launch Direct to Home (DTH) services in India. From a mere one percent or Rs. 15 crore in 1992 the advertising revenue collected by satellite channels have gone to Rs. 115 crore in 1993. By the year 2000, India was expecting to have 100 channels at least 70 percent of which to be pay channels. And by that time according to some estimates, advertising revenue on television grew to Rs. 3,000 crore from Rs. 1,160 crore in 1995. Gujarat State has high, Karnataka is in middle and Uttar Pradesh has lower percentage of cable reach.

PROMOTION OF IT - GOVERNMENTAL INCENTIVES:

With the formation of a new ministry for IT, Government of India (GOI) has taken a major step towårds promoting the domestic industry and achieving the full potential of the Indian IT entrepreneurs. Constraints have been comprehensively identified and steps taken to overcome them and also to provide incentives. Thus for example, venture capital has been the main source of finance for software industry around the world. However, majority of the software units in India is in the small and medium enterprise sector and there is a critical shortage of venture capital kind of support. In order to alleviate this situation and to promote Indian IT industry, the Government of India has set up a National Task Force on IT and Software Development to examine the feasibility of strengthening the industry. The Task Force has already submitted its recommendations, which are under active consideration. Norms for the operations of venture capital funds have also been liberalized to boost the industry.

The Government of India is also actively providing fiscal incentives and liberalizing norms for FDI and raising capital abroad.

An IT committee has been set up by the Ministry of Information Technology, Government of India, comprising Non Resident Indian (NRI) professionals from the United States to seek expertise and advice and also to step up U.S. investments in India's IT sector. The committee is chaired by Minister of Information Technology, Government of India, and the members include Secretary, Ministry of Information Technology and a large number of important Indian American IT entrepreneurs.

The group will:

* Monitor global IT developments and refine Indian IT policy to meet global requirements. Specifically, this will help angel investors, venture creators and incubation;
* Promote the growth of human resource development in the IT sector with the aim of creating quality-based education;
* Promote R&D in the sector by identifying thrust areas and drawing up a blueprint for action.

India's most prized resource in today's knowledge economy is its readily available technical work force. India has the second largest English-speaking scientific professionals in the world, second only to the U.S. It is estimated that India has over 4 million technical workers, over 1,832 educational institutions and polytechnics, which train more than 67,785 computer software professionals every year. Government of India is stepping up the number and quality of training facilities in the country to capitalize on this extraordinary human resource. It is the knowledge industry that will help take the Indian economy to a sustained higher rate of growth and the policy makers are fully aware of this.

Computer

Rapid changes in the technology have helped cut costs dramatically and make the personal computer a lot more affordable. Moreover India has agreed to bring down the duty on 217 tariff lines to zero level by 2005 as per the requirements of the Information Technology Agreement (ITA). The agreement aims to expand the world trade in information technology products. The agreement covers main categories of products such as computers, printers, scanners, monitors, hard disk drives, power supplies, semiconductor manufacturing equipment, and software products such as diskettes and CD-ROMs. (Express Computer 1997)

As a result the concentration of the industry from the corporate board room has shifted to the household bedroom. The industry estimates reveal that a total of 2,50,000 personal computers were sold in India in the first half of 1996 of which 10 to 20 percent were sold to home sector. Within the home segment, the product is essentially aimed at school-children and college-going teenagers. Computer education has increasingly become a norm in private schools and selected government run schools across the country has also begun to use computers under the Computer Literacy and Studies in Schools (CLASS) programmes during the eighth plan.

The US based Intel Corporation has helped in setting up of cyberskools in New Delhi's National Science Centre and in Mumbai's Nehru Centre. For the first time students from the less affluent schools are able to get a hands on experience on a computer which also offers multi-media facilities. In Mumbai's Cyberskool at least 50,000 Mumbai children are expected to get a chance to use computers free of charge within a year (India Today 1995).

With all the given facilities educational computing is a rapidly growing field. Computers can play a vital role in educational management. Educational computing is going to be part of educational management in the twenty first century.

Computer helps in planning, organizing, leading and controlling to achieve educational goals and also promotes process of meeting educational needs. (Rajyaguru 1998)

The introduction of bilingual computing has brought computing and communications closer to the common man by communicating in local languages. Bilingual communication is claimed to be popular in government department. It has also proved very useful in the educational field where use of native language is critical (The Economic Times 1997).

IDC expects PC sales in India to accelerate in the future. Its small but high-potential PC market is dominated by thousands of cut-rate unbranded computer assemblers operating out of tiny shops spread across the country. These unbranded assemblers, who compete with big names by putting together computer components, have over the past several quarters expanded market share despite the entry of global majors like Hewlett Packard and Dell.

Local assemblers performed well in the consumer market as they were able to provide a greater cost advantage and reach than multinational and large Indian branded competitors. The share of local assemblers and small regional brands rose to 69 per cent in 2003 up from 66 per cent a year-ago, leading local brands include those made by Wipro, HCL Infosys and Zenith Computers.

Software Production

The Indian software industry has grown from a mere US $ 150 million in 1991-92 to a staggering US $ 5.7 billion (including over $4 billion worth of software exports) in 1999-2000. No other Indian industry has performed so well against the global competition.

The annual growth rate of India's software exports has been consistently over 50 percent since 1991. As per the projections made by the National Association of Software and Services Companies (NASSCOM) for 2000-2001 (April 1, 2000

- March 31, 2001), India's software exports was around $ 6.3 billion, in addition to $ 2.5 billion in domestic sale.

Indian Software Industry 1995-2000

(US $ million)

	1995-96	*1996-97*	*1997-98*	*1998-99*	*1999-2000*	*2000-01**
Domestic software Market	490	670	920	1250	1700	2450
Software Exports	734	1085	1750	2650	4000	6300
Indian Software Industry	1224	1755	2670	3900	5700	8750

(Source: NASSCOM Report)*

Today, India exports software and services to nearly 95 countries around the world. The share of North America (U.S. & Canada) in India's software exports is about 61 per cent. In 1999-2000, more than a third of Fortune 500 companies outsourced their software requirements to India.

NASSCOM's survey during 1999-2000 indicates a reversal in the mode of services offered by India. In 1991-92, offshore services accounted 5 per cent and on-site services 95 % of the total exports. However, during 1999-2000 offshore services contributed over 40 percent of the total exports.

The NASSCOM - McKinsey report on India's IT industry

According to a NASSCOM-McKinsey report, annual revenue projections for India's IT industry in 2008 are US $ 87 billion and market openings are emerging across four broad sectors, IT services, software products, IT enabled services, and e-businesses thus creating a number of opportunities for Indian companies. In addition to the export market, all of these segments have a domestic market component as well.

Other key findings of this report are:

* Software & Services will contribute over 7.5 % of the

overall GDP growth of India

* IT Exports will account for 35% of the total exports from India
* Potential for 2.2 million jobs in IT by 2008
* IT industry will attract Foreign Direct Investment (FDI) of U.S. $ 4-5 billion
* Market capitalization of IT shares will be around U.S. $ 225 billion

Projected Revenues – 2008

($ US billion)

	India Based	*India Centric*	*Sub total (International)*	*Domestic*	*Total*	*1998*
IT Services	23	7*	30	8.5	38.5	2.1
Software Products	8	2	10	9.5**	19.5	0.6
IT-enabledService	15	2	17	2	19	0.4
E-business	4	1	5	5	10	0.2
Total	50	12	62	25	87	3.3

Exports of $50 billion in 2008

* Legacy/client server, ERP and package work and Internet all have different proportions of work outside India where revenues are not export revenues.

** Resale of imported products included.

Success in HighTech

India's success in the high tech sector was no accident. Throughout the 1990s, large numbers of educated, relatively low-waged, English-speaking engineers gravitated to IT centers in Bangalore, Bombay, Delhi, Madras, Hyderabad and Pune, where foreign and domestic investors had set up small software plants.

India's software exports grew by 68% in 1998/99, totaling $2.65 billion. Some $200 million of venture capital is currently available for Indian technology startups. Of particular interest are projects involving wireless and internet technologies and services call centers and medical record transcription services and technically proficient, English-speaking pool of skilled workers.

All of India has not shared in this boom, however. Economic growth has been unevenly dispersed. Selected states in the south and west of the country have benefited enormously from the technological revolution. But others have not and they remain largely impoverished. However the latest development of entrepreneurs in the satellite towns of Delhi particularly NOIDA and Gurgaon has introduced the software profession to the Northern part of the country.

Over the past year, the Bombay stock exchange has been up more than 75%. The key drivers of this increase are software companies. In fact, India now possesses 3% of the global software manufacturing market, and this number is growing dramatically. Although software services account for just 1.3% of India's GDP, the industry is growing more rapidly than any other in the country and is now an agent of profound corporate and economic change.

Today, the Indian software industry employs 400,000 software engineers in about 1,000 companies. These workers are the best and the brightest graduates of India's elite universities and technology institutes. Many are now multi-millionaires. As of September 1999, the market capitalization of India's Information Technology industry reached $24.3 billion, up from $13.6 billion just six months earlier. But none of this would have been possible if the Indian economy has not begun to emerge from a two year recession.

The industrial production growth has improved, housing starts are up, and the fiscally prudent government appears to be stable. Analysts at Credit Suisse First Boston forecast an average growth rate of 7.5% over the next five years in India. The World Bank cautions, however, in its most recent report, that this goal will be achieved only if serious economic reforms continue to be implemented on both the national and state levels of government.

The Government of India has pledged to triple foreign investment in India. In fact, the finance minister has stated that he hopes to attract $10 billion in foreign direct investment in each of the next five years. This is more than triple the annual average of the past decade.

In recent months, onerous foreign-exchange controls have been removed and new laws have opened the insurance sector to foreign investors. The government has also promised to encourage competition in the banking industry in the near term. In addition, in March 2000, the government passed legislation relaxing the tax burden for foreign venture capital firms setting up in India.

Serious problems remain of course. The public service remains painfully slow in implementing new legislation. Infrastructure is often poor, there is a lack of agricultural deregulation, and the national fiscal deficit continues to drive up the cost of capital. Regional economic inequality is pervasive. Six southern and western states have attracted most of the $18 billion in FDI that has come into India in the past decade. Many of the remaining states have made little progress.

As problematic as these issues are, the software industry has emerged largely unscathed. As a new economic sector, it is relatively free of state involvement. In the absence of a stifling national or state bureaucracy, software entrepreneurs are succeeding against global competition. Today, strong exports, professional management, and top technical talent characterize India's information technology industry. Infosys, the first Indian software company to list on the US-based Nasdaq exchange, has seen its share price soar. It is now in the Nasdaq top 20.

In 1999, Satyam Infoway, one of India's new internet service providers, became the second company to list on the Nasdaq. Others, including internet portal Rediff.com and Zee Telefilms are poised to follow and Nasdaq recently announced that it would open up a representative office in India to facilitate future listings.

Furthermore, prominent US and European firms such as Cisco, Microsoft, Texas Instruments, Oracle, Siemens, and SAP are recruiting Indian engineers for their research and development centers in India.

The rapid success of the Indian software industry has been remarkable. But the industry remains in its infancy. Fewer than three million Indian households own a personal computer, out of a population of over one billion. Furthermore, there are less internet connections in India, but it is estimated that there are four internet users for every connection.

Undoubtedly, internet usage will increase when cable TV access is increased in India. Currently, thirty million Indian homes have cable service. In fact, several international companies including the UK-based WorldTel have negotiated or are negotiating with various Indian state governments to set up community internet cafes.

We expect this trend to continue. India's export-led software development industry has made it the model to emulate for the modernization of the rest of India's otherwise lackluster economy. Indian IT products are inexpensive by world standards. But they also stand out on the basis of quality, speed, reliability, and innovation.

The central government and almost all of India's state governments have created an IT development policy, including steps to encourage the use of computers in government. Ten years ago, few observers would have predicted that the Indian economy could have been transformed in this fashion. The country has very far to go of course, to eliminate its widespread poverty, and to promote widespread economic development. But it has taken a major step in the right direction by nurturing its IT industry. In this sphere at least, it is a world-class competitor.

Internet

India's first high speed information highway was set up by the National Informatics Centre connecting networks in 150 countries commissioned on September 20, 1994. Today India has many significant networks, all of which have connectivity to INTERNET either directly or via other international networks. The other popular networks in India include Educational and Research Network (ERNET) set up and managed by Dept. of Electronics, Scientific and Industrial Research Network (SIRNET) set up and managed by Indian National Scientific Documentation Centre (INSDOC) on behalf of the Council of Scientific and Industrial Research (CSIR), National Informatics Centre Network (NICNET) set up and managed by National Informatics Centre, Indonet set up and managed by CMC Ltd. There are several others like I-net which is a public data network set up and managed by the Dept. of Telecommunications (DoT), rural area business messaging network (RABMN), a satellite based network set up and managed by DoT, I-net a private electronic mail network and UUNET-IN, the Indian component of the International Unix Users Network (UUNET) set up and managed by a private company.

Most of the Indian data networks provide electronic mail and file transfer services predominantly. Some networks support other network services like remote log in search and retrieval of databases. The transfer of full text document consisting of pictures, figures, diagrams and graphs have not yet become common place.

In addition to the above wide area networks and library net works are being evolved in major cities of India. Among these are the Calcutta Library Network (Calibnet), Delhi Library Network (Delnet), Madras Library Network (Malibnet), Pune Library Network (PUNET), Bombay Library Network (BONET), Ahmedabad Library Network (ADINET) etc.

A nation wide network known as Information and Library Network (INFLIBNET) planned by the University Grants Commission has interconnect these library networks including Delnet, Malibnet and BONET. Calibnet, is the first library network to have been initiated in the country in 1986, is yet to become operational in the practical sense. Eventually all the networks will become part of the global networks. Superposed on the existing National Informatics Centre Network (NICNET) which already has about 700 satellite earth stations linking 500 cities and towns as well as important plan projects, the national information highway connects 14 cities - Delhi, Pune, Hyderabad, Bhubaneshwar, Lucknow, Patna, Calcutta, Jaipur, Ahmedabad, Chandigarh, Bangalore, Bhopal, Mumbai and Kanpur and will grow to criss-cross the country to link more cities raising long distance information transfer capabilities.

India had less than 50,000 users of Internet as compared to the US where more than 20 million people cruise Internet prior to 1995. Most were in academic institutions. Since August 1995, when INTERNET was made available commercially for the first time, the number of individuals and corporate users of state owned Videsh Sanchar Nigam LTD's Gateway Internet Access Service has grown to over 3,000. From a narrow bandwidth of 128 kilobits per second the VSNL upgraded its services in most of the metros to 512 kilobits per second which is four times faster. Despite VSNL improving its operations the growth is at the moped speed compared to the rest of the globe's Formula one speed. Mainly three reasons (India Today 1996). for this lagging growth are:

1. the negligible number of users in India
2. the high costs of setting up of a web server.
3. limited band width space on telecom lines out of India

Experts believe that the real key to the spread of the INTERNET will be when VSNL, the public sector controller of electronic gateways out of India, gets competition from private Internet service providers. They are of the view that the government needs to consider the INTERNET as part of its core infrastructure and in addition there is a need to scale down tariff as it could well prove to be the incentive for logging onto the INTERNET.

* A recent study by the Gartner Group has suggested that

the country has topped the list of Internet users in the Asia Pacific region for 2001. India has an estimated 3.1 million regular Internet surfers, although the number of registered users would hover at just about 1 million.

* A study by India's Manufacturers Association of Information Technology (MAIT) has revealed that the number of Internet subscribers has increased to 1.12 million during the 2000 - 2001 period from just 651,000 in the previous year; the home segment registered a whopping compounded annual growth rate (CAGR) of 215 percent.
* The number of active Internet subscribers increased to 1.12 million by March 2001, leading to 67 percent penetration among PC-owning business establishments and 54 percent penetration in PC-owning homes," the annual survey found.
* IDC India predicts that the number of Internet users will grow eight-fold to 37.5 million by end-2005,representing a CAGR of 53 percent for the period 2000 - 2003; the research firm had estimated that there were 4.47 million unique Internet users in India in 2000. India is expected to be next only to China in the Asia Pacific region in terms of total number of Internet users by end-2005.

IDC also forecasts that India's home and small business segments will drive the growth in the Internet user base for the next five years. For the period 2000 - 2005, the Internet user base in the home segment is expected to witness a CAGR of 87 percent, while that of the small business segment is expected to grow by a CAGR of 72 percent.

Despite the differences in actual prediction figures, all agencies have agreed on one point - India is expected to see the highest growth rate in the region's Internet market in the next five years.

Seeking to promote the spread of the Internet, the Planning Commission indicated telecom operators must get the required bandwidth and the last-mile connection to achieve that aim. The use of cable network and DSL technologies may be actively promoted to provide higher bandwidth to Internet users, it said.

For dial-up Internet users, telephone call charges are a major element of cost, with the higher local call charges and multi-metering of local calls discouraging its usage. Call charges for Internet use need to be brought down substantially," added the Planning Commission's report.

Electronic Mail

Electronic mail started in India in mid - 1992. It went slower in its penetration than expected. However, later it struck up a decent growth rate of 35 percent to 40 percent per annum. Views are expressed that in 1997-98 there will be escalation in subscriber numbers by at least 20,000 for E-mail service alone.

Sprint RPG, one of the significant leaders in the industry, claims to have around 3,000 subscribers on the network with 19,000 mail boxes, Wipro BT claims 5,000 mail boxes on its system. In India E-mail is seen more as a business application platform than a basic messaging tool. As an incentive training as well as refresher classes are offered to users on a regular basis.

The Videsh Sanchar Nigam Ltd (VSNL) is currently the sole provider of Internet services in the country and its monopoly over the service contend the E-mail service providers. In the case of VSNL E-mail comes as a part of the Internet service and there are no separate charges for it. VSNL currently has 3,500 customers on its GEMS-400 E-mail service and 20,000 customers on GIAS who use E-mail through the Internet.

E-mail in India is seriously challenged for the first time as Internet comes in the picture with free E-mail as a part of its package. Moreover, the government is considering allowing private operators to offer Internet services nationally. The experts have diverse opinions on whether e-mail as a stand alone service will sustain its momentum and grow or will be getting absorbed as a part of larger communication package in near future. Some feel that the future of the E-mail as a sole service is bleak. While several others believe that the Internet can not take place of E-mail as it has two major drawbacks of reliability and confidentiality. They are predicting that there will be a clear cut division of users. The individuals are expected to utilize Internet for their messaging needs while the corporate and the heavy users will stick to dedicated E-mail services. The users will go for sole E-mail service application where response time is critical and users need to communicate across mail system. Thus, at present there seems a possibility that the two forms of E-mail communication will co-exist in the country (The Economic Times 1997).

The Communication Media

The Ministry of Information and Broadcasting remained the real decision-making body for All India Radio and Doordarshan for a long time, though a fair amount of freedom was permitted in the selection and production of entertainment programmes. The Prasar Bharati Bill was introduced in 1979 and once again in 1989 in a revised form to grant an autonomous status to the broadcast media (Keval Kumar, 1994) which was finally passed in1997. The ministry is now seeking to regulate all forms of private broadcasting, including free-to-air channels, as well as cable operations.

All India Radio covers 90% area of the country with 97% of population. Approximately 104 million homes possess about 111 million radio sets. For the task it has 72 Local Radio Stations, 105 Regional Stations and 32 Vividh Bharati Centres. There are 148 Medium Wave, 51 Short Wave and 94 VHF/FM transmitters (Doordarshan 1996).

On August 15, 1993 a Frequency Modulation (FM) Channel was launched in Mumbai with nine hours of radio time leased to private producers like Times FM, Radiostar and Radio Midday. According to an 'upmarket survey' by *MARG", there are 1.95 lakh FM sets in Mumbai, compared to 7.24 lakh transistor sets and 7.42 lakh "two-in-ones". This would give a potential audience of one million Cities with FM broadcast include Mumbai, Calcutta, Chennai (Madras), Delhi, Ahmedabad (India Today, 1994). Recently AIR has diversified to the areas like Radio Paging (Doordarshan 1997).

The Government is very keen to introduce regulations as it feels that foreign channels have invaded "Indian culture" and, therefore, it is acting in the national interest by putting restrictions on them. This has led to prepare a Broadcasting Bill. The Ministry also wants to stop foreign broadcasters from introducing in India a new technology, Direct to Home (DTH) broadcasting by an ordinance to make it illegal for people to own Ku-band dishes unless a license is obtained from the Government for this purpose.

Television is preferred in comparison of radio for it has both audio as well as visual appeal. Television has become a common sight in almost all middle and high class families in the country attraction it members across the age groups. It has sufficient material to satisfy almost every section of the society fulfilling their entertainment and developmental needs.

In India it has been found in a recent survey that 192 households have access to television whereas only 42% of the households own it. There are 59 million TV sets about half of which are colour and 30 million are Black and White. Television commands a 72% share of the average 13 hours spent on a traditional media in the country..

The number of households with cable and satellite access has jumped from 29 million to 40 million from 1999 to 2002 with 13% increase. The sale of TV sets has also escalated at the rate of 25% during the last five years.

Media Policy

The policy decision regarding broadcasting are looked into from a holistic perception of national interest and social impact. Therefore, any national media policy incorporate basic issues. A monopolistic control of various different media would yield disproportionate bargaining power that may not be in the best interests of the nation. Hence, certain guidelines should be evolved on cross media ownership and foreign equity participation to bring out a level playing field for all players in the field (IIM, Calcutta 1996, India Today 1995)

Communication/ Information work is, in fact, spread over several ministries and departments in the government sector and many agencies in the private sector. As a result hardware projections, planning and design are not based on either (a) utilization assessment or (b) software capability. Therefore, an appropriate forum should be created to co-ordinate the various financial and structural problems in the field of communications systems (Sondhi 1983).

The Paswan Committee for National Media Policy presented its report on the 29 March 1996, which covers television, radio, film, advertisement and press. It states-there should be a regulatory body to oversee both public and private telecasting/broadcasting. This regulatory body may be set up to ensure adherence to the programmes/advertisement code and other stipulations. This body may develop an effective mechanism for public grievance redressal also.

As the revolution in consumer electronics sweeps the world, video and audio cassettes are being increasingly used. It is estimated that there are a million video cassette recorder both domestic and imported now in use. The boom in this industry came about when custom duties were modified during the 1982 Asiatic game so that sports fans could record events for later viewing. The use and impact of these mobile technologies for education research and development purposes are of much interest and are extremely popular).

Mobile audio-visual media including cassettes and films have come into use in development projects, because of their versatility, mobility and adaptability. Mobile media are specifically targeted to local situations and are easily reproduced and distributed. They lend themselves well to discussion groups, investigation forums and to repetition, yet carry the credibility of the electronic media and the excitement and liveliness of oral communication.

In the field of education, open university like Indira Gandhi National Open University (IGNOU) has produced a large number of videos and audios. The video equipments are still out of the reach of most of the students that is why audio and videocassettes are kept at the study centres. This provides flexibility to play and replay at the will of the learner. The students avail this facility for their study purpose at the near by study centre (Haider 1998).

Telecommunication Services

Telecom services have been recognized the world over as an important tool for social and economic development of a nation and hence telecom infrastructure is bound to be central to the release of the socio-economic objectives in India. Accordingly, the Department of Telecom has devised strategies for accelerated growth of telecom services to the tune of 15 to 20 % in the urban areas to meet the growing demands and taking the services to rural areas as a developmental infrastructure.

Telecom services are emerging as the third largest telecom market in the world. The Indian Government plans to wire the country with a National Information Highway (NIH) by interlinking the existing networks. The NIH could cost up to Rs.4, 000 billion depending on the sophistication and its size. Such information highway would enable Indians to access high speed interactive multimedia and two way communication facilities. NIH has brought nearly 30 Indian cities into its own information superhighway and will expand to cover 70 cities within a year.

India has a network of telephone exchanges with a capacity of millions of lines and telephone connections. Besides new value added services such as cellular phones, radio paging, VSAT services, Electronic Data Interchange (EDI), voice mail, video conferencing, facsimile, Remote Area Business Messages

Network, Packet Data Switching Network, Electronic Mail and CB radio have also been introduced.

The DoT had planned to connect all villages by telephone lines by 31st March 1997. During 1994-95 it was proposed to provide telephone facilities to 50986 number of villages. Out of this connectivity was achieved in respect of about 16,000 villages up to Dec. 31, 1994. DoT had also provided STD connectivity practically to all the District Head Quarters.

The two basic thrust areas of the 8th Plan (1992-97) were rapid extension of telecom network and transforming it into a modern and most efficient one. Accordingly it is envisaged to achieve provisions of additional 7.5 million phones in 0.36 million villages, STD facilities to all exchanges by April 1997 and one PCO for every 100 households in urban areas. Besides connecting all District Head quarters by digital network, introduction of value-added services are also planned for (Manorama Year Book 1996).

The package essentially entails lower call charges, rentals and registration rates besides higher commission to village panchayats for public phones installed on their premises. This enhanced communication is also being extended to the PCO franchise given phones under the Panchayat Sanchar Seva Yojana landed by the Department of Posts.

For the country's 0.45 million PCO operators, a three tier royalty structure will come into effect, the rural areas will be paid 25 % commission, hilly areas 20% and urban franchises will be paid commission at the rate of 16% on turnover. The group dialling scheme has been further liberalized to make it really effective. Group dialling facility upto 30 km in rural and in hilly and tribal areas it is up to 20 km (Manorama Year Book, 1996).

Large number of old and obsolete equipment in the network is main trouble shooters. Heavy dependence on operator assisted services, high fault rate due to vulnerable outdoor plants and frequent damage of U/U1 cable plants due to vandalism also bring down the efficiency of the system. The limited resources result into a long waiting time for new telephones and the services provided as social obligation suffers cuts whenever there are more pressing demands on resources. Transmission of educational programmes has been one of the high priority areas for Doordarshan.

Satellite News Gathering and Dissemination

Satellite News Gathering using INSAT system enables on-the-spot real-time news coverage. With the help of Outdoor-Broadcast (OB) SNG terminals, Prasar Bharti, covers important events in different locations for transmission via satellite to a central station at Delhi for rebroadcast over DD channels.

Press Trust of India (PTI) is implementing a system to provide its news and information services at higher speed and increased volume and variety directly to a wider range of media and other users by utilising the broadcast facilities of INSAT-3C satellite.

Radio Networking

Radio Networking (RN) through INSAT provides a reliable high-fidelity 10/15 kHz programme channels for national and regional networking. At present, 209 All India Radio (AIR) stations have been equipped with S-band receive terminals and 37 with C-band terminals. RN system primarily uses CxS band transponder in SCPC mode. The RN carriers are injected at a low level into the high power CxS band transponders along with the TV carrier. The programmes received on these S-band receive terminals are rebroadcast by terrestrial transmitters. Interactive exchange of programmes is also possible between any two or more uplink stations.

There are 50 RN channels at present _ 40 operating in S-band and 10 in C-band. Single channel captive uplink earth stations have been provided at 20 major programme producing centres (Srinagar, Ahmedabad, Bhopal, Cuttack, Patna, Guwahati,

Shillong, Thiruvananthapuram, Hyderabad, Bangalore, Jaipur, Shimla, Lucknow, Imphal, Kohima, Agartala, Aijwal, Chennai, Borivili and Hanagai). The captive earth station at Broadcasting House (BH), Mumbai, providing uplink of two Vividh Bharati channels.

The earth station at BH, Delhi, has been augmented to provide uplink for 7 RN carriers in CxS band and in CxC band. Four RN carriers are uplinked from Sikanderabad station of DOT for national networking. C-band RN carriers are being received by 37 AIR stations.

Four transportable uplink terminals have been acquired by AIR for coverage of events taking place at remote locations and for relay of programmes directly from the spot via INSAT. These terminals are capable of uplinking CD quality music channel from any remote locations to a central place such as Delhi.

The geo-stationary satellites are placed in an orbit, about 36,000 km over the equator at which altitude, the satellite has an orbital period of 24 hours and hence appear to be stationary with respect to any point on the earth. Thus, they can be used as a stationary platform for telecommunication, television broadcasting and meteorological services.

The Geo-stationary Satellite Services in India were commissioned in 1983 with the launch of INSAT-1B. Today, INSAT is one of the largest domestic communication satellite systems in the Asia Pacific Region with five satellites, INSAT-2DT, INSAT-2E, INSAT-3B, INSAT-3C and KALPANA-1, in operation. INSAT system is a joint venture of the Department of Space (DOS), Department of Telecommunications (DOT), India Meteorological Department (IMD), All India Radio (AIR) and Doordarshan. The overall coordination and management of INSAT system rests with Secretary-level INSAT Coordination Committee (ICC).

INSAT-2 Series

Of the five satellite built by ISRO under the INSAT-2 series, INSAT-2B, even after completing nine years, is continuing to provide Satellite Aided Search and Rescue Services and Data Relay Services. The last of the series, INSAT-2E, was launched in April 1999 and continues to provide service. It is positioned at 83 degree east longitude. INSAT-2E carries the following complement of payloads:

Seventeen C-band and lower extended C-band transponders with 36 dBW power and zonal and global coverages. The zonal coverage channels use 32 W Travelling Wave Tube Amplifiers (TWTA) and global coverage channels use 60 W TWTAs.

A Very High Resolution Radiometer (VHRR) with imaging capacity in Visible (0.55-0.75 microns), Thermal Infrared (10.5-12.5 microns) and Water Vapour (5.7-7.1 microns) channels, providing 2x2 km, 8x8 km and 8x8 km ground resolution respectively.

A Charge Coupled Device (CCD) camera in the Visible (0.63-0.69 micron), Near Infrared (0.77 - 0.86 micron) and Shortwave Infrared (1.55-1.70 micron) bands providing 1x1 km ground resolution.

Under an agreement with the International Telecommunications Satellite organisation (INTELSAT), eleven 36 MHz equivalent units of C-band capacity on INSAT-2E has been leased to INTELSAT.

INSAT-2DT

To partly augment the capacity of the INSAT system consequent to the loss of INSAT-2D in October 4, 1997, an in-orbit satellite, ARABSAT-1C, was procured from ARABSAT Organisation which is a regional inter-governmental satellite consortium of Arab States. The satellite, designated as INSAT-2DT, is located at 55 degree east. It has 25 C-band transponders and one S-band BSS transponder. The transponders are mainly used by Doordarshan and BSNL.

INSAT-3 Series

Of the five satellites, INSAT-3A through INSAT-3E, planned under INSAT-3 series, INSAT-3B and INSAT-3C have already been launched. INSAT-3B was launched by Ariane-5 launch vehicle in March 2000. It is colocated with INSAT-2E at 83 degree east longitude. INSAT-3C was launched by an Ariane-4 launch vehicle on January 24, 2002. It is positioned at 74 degree east longitude.

INSAT-3A, with communication transponders in C-band, Extended C-band and Ku-band, meteorological instrument comprising Very High Resolution Radiometer, Charge Coupled Device camera, Data Relay Transponder and Search and Rescue payloads, is awaiting its launch by Ariane from Kourou, French Guyana. INSAT-3E is scheduled for launch in 2003It will carry communication transponders in C-band and Extended C-band. INSAT-3D, which is an exclusive meteorological satellite carrying advanced meteorological payloads — a six channel imager and 19- channel sounder — is under development.

Information Technologies and Telecommunications

Development of digital techniques and convergence of information processing and telecommunication technologies have revolutionized the field of information management world-wide. Telecommunication processors such as modems, multiplexers, concentrators, front end processors, EPABXs and other similar devices perform a variety of support functions between the terminals and computers in a telecommunication network. The electronic exchanges are all central processor controlled switches. Also computers have simplified many vital support and control functions of operations and management of telecommunications services. Many new services such as voice mail, electronic mail, cellular phone, radio paging video text, interactive data communications system have become technically feasible due to introduction of computers in the field of telecommunications. Department of Telecommunications under its scheme named "Communications Information System for Department of

Telecom" (CISDOT) has adopted an integrated computerization plan for efficient management of information and various support functions (Banerjee, 1992).

Pager

Pager is considered common man's cellular phone, offering one way wireless communication. It was almost a non-existent concept in the country till the beginning of March 1995, when the first paging operation by Modi Korea Telecom began in Chandigarh. At the end of the first quarter of 1996, there were around two lakh pagers in the country and this figure was expected to rise to five lakh at the end of the year. Compared to India in US there were only 1,40,000 pagers operational in the first decade and Thailand had around 1,20,000 after a decade.

Cellular Phones

October 1995 is considered as the benchmark for the start of cellular services in India. In 1995, a study conducted by JP Morgan (the leading US Bank) indicated that around 10 lakh Indians were keen on fastening pagers on their belts, while another six lakh were willing to converse through cellular phones. The study added that the number of people with pagers could vault to 70 lakh and those with cellular phones to 25 lakh by the turn of the century. Another Industry report, by the Mumbai based Infac, forecasted a less optimistic demand for cell phones- around 1.3 lakh but it shared JP Morgan's long term view. By March 1996, Delhi was expected to have 75,000 to one lakh subscribers and Mumbai 1.3 lakh (India Today 1995, 1996). Now, cellular phones have exceeded the number of land lines in case of the new subscriptions.

Cellular phones are ringing in a new culture in coffee shops and cars, at wedding receptions, discotheques, restaurants and bars of the metros and even in the Parliament House of the nation. With cell phones a small but growing number of Indians is discovering a new feeling of power. For many, cell phones are the tools for business promotion but for some they are simply the newest must have toys. The status battle has moved to a higher level involving usage of the latest instrument launched in the market. Today the major players of the handsets include Nokia, Motorala, Ericsson and Siemens. Rs 500 crore Bharati Telecom Group has the largest cellular subscriber base in India. The foreign stake is limited to 49 percent. Standard rate is Rs 1.40 per 10 seconds (India Today 1996, 1997).

The service has started in cities other than the four metros like Ahmedabad and Bangalore. Once the service starts in the non-metro areas, roaming facility will be extended. International service will also be made available after the government works out arrangement with countries that use GSM (Global System for Mobile Communication) technology. Today the average cell phone subscribers across the country consists of traders, businessmen and self-employed professionals such as lawyers and doctors. For the coming years, the service providers plan to target corporate clients heavily.

However, the picture is not so rosy as it appears. The most formidable hurdle for the mobile services can be traced to the telecommunication industry itself. The problems dogging the wired network are expected to spill over the new technology that will have to bank heavily on the existing system. Moreover, the mainline business is under pressure with the entry of multinationals. The growth of the cell phone market has been slower than anticipated. At the macro level, structural limitations have proved to be impediments to growth. The first of these has been the high import duty on hand sets that placed them on a high price band. Second, the network operators have had to pay high duty on the import of network. The costs of networks are the highest in the world. Therefore airtime for users has tended to be high. Network operators are widely applying discount tactics now in order to garner full airtime usage, essential to recover their instrument costs.

A lot of potential consumers have also been waiting for the hand set prices to come down anticipating this will happen as it has in a number of other product categories. Ultimately, the success of the cellular phone in India will depend on continued efforts on both fronts - the handsets as well as the network service. When the volumes on both fronts cross the critical penetration level, this service market can move onto another platform more akin to the developed markets. When what level will be crossed, is still an open question (The Economic Times 1996).

FAX

A Facsimile Service was set up for the first time in Chennai (Madras) enabling the simultaneous printing of a newspaper at Chennai and Coimbatore. It was extended to Bangalore later on. India's overseas Communication Service was initially working through four centres one each in Mumbai, Calcutta, Chennai and New Delhi.

Today this service has become as common as regular telephone service in metros and cities. But it has not got rooted in the rural sector yet. Charges are levied by the Telecom Department from the private operators for using the fax service for commercial purpose. (India - An Encyclopaedia Survey 1984) (Chopra 1984).

Older Media with New Look

The publishing industry in India is highly competitive. A large number of newspapers and magazines are launched every year for the readers and the advertisers. As a result of this, competition in the industry has not lagged behind in absorbing modern technology. In fact, some of the first application - specific computers, the photo composing machines was brought in by this industry and the industry has also been quick to automate the various functions. Significant level of computerization has been achieved by the leading print organizations. The top five publishing companies viz. The Times of India, Hindustan Times, The Statesman, Indian Express and Living Media have a total installed base of 1,000 PCs and 17 medium ranged computers. At an average of 200 PCs per organization, it is clear that the industry is serious about mechanizing so as to able to provide services to the readers and the advertisers. The application of information technology in newspapers and magazines are mainly in two areas - production and commercial.

The IT scenario of the country has drastically changed during the last few years. It has been possible with the availability of computers, Internet connection, telephones (both land lines and cellular) at low cost.

3

Educational Technology

Technology and education are the subjects of considerable professional interest to academics as they are in the business of communication of idea. The related technologies provide services to individuals, groups and the society at large. Such a position is not only assumed but continues an integral part of the natural process.

Technology is defined as " a science and techniques of methods of doing or getting things done, related to an art, science or a particular profession." Technology has also been defined as the science of "industrial arts" and it is also defined as the application of science to the needs of an individual and society. Technology is a scientific way of developing new techniques, and a systematic way of evolving and applying these techniques.

Technology is thus a method of designing techniques. Information technology is a collection of technology based on computer and telecommunication and the technology employed in education is popularly known as Educational Technology, which may be defined as "an application of scientific knowledge about learning and the conditions of learning to improve the effectiveness and efficiency of teaching and training, John Leedham (1973) offered a definition of the term "educational technology" by giving a special consideration to the adopted role of the teacher. According to him," educational technology concerns the systematic use of modem methods and technologies in teaching and learning. It involves teachers in a variety of roles-some of which are traditional, some still emerging."

The term educational has been used in the recent times in place of 'instructional' to signify services to both teachers and students for teaching and learning. The Instructional Material Centre (IMC) and the Educational Media Centre (EMC) are conceptually parallel. Both develop from efforts to merge audiovisual services to individual students. The IMC came first initially called the audiovisual department or center. It was supposed to support group instructions with different kinds of media and its basic function was to furnish materials to faculty for teaching groups of students. As materials and equipment were developed for individual use, the later service came into being and IMC became the EMC.

Media is the channel used for the transmission of a message as in the distinction between print sound and vision. The channels are printed messages, visually on a paper or on a screen *which* can be writing, graphics or photographs: still pictures which are transparent for projection or previewing: sound discs, moving pictures as in a live television broadcast or recorded on a cine film or videotape.

It can be observed that educational technology has three important components:

a. Defining of educational goals in specific clear terms:

b. Designing of instructional: strategies and learning sequences: and

c. Evaluation of outcomes so as to obtain indicators of success or worthlessness of educational strategies.

The process of educational technology can be defined in the following components:

a. Different students learn in different ways, and at different rates:

b. Different kinds of skills- abilities, knowledge and understandings are required in different ways:

c. The various elements of instruction themselves have different learning characteristics:

d. The elements in learning process should not be considered apart from each other as each has some bearing on education:

e. As far as possible any learning system should be self-correcting which means it should have some built-in arrangement and evaluation and feedback, which can be used to improve it.

HISTORICAL PERSPECTIVE

Educational technology is as old as the human civilization but it was given different names. It started when the man learnt to carve symbols on the walls of the caves, which were their first settlements. With the advancements in recording and preservation of the acquired knowledge, the techniques changes and a major boost was experienced when the scripts for languages were discovered and used to preserve the available skill.

The history of educational technology is essentially linked with the development of new modes of communication of ideas and their application in education. Hare cited the gradual development of new media over the period with first a photograph then the phonograph followed by the silent film, the radio, the talkies and subsequent television. The demonstration of electronic media in March 1970 was a landmark. It enabled an individual to watch television programmes of ones own choice and that too at the time and place of the preference. The active participation of Europe's publishing houses at the end of the 1960 in discussions with television, videocassettes and videodiscs, these publishers formed audiovisual divisions and companies.

The term educational technology was almost unknown to India till early sixties. It was used a synonym to audiovisual aids in the academic circles The advent of teaching machines, radio, television, tape recorder, computer and Internet provided a new dimension to the role of audiovisuals. The Department of Teaching Aids was established in New Delhi in 1940's which later merged with the Centre of Educational Technology (Established in 1973) to form the Central Institute of Educational

Technology (CIET) in the National Council of Educational Research and Training in 1984

The educational mass media has its practical origin from radio before World War II. British Broadcasting Company was the first to broadcast programmes for schools in 1924. They were aimed at supporting the classroom teacher. As radio is having the capability of reaching large audience simultaneously with ease and not much cost. Japan introduced school broadcasting in 1931, which was followed by Australia and New Zealand in 1932.

In India, school broadcasting first started in 1938 followed by Tanzania in 1954 and Kenya in 1963. The first radio programmes were broadcast successfully in England in 1920. School broadcasting as a part of educational broadcasting began in 1924. At present, there is a huge network of local stations operating in almost all the countries of the world.

Highly developed societies concentrate on the mechanical use of audiovisual materials in libraries. Although in the less developed countries. A/V does play an important part in educational programmes. In the Government library scheme in South Italy-television is used to reach the widest audiences. India's employment based literacy program uses audiovisual as much as possible. In such countries where there is a library service, it has an important role to play in backing up the new found literacy. The Indian Library Association encourages the training of librarians in the use of audiovisuals.

There have been several efforts to format and standardize the descriptive catalogue of media materials. The audiovisual standards to an extent are reflected in the National Information Centre for Educational Media (NICEM), Bibliographies are available in book form. The printed catalogues are available since 1901 in the Library of Congress. The structure of all MARC formats for various media are identical but the content descriptors can be varied to extract the homomorphic transformation of different kinds of representation, film and strips, videotapes, pictures, transparencies, slides. Audiotapes, music, phonorecords, maps, serials, books etc. 4.

The year 1984 has great significance in the history of educational technology since two pioneer organizations i.e. INSAT/TV Project (lately transformed to Countrywide Classroom of the University-Grants Commission} and the Indira Gandhi National Open University (IGNOU) at New Delhi came into existence. The effective utilization of radio and educational television programmes started since then. As these organizations grew, the materials produced by them in the form of audio and video films as well gathered for academic support from other agencies were also collected.

Along with social change has come the technological change. Society is rapidly evolving from the industrial, machine age of the electronic era. There is a continuing logarithmic increase in the use of automation in just about every human activity. It is as astounding to ponder that in less than three quarters of the last century, man was able to proceed from the first heavier-than-air flight to walking on the moon not as dramatic, put perhaps more important, is the progress in medicine and healthcare. Many of the killer epidemics that plagued man in the past are today virtually nonexistence, in achievement not with out price that world, for the first time, is faced with the critical problem of global over population, which generates a whole new set of survival problems. We are now witnessing the emergence of genetic control and manipulation and of biochemical regulation of the brain and intellect

The very purpose of educational technology is to facilitate and improve the quality of human learning. In order to solve the various problems of education, technology consisting of various media of mass communication and modem testing and evaluation techniques are essential. Specially, in developing countries like India, it has to be mastered and utilized by the educational administrators if they have to keep pace with each other and catch up with the developed nations.

Educational technology is concerned with providing appropriately designed learning situations which hold in view the objective of learning and the purpose of educational technology is to improve the quality of human learning. The uniqueness of educational technology is characterized as:

(i) Use of broad range of resources of learning:

(ii) Emphasis on individual learning, and

(iii) Use of systems approach.

The effectiveness of educational technology depends on:

(i) Ability to achieve goals:

(ii) To maintain itself internally; and

(iii) To adapt to its environment

The following are the reasons for application of educational technology in education:

(a) Print media is easy to carry and it can be used according to the convenience of students. Newspapers are specifically useful for maintaining contact between scattered people.

(b) In the broadcast media, radio has enormous potential. It can cover very large audience and can reach isolated spots. Radio is within the reach of masses and should be used as a home-based means of imparting education. It supports to correspondence students by way of classroom materials and information services of various kinds

(c) TV makes it possible to use broadcasting for visual presentation. TV broadcasting is an important component in the distance education and gives the individual strength in encouraging representations by individual learners. Recently, a channel of Doordarshan has been dedicated for imparting instruction to the distant learners.

(d) Audio and video cassettes are the media which would be crucial for distance education

(e) Through the teleconferencing, the counseling sessions are arranged for students to bring the factor of two way interaction

(f) Telephone teaching can provide two-way interaction between learners and teachers

(g) Video disks can be linked to the computers and the learners can interact with the materials at their own place and choice.

(h) The most convenient means at least in principle of getting textual information to member institutions is by fax. Since this arrives the same way in which the message is sent.

A variety of subjects of high quality make the involvement of media a must for education.

Multimedia like audio, videocassettes, telephone teaching, radio broadcast, computer learning material etc. are used at home or at the educational institutions in various parts of the country to have a face to face contact with educators to clear doubts. All theses media are educationally sound and reaches to the masses at a greater extent.

The report on President's Commission on Instructional Technology has great significance with regard to the assessment of impact of technology on education. It represents the largest and the most comprehensive study ever undertaken on the relationship of man, media and machines as well as the process of educational technology. The report provides a strong foundation not only for the continued education of educators in media utilization but more significantly for the public education of all citizens. Radio, television and graphic press can be employed in the process of communicating to the general public and the possibilities for improved education. Briggs has identified the significant contribution of the report, which can be taken as characteristic problems and trends in the current status of educational media and technology;

(a) Why should not continue to bolster outdated curricula by use of new media

(b) A system model for the design of instruction should govern media decisions with specific kinds of learners in mind.

(c) The new media can help bridge the gap between school and the real world.

Now, information is available in various forms of document and these forms kept changing with technologies available with time. As a result of advancement in knowledge and information, newer type of information media emerged and suitable methods need to be designed to organize their collections. A major breakthrough in this direction in the history was the invention of printing press but the invention of computer has broken all records of generation and distribution of information. The educational media with the help of telecommunication links can reach the unreached and is proving to be the most effective device in the education and learning process.

The educational institutions are given due consideration to the production and distribution of information contained in the non-print media. The area includes graphics, photography and film production, audio and videotape recording and reproduction or any combination of the above said media. The sphere of educational media is so wide that it is not possible for a researcher to carry out a comprehensive study since the varied nature of media products and services offer a range as well inconvenience in it

Retrieving electronically stored information will become the business of common man. It will include determining what data are to be entered into the information bank, to what media format the data are to be committed, and what information is to be rejected or discarded. The system will include a feedback with a two-way flow of information between the smallest library and the largest information bank. Obviously such a system will involve a highly sophisticated electronic network managed by a capably trained professional.

The following are the needs and challenges for educators in view of the technological developments:

(1) Increased training in the use of audiovisual materials, but far more important will be the need for imagination, initiative and special planning.

(2) More intensive need for studies of needs for audiovisual materials: their usefulness, effectiveness and relationship to the requirements of teaching and library services.

(3) Expansion of technological research and automation to permit a greater degree of use through self service and through mass service.

(4) Greater coordination of the various audiovisual forms with one another and with print materials through more intensive programming.

(5) Development of more bibliographic coverage and methods of organization of audiovisual materials for use.

The advent of teaching machines i.e. radio, television- tape record, computer and language laboratory provided a new dimension to the role of audiovisual aids. Technology in education lays stress on the concept of service like technology in the service of farming or agriculture or science in the service of mankind. It is concerned with the use of technical advancements in terms of various equipments materials and machines for educational purposes. It is involving audiovisual equipment, hardware and sophisticated electronic devices such as radio, television, film, projectors, tape recorders etc.

There are two technologies, which have contributed emerging educational media viz. video and computer. There are of course varieties of modes in which these two are presented as different instructional media.

VIDEO IN EDUCATION

Video in education includes-:

(a) Videocassettes with VCR/VCP and Television

(b) Broadcasting video programmes, live or recorded and distributed through microwave stations to satellite coupled with direct receiving sets (DRS) or relay stations e.g. SITE and UGC's Countrywide Classroom or school telecast of CIET

(c) Closed Circuit Television
(d) Able TV
(e) Community Antenna
(f) Interactive Television
(g) Telex, and
(h) Videotext

COMPUTER IN EDUCATION

Computer technology offers the following in the field of education:

(a) Computer Managed Instruction
(b) Computer Assisted Instruction
(c) Computer Based Education
(d) Intelligent CAI
(e) Artificial Intelligence
(f) CAD/CAM
(g) Expert Systems
(h) Microprocessor Based Educational Kit for Laboratories and Workshops

A combination of varieties of motion pictures, slides, computer data, text, music, speech etc. are using computer and laser technology.

These technologies are particularly relevant for distance education because of the inherent simplicity of audio as a communication medium, its capacity to invoke the imagination of listener, promote his/her active participation in the learning process, its easy reach economy etc.

The audio formats usually employed in education are:

(a) Talk by eminent experts

(b) Discussions regarding controversial/complex problems

(c) Question answer series containing frequently asked questions (FAQ) on a given subject

(d) Audio updates as quick revisions for the printed lessons

(e) Language learning

(f) Features/drama on historical topics

Universities have also started producing 'blind friendly' lessons. These are audio transformations of the print materials so that the audio is self sufficient in itself for the independent use of visually impaired. Such audio transformations are also found useful for the course in which the literacy level of the target group is generally very low.

Alongside the non-broadcast use of audio in the form of taped lessons, radio broadcasting is equally popular means of serving the need of education. The reach of radio now extends to all nooks and corners of the world.

While radio broadcasts are useful in their own way. the fact of broadcasting is a one-way medium limits their use in the educational context. Phnoe-in-programme through radio can overcome this limitation to a large extent. Once radio counseling takes root, it can be used as an alternative to face to face counseling.

Video, television and other audiovisual media have obvious application for education because of their ability to carry both visual and oral messages to recreate a classroom atmosphere for the learners. Even though much costlier than audio-based media, they are pedagogically very effective and in fact unavoidable whenever the subject matter involves visual portrayal of real events, explanation through graphic animation etc.

Videotapes deal with topics/concepts requiring visual exposition that cannot be adequately dealt through print or audio media. They are also used to record renowned authorities and scientists in their respective areas of specialization, to serve as reference material for the students. Production formats for video vary depending upon the subject matter and target groups involved. In the simplest case, their video lectures containing the teacher's image and voice, the occasional visual inserts relevant to the topic. On the other hand. documentaries, which portray real life situation, on location-visuals and dramatized portrayal recreating a particular historical period are also produced.

Videos for natural sciences are helpful for demonstration of science practical, magnifying view of microscopic objects, graphical explanation of process, reactions etc.

Educational videos produced for different courses through the various production agencies like IGNOU, EMRCs/AVRCs/ MCRC/CIET etc. are trimmed and capsuled to suit the telecast mode of the television. IGNOU's video programmes are telecast daily from 6.30 to 7.a.m and through the primary channel of Doordarshan.

Interactivity is the foremost requirement for video-based technologies as in the case of audio-based technologies. This consideration has prompted to start the Training and Development Communication Channel with the help of Indian Space Research Organization (ISRO). This is one way video/two way audio teleconferencing system, with the teaching end of the EMPC studios and learning ends located at all the regional centres.

Computer can do all the things to facilitate qualitative learning. Software techniques programs are stored and transmitted through input devices including computer-based training.

Objectives of Computer Based Media

The objective of using computer based media in distance education as suggested by J. Rama Naidu are:

(1) To make distance education more effective
(2) To strengthen and sustain interest in learning
(3) To cater to individual differences in learning preferences and abilities.

(4) To provide feedback

(5) To help the learners solve their problems easily.

(6) To improve the standards of distance education.

(7) To inspire or initiate teachers to change their method of teaching by exploring different possibilities

(8) To bridge the distance between the teacher and the student.

In recent years, penetration of computers and computer networks even in the developing countries has been phenomenal. Even though individual ownership of computers in the country is negligible, their instructional availability and usage is well neigh universal with even small size establishments generally using one. In the beginning use of computers was restricted to scientific and administrative functions but of late it was extended to the library services. Their use as a "surrogate teacher' and as a medium in the mainstream of the multimedia academic packages has started more recently

Some institutions have started producing and distributing courseware on CD ROMs. IGNOU produces entire duration course on CD ROMs for BCA and MCA programmes so that students may use them as and when need as an alternative to the printed text. Apart from the huge storage capacity (One CD ROM can contain the material of whole programme) they ca be used in an interactive way enabling the *power* points sides and streaming audio and video can provide a model of just in time or on demand multimedia lectures. CD ROMs produced by IGNOU are used by students in the standalone modes since computer students are expected to have better understanding and involvement with the latest technologies.

Multimedia is not a machine or system or a newly discovered principle. It is defined multimedia as an objective describing a multi sensory approach to the disbursement and acquisition of information: text and pictures, still graphics and motion video. Pictures and text manipulated with buttons and slide bars.

A videodisc is similar to CD that holds still images, video segments and sounds. The advantages of video disc over video tape or videocassette is its high quality of images- still frames, fast access to any part of disc, freedom from wear and expansive mass production. When combined with computer, videodisc becomes a powerful audiovisual database if interactive teaching and learning. Information on disk cannot be changed by the user. Disadvantage is the playback only and its high production cost.

The constant linear velocity (CLV) is primarily used for linear playback application such as movies, musical performance and so on. These discs may be recorded with one frame per track near the centre of the disc and up to three frames per track near the outside of the disc. Due to this quality, CLV videodisc must be played at the speed varying from 1800/rpm (revolution per minute) near the centre to 600/rmp near the outside. Thus it plays at a speed of 30 frames per second- required to be compatible with National Standard Television Committee (NTSC) video, and therefore, displayable on standard television sets. The CLV videodisc permits a forward and reverse scanning as dual channel audio and chapter stops. But CLV is relatively limited in its interactive potential.

Microcomputers are often considered to fall within the domain of educational media because they are similar to other machines and software systems already located there and it is presumed that the audiovisual professional is more likely comparing with others to know administer them. Microcomputers can be found in a variety of other places as well such as departments as systems, cataloguing, children and public service often find themselves.

Internet is being used by academic institutions as a delivery system for the courses. Despite the constraint of poor individual computers and Internet connectivity. It is being recently used for the following purposes:

(a) Downloading/browsing rapidly changing information such

as schedules and announcements, assignment or even short samples of course materials.

(b) E-mail for operational and academic support- and communication with fellow students.

(c) Using FAQs to answer the queries: both academic and otherwise

(d) Using chat to interact with teachers and fellow students

After the invention of the printing press and computer. Internet is the next paradigm shift in human life. It has provided a powerful medium of communication for individuals of different tastes. And education is no exception. Virtual universities are being established all over the world and the beginning has already been made in India with about all major cities organizing such institutional support to the students. One can enroll with such universities for the desired academic course without being physically present.

With increasing convergence between computer and communication technologies and the spread of telecommunication networks, present day universities are expected to gradually transform themselves as virtual universities where all functions of the university will take place electronically over the digital links and networks,

The importance of non-book materials as carriers of information has got a wider recognition along with the technical aids to retrieve information from them.

It is often said that a picture is worth a thousand words as it may communicate a huge mass of ideas, which may mean differently to different people. Photography emerged as an appropriate medium for such presentation, which coupled with the technology of sound proved to be the greatest and the most significant form for presentation of ideas.

Audiovisuals

The present day photography is the result of the early

observations by alchemists and chemists based on the action of light on the photosensitive materials. The technique developed towards the end of the 18th century when the demand for the pictures grew. A major advancement in photography took place with substitution of glass for paper as a carrier for the light sensitive material. In 1851, once the manufacture of photographic materials was established as a commercial industry, the photographic techniques followed steady growth. In 1912 Kodak Company introduced flat film in place of glass plates for making negatives. The technique was advantageous for manufacturers. A few years later, the development in new sensitizing dyes made it possible for preparing panchromatic materials of improved quality.

Photography coupled with sound heralded a new era in field of communication of ideas. It followed the invention and application of a variety of technologies for recording and presentation of information. It began with the art of sight and sound which later transformed into tape slide shows. But with further improvements in synchronization of sound with the moving images, the present day cinematography took its birth.

The development in photography and cinematography brought significant changes in the world of learning. Now more sense organs were involved in the perception process. The human nature is so that the maximum of ones total knowledge is perceived through the senses of sight and sound and the new media of communication available as a result of these advancements exploited this potential of man to its fall, facilitating learning at a higher speed and with a greater ease. The trend was on for about thirty years in India from the mid of the last century. The celluloid medium was primarily adopted for entertainment but soon it became equally popular in the academic circles. Film became the medium of instruction within fifty years of its existence.

Motion Pictures

Motion pictures are now available on cinematographic film as well as on video. Their basic and common characteristic is the movement of picture on the screen. The movement is achieved by running a film or video through a projector or player at a speed of 24 frames per second. The stills are recorded in a situation where all of them are comparatively similar and differ only at the point where movement has to be visualized. Motion pictures include silent and sound films as well. Nowadays, nearly all of them are being recorded in color.

Motion pictures are being accepted increasingly by the academic circles as a learning aid as well as the medium for preservation of information. In India, we always need good instructional and enrichment films available in the international market. But there are hurdles in their import Even for the academic and research purposes. This requires urgent attention of all concerned so that motion picture can also be imported like books for the purpose of education and research. Moreover, just as there are renowned authors so are there well known filmmakers who have a series of worthwhile films to their credit and which could be an intrinsic part of every library.

Cinematographic film consists of a transparent flexible support or base on which is laid a photosensitive adhesive emulsion. They are now available in different widths ranging from 8 mm to 70 mm. The more the width the higher is the cost of the film. They are used for varied purposes depending upon the cost and the quality of the film. The super 8 mm is used very rarely as the infrastructure for production on this format is not generally available. But this is certainly the cheapest cinematographic medium available so far. The 16 mm film is used by most of the institutions for education and development. This has advantage over 8 mm because of comparatively higher resolution being suitable to be magnified on slightly larger screen.

Both the 8 mm and' 16 mm films are used depending upon the size of the audience as well as the cost of the production involved. The 35 mm and 70 mm films are normally used for entertainment and commercial purposes. 'They are suitable for larger gatherings like the audience of feature films in cinema halls. The advertisement agencies produce ads on these formats. The advantage of their having larger width is that the picture contain: very high resolution and does not blow up while magnified on larger screens. Sound for cinematographic films can be recorded magnetically or optically depending upon the circumstances.

Computer

Computer is regarded as the greatest invention of all the times. It facilitates the storage, processing and distribution of information much easier with its vast memory speed and accuracy. The advancements in calculator, which was invented to carry out mathematical calculations led to the invention of computer.

A more visible change took place when calculators acquired the capability of processing textual data proceeded by the capacity to process information available in varied formats. Further improvements in computer design during the 1960s enabled the integration of text and graphics, a move that encouraged the development of computer based training programs. Such use was however limited, as programming was costly, slow and cumbersome, and the computing relied on a mainframe, or central computer to do all the work. The release of the first microcomputers during the late 1970s saw computing become more portable and affordable. Ease of use took a quantum leap with the introduction of the Apple Macintosh computer in 1984. Operation of the computer and its programs became more intuitive, largely as a result of research in the area of human-computer interaction.

The adoption of computers in the area of vocational training also increased, with some industries recognising that the technology offered benefits that were largely centered on efficiency gains. This was particularly the case in industries such as finance and insurance, manufacturing, health care, and the armed forces where training was a critical but costly component of operation. These types of organisations, with large staff numbers requiring training to an industry standard, or with staff located across national and international borders, found cost savings could be achieved by using technology to distribute training programs to the workplace, rather than bring staff to a central training centre. Computer programs could deliver training at a time and place convenient to all parties, provide flexibility in terms of progression and pace, generate and score tests, record all interaction between the learner and the system and produce detailed reports of this interaction. These attributes were welcomed in organisations where staff development programs were valued as a means of motivating staff and maintaining the standard of service. These programs are commonly based on competency standards that clearly define objectives, and set standards of performance that may be observed and measured against defined criteria.

The notion of providing training when it was needed to where it was needed was extended through the development of performance support systems. These systems allowed an employee to use a computer as both a tool and a tutor - the tutor would provide step by step assistance in the performance of specific computer related tasks, in much the same way as help "wizards" incorporated within many Microsoft products try to anticipate users needs in designing a new spreadsheet or database.

Computer based training has also been a logical choice where there was substantial risk in allowing a novice to train in an operational environment. It is safer and more cost effective to allow the operator of a steel rolling mill to practice the procedure using a computer simulation, or a pilot to manage an engine failure without leaving the ground. Submariners crewing the Australian Navy's new Collins Class submarines were expected to develop a familiarity of the control systems prior to the vessels delivery, again through the use of computer simulations. Adoption of computers in education has not always met with similar success. The reasons are varied, and these will be discussed in the next section. Computers can be an asset in education, but the knowledge of appropriate applications, limitations and advantage needs to be clearly understood.

Electronic Media

The electronic media has the capability to store, manipulate and transfer information in the form of text as well as audio visuals. It is also possible to combine both of them. Multimedia is and hypermedia can be cited as examples. The electronic media is useful in learning both in a classroom situation or individually. It includes information networks and CD ROMs. the information is recorded electronically, hence greater speed, accuracy and memory is available to the users. It is presumed that within the coming decade, the electronic media will supersede all the available media for storage, management and dissemination of information. This will particularly affect the educational institutions as it is more effective and economic both in terms of money and time spent in learning. It will also affect the nature of classroom instruction. A new learning culture is in the offing, which can be seen in the open system of education where attendance in class is not a prerequisite to earn a degree.

The advances in electronics and telecommunications brought newer technology capable of accommodating very large quantities of information in a very little space. Magnetic tapes, CD-ROMs, multimedia and hypermedia are a few examples. The capacity may be doubled if the stacks are partitioned according to the size of the disc and not the size of books which require more space. CD ROMs have the capacity to record and display large amount of information through computer system. The information contained in them can be manipulated and produced in varied sequences. They are easy to consult and make the searches convenient. The Microsoft Corporation has come out with a set of two CD ROMs that contains information equal to about twenty encyclopedia and the information it holds can be searched through various options.

CD ROMs have an edge on print as well as online resources. On the one hand they save a lot of physical space required for their print counterpart while on the other hand they allow to work on huge resources independent of online connectivity that is far expensive. The ever-increasing cost of Internet connectivity also suggests that CD ROM technology is more suited to education and research. Document in an ever-increasing number are being directly published on CD ROMs without involving prints. Now experts believe that the shift from page to screen once a fantasy is approaching reality now. Students in many university use textbook that exist online. Similarly there are CD ROMs, which hold valuable academic information and are the only sources of information in certain areas of study like medicine and technology.

In the electronic media, search time has been reduced miraculously. Bulky reference tools like the *Chemical Abstracts, Dissertation Index, Index to Higher Theses*, encyclopedias and dictionaries, etc. can be searched within a fraction of a second by just pushing the keys of a computer. Further, the search is very easy as most of the databases are user friendly. Any of the related words can be taken as 'Search Term' and fed into the system for retrieval of information. This is followed by appearance of a detailed list of documents available on the same topic from which one can select the most relevant and pinpointed information and even download it in the memory of the computer or on auxiliary memory for future use. There are some restrictions. Words, which can create hindrance are debarred from the retrieval process. They are called stop words. This is achieved by maintaining a separate file for them.

Another advantage of electronic media is the updating of the reference tools. Unlike the printed medium, which requires repeating the whole mechanical process for improvement or updating, the information is updated instantly in the electronic media. This is achieved with the push of a button. In fact, the agencies dealing in the electronic sources of information enter into an agreement with the consumers. The same discs can be sent to the agencies and returned updated. Now, with the Electronic Mail facility, updating can be carried out instantly on line. 'This practically involves no time and saves expenditure as well. In the print as well as the celluloid, mass copying leads to deterioration of prints by way of generation loss. But in the electronic media, the same text can be generated again and again without any loss or deterioration in the quality of the original or its copy.

In a tropical country like India the fluctuation in temperature and humidity leads to deterioration in the quality of print as well as celluloid by way of chemical reactions. This process of degeneration goes on with the passage of time. It is very difficult to maintain quality of print beyond a century and of celluloid beyond a decade. The solution lies to some extent in erection of specialized dehumidified chambers and providing air conditioners but this too is not practicable for many other reasons such as frequent breakdowns in supply of electricity and the huge expenditure involved.

Multimedia

Multimedia represents the convergence between computers, digital video, digital audio and sound synthesis. It has initially culminated the re-evaluation of the ways in which we communicate information combining still and moving images, sound, text and audio. Day to day applications of multimedia can be visualized considering information activities around us. Multimedia is being increasingly adopted for education and training, reference, business, entertainment etc.

Multimedia is widely acknowledged as an environment with great potentiality for education. It is able to assist both the people and teachers in new ways since for teacher it provides a means of putting across information and ideal and for students it can represent a one-to-one teaching environment which moves at the required pace.

Distribution of multimedia lessons, lectures and courseware on CD ROM or CD-1 discs adds another dimension to multimedia in education providing a vehicle of information to the students to take home. Its potential is enormous for the rural communities and isolated geographical regions where schools are inaccessible. The Open University teaching will certainly depend more upon the means and methods presented by advances in multimedia in the time to come.

As projected in the past we have now libraries without space. An information specialist sitting comfortably at his place of work just connecting his computer can establish contact with the desired number of foreign databases and an interaction can follow for the desired information. These services are being offered now on commercial basis too. The information thus selected can be downloaded on computer for further use.

Pupils traveled long distances in the past in search of information. Now information is knocking at their doors. The electronic devices have made it possible to transfer information at the speed of light. Pictures and sounds too are being transmitted from one place to the other. What is important today, is the selection of information and its dissemination for application. The quantum of information available is so much that everybody can have enough to learn individually. This is because of the coordination of efforts at the global level and presentation of this vast amount of information in a way that makes it convenient for the users to determine what is relevant to their needs.

Many academic institutions in the West have made database search an integral part of their educational process. Now thanks to the power of CD-ROM technology, information on nearly all the disciplines of education is available within reach of virtually every academic institution, its teachers, students and researchers. One can search as broadly, as deeply and as long as he or she wishes. The Indian National Scientific Documentation Centre is providing professional expertise in this regard to the academic and research institutions in India. Some other agencies like the Videsh Sanchar Nigam, the National Informatics Centre and the Faxon Informatics, Bangalore also coordinate in subscribing to these services. The data available from these agencies reveals steady growth in demand of the On-Line Information Services by the academic institutions in India.

The electronic media allows portability as well as durability. Information recorded digitally can last for centuries virtually with no effect of humidity, dust or temperature. The quality of recording is not affected because the information i , not recorded on the surface but within the medium itself. The electronic media seems to be ideal for preservation of manuscripts and other valuable records. There are two ways of recording from paper on to the digital media-one is the transfer of text page wise and the other is that the contents of rare manuscripts may be entered word by word. Thus, not only the life of the documents increases but also they can be retrieved rapidly and made available to the researchers.

The present situation has become an ideal one for adoption of multimedia in education as in the words of Bill Gates "For the first time, all kinds of information-numbers, text sound video-can be put into a digital form that any computer can now store, process and forward. For the first time, standard hardware combined with a standard software platform has created economies of scale that make powerful computing solutions available extensively to all kinds of companies" (Business @ the speed of thought: Penguin Books: London (1999).

The confluence of satellite and multimedia resulted in making the communication technology available at an unimaginably lower cost to the betterment of the common man although it originated in labs for scientific researchers. Now, Internet services are primarily based on these technologies.

The Internet

Internet has emerged as the most powerful medium for storage and retrieval of information. It works round the clock and connects every nook and corner of the globe. With an unprecedented growth in the quantum of knowledge worldwide and the easy accessibility, Internet has become an unavoidable necessity for every institution of higher learning and research. Internet is continuously growing internationally. Within a short span of ten years, its services have been spread among all the nations of the world. In 1991 it was within reach of 73 countries but within four years of its existence Internet reached 148 countries. The number of Internet users is also increasing tremendously as they are almost doubled after every two years. In the meanwhile Internet widened its scope. Now it is used for storage, manipulation and dissemination of textual data as well as the multimedia.

Internet became more popular by its feature of the World Wide Web in 1991, Tim Berners-Lee, a young scientist working in European Particle Physics Laboratory (CERN) produced Internet's first browser. According to him, "the dream behind the Web is of a common information space in which we communicate by sharing information. "By its application, someone could scan every document or photo or video on the net. It gave an opportunity to share the resources by individuals and organizations on the basis of mutual understanding. In the past ten years, it has been so popular that the number of Internet users has jumped from 600,000 to 140 million and it is expected to grow further to 350 millions within the next three years.

With the increasing dependant on micro literature for research in the universities and the availability of improved technology for information handling, the traditional library practices of classification and cataloguing are proving to be less relevant. As the information needs of users even in the academic institutions are satisfied with some alternate means. The growing use of Internet by medical and engineering institutions is a clear indication of what is in store for the libraries of the future? PUBMED, a service of the National Library of Medicine provides access to over 11 millions of citations back to the mid 1960s and additional life science journals. It includes links to many similar websites providing fall text articles and other related resources. The service is available free of cost. Journals are the most pertinent sources of information for research in the universities. They are available in plenty on Internet. Moreover a large number of them is free of cost and if priced they cost less compared to their print counterpart. After the print media, journals could not figure in any other format except the digital media. The audiovisuals remained short lived and barring a few political ones no worth mentioning journal could surface in the audiovisual media.

Internet has also democratized the process of higher education in the true sense librating it from the clutches of the few knowledgeable and powerful without whom research was a distant dream for the students. It has affected almost every sphere of human activities. In the field of education, the work of traditional gurus has been taken over by Internet now, which provides information on the latest advancements and researches taking place in the various disciplines of study. It also supports farther activities of collecting data, analyzing and synthesizing it. Moreover it presents the events in international perspective hence the research work is supposed to be unique whereas the chances for repetition were higher in the past when things were perceived in the limited geographical limits.

Virtual Universities

With increasing convergence between computer and communication technologies and the spread of communication networks the present day open universities are expected to gradually transform themselves as virtual universities, where almost all functions of the university take place electronically over digital links and networks.

In Indian universities have started a beginning for which the following possibilities may be forecasted for the time to come:

* Pre-eminence of the printed text as the master medium of instruction will gradually yield place to multi-media instruction through CD-ROMs and such other devices.
* Audio and video programmes which are now tape-based will enjoy disc based digital storage techniques for deterioration free preservation and random on-demand retrieval through network
* Broad-band digital communication through satellite will be used for synchronous and asynchronous interactivity between teachers and students and among students groups located in different places.
* Internet will play an increasingly central role in the university functioning right from student admission, programme delivery, counseling and assignments to final evaluation and certificates.
* The present day study centers would transform themselves to function more as kiosks offering information and communication terminals to students rather than as places where face to face counseling is conducted. A medium of face to face component may still continue, but more for social interaction than academic purposes.

Nanotechnology

Technology converts sunlight into energy, cleans the oceans and beaches and provides barren land the fertility. Nanotechnology is the technology of far future. It will be employed to do wonders for the coming generations of mankind. Now we are well ahead in the age of Nnotechnology after passing through a long journey through the Stone Age, Bronze Age, Iron Age and recently the Silicon Age. In the age of Nanotechnology, materials are just getting smarter day by day. The smarter materials will bring the near-perfect future that now we envision in our dreams. Machine will perform functions with more accuracy, least dependents and at a greater speed that we nowhere see in the developing countries today.

Nanotechnology can be said to be the brainchild of a physicist Dr. Richard F. Feynman who in 1959 gave a now-famous lecture at the California Institute of Technology in Pasadena. The talk outlined the theoretical concept of manipulating atom to build molecules. To substantiate his claim, Dr. Feynman explained the principles of physics which do not deny the possibility of manipulating things atom by atom.-the idea of using small machines to make even tinier molecules and so on down to atomic level itself.

It is presumed that nanotechnology will be applied to construct every item of human need on smarter lines atom by atom hence the idea of nanorobots to heal human ills, cell by cell and to transport him safely giving and acting on add condition suitably. In 1986, a technologist J. Eric Drexler published his work Engine of Creation which proposed the building of molecular machines atom by atom, through the use of' assembles'. He virtually proposed the unlimited potential of nanotechnology to construct anything. The assembler he proposed was a nuclear robotic arm.

Though we have not reached the omnipotent stage of evolution in this new technology, we still have plenty of applications from biosensors of human body to intelligent systems embedded in real-time assessment and maintenance of automobiles and spacecrafts through their super telecommunication and decision making systems. Its application in processing of the given piece of information is bound to be far quicker and beneficial in all spheres of activities including education and research.

In India, the scope of nanotechnology is quite evident as the country has another incubator in the form of IndiaNano (www.indiaco.com) . A team lead by the president and CEC of this concern is working to bring the nanotechnology revolution.

The firm has tied up with several US companies that are predominantly working on nanotechnology products.

IndiaNano is an initiative support by US and Indian research organizations, investment firms and co-operations, aimed at developing a platform for collaboration between academia, corporates, government, private labs, entrepreneurs, investors and service providers. In order to harness the benefilts of advances in material and manufacturing, electronics, medicine and healthcare, environment and energy management, chemicals, biotechnology, agriculture, information technology and national security that have been enabled by the breakthroughs in nanotechnology. More specifically, nanotechnology would:

1. Assist the government and the private sector in developing a national research and commercialization strategy.
2. Provide a unique and beneficial platform for initiating and exploring relationship between entrepreneurs, start-ups, and investors in the US, Europe and Asia and research organizations, co-operations and entrepreneurs in the country.
3. Helps raise funds for long term nano-sclae research and development in India
4. Provide researchers, students and engineers in India the opportunity to learn from the practical experiences of entrepreneurs and specialists through week-study, programs, internships etc.
5. Provide worldwide science and engineering community with a broad view of this field in India.
6. Identify promising areas for future research and commercial development in India.
7. IndiaCo. Is working on to have some tie-up with the Indian government for setting up an incubator for nanotech but the firm will lead this initiative as separate initiative under its cluster for incubation. IndiaCo is closely involved with

several companies with the US that are predominantly working on monotech products. In future their number is expected to rise in India.

High Technology

The communication revolution is the result of advances in microelectronics; a branch of electronics engineering. It has brought transience and rapid social change. Microelectronics centers on semi-conductor chips and their uses in computers, telecommunication and many other types of electronic equipment. As a result of semiconductors, computers have shrunk in size and cost over the last five decades of its existence.

A High-technology industry is an industry at the cutting age of technology whose core technology changes rapidly. The two popular examples are microelectronic and biotechnology. It is typically characterized by a high proportion of scientists and engineers in total employment and up to 10% of sale transactions on research and development activities of the industry. It is imperative to remain up dated of the state of affairs and made investments to grab the future needs by way of orientation and experimentation, which involves risks as well. The essential of this industry is brainpower and that must be boosted at every point of time so that it passes through the test of time.

India produces about 15000 engineers every year and a fair quantity of this manpower is employed in the related field. One result is the manpower boom in export of computer software from within the country and also the employment of engineers abroad.

4
The Broadcast Media

In the early times, it was smoke that communicated meanings to the responders at the other end. Now, information is transferred to other places in a number of ways. The telecommunication has brought a revolution in the ways of sending messages at distant places virtually without involving any considerable amount of time.

Wire remained the main career of messages for the last two centuries and improvement in wire-based technology increased efficiency of transmitting messages across the geographical boundaries of the nations. Different materials were used to manufacture them ranging from copper, aluminum, steel etc. Recently fiber optics has taken a lead over all the existing wire-based communication devices. Satellite communication developed during the 20th century. It has turned the entire world into a global village. Satellites relay or transmit information such as TV, phone, weather, military intelligence, and data. Communications satellites provide a worldwide link.

Broadcasting started with radio communication during the first half of the twentieth century. It has now developed enormously. Earlier, broadcasting was a very difficult affair because of the cost involved and the strict control of governments on broadcasting agencies. But, with the emergence of private television channels, and Internet, popularization of ones ideas or the publicity campaign by government and individuals has become much easier.

GROWTH OF BROADCASTING

Advances in technology and increased competition have created new opportunities and new challenges for radio and TV broadcasters. The steady advance of technology makes it easy to lose light of the great progress made from one decade to the next in broadcast equipment design. The advance of technology generally can be divided into decades.

The Decade of the Sixties

From the standpoint of broadcast equipment, this was the decade of color television, videotape, stereo FM and remote transmitter control. The color TV conversion process often was slow, as local stations replaced or modified pickup, playback and transmission equipment one piece at a time. By the early 1960s, the switch to color programming was gaining steady momentum. By the fall of 1965, almost all of NBC's prime time schedule was produced on color film. CBS was a year behind in reaching that point, and ABC followed in the 1967 season.

Tape recording technology continued to progress, with the widespread use of color videotape machines and unique production devices like the Ampex SloMo disc recorder. The videotape cartridge system emerged in the middle of the decade offering stations a simple, and usually reliable method of spot playback.

Television broadcasters stretched the limits of portability with the large cameras and recorders of the day. A TV camera was placed aboard the Ranger 7 explorer to the moon in 1964, and in 1968 CBS made history by using a portable minicam for political convention coverage. Newsgathering hasn't been the same since.

Program relay by satellite emerged from the laboratory to the field during the '60s. The young technology provided viewers fascinating images from far-away lands *live*. A new and useful device called the character generator made its debut in 1964, finally giving broadcasters an alternative to studio cards "supered" over video.

Attempts were made at automating radio and TV stations using a variety of schemes. Although the hardware worked, it left much to be desired and rarely lived up to its promises of flawless execution and reduced personnel count. The idea was right, but the technology was too primitive to meet the expectations of station managers.

The conversion of FM radio stations to stereo operation was a lengthy process that spanned most of the decade. While operation under the new mode of broadcasting was authorized to begin on June 1, 1961, it was not until 1969 that most stations had converted to FM stereo. The delay in implementing the new technology was primarily because of the lack of profitability of FM broadcasting at that time.

Many radio and TV stations converted to remote-control operation of their transmitters. Advances in transmitter design and remote control technology helped this process along greatly. Station coverage area improvement and studio facility relocation were two of the reasons for increased interest in remote-control operation during the '60.

The Decade of Seventies

With color television, stereo FM and transmitter remote control in full swing, broadcasters looked for more efficient methods of operation during the 1970s. Radio station program automation became feasible from a technical standpoint, and managers saw in the technology a way to improve their on-air sound and reduce staffing requirements. Earlier attempts (some dating back to 1959) were made at program automation for radio and TV, but it was not until digital circuitry had been perfected that the system controllers were smart enough and versatile enough to handle sophisticated formats. FM radio became the home for most radio automation systems.

FM during the early 1970s was rarely a money-making proposition. The FM side of a combo station was usually treated as a stepchild until the end of the decade, when station owners found they could make money — lots of it — from the listeners that were flocking to the FM band. FM began its rise to dominance, and AM began its decline to a secondary status.

The '70s ushered in a milestone in TV broadcasting: ENG. News reporting "live from the scene" became commonplace on the evening TV newscast as ENG began to grow and mature. Improved satellite relay and distribution systems helped give broadcasters a look of immediacy they had never seen before.

Satellite distribution of network radio began in 1979 when the Mutual Radio Network and National Public Radio went up on "the bird". During the same year, the Public Broadcasting Service began regular transmissions over its all-satellite distribution network. These pioneering efforts pointed the way for radio and TV network distribution during the 1980s.

Quad VTRs were in use at virtually every television station in the United States at the beginning of the '70s. As the decade wore on, however, users began to ask (or even beg) for an improved format. Three one-inch formats were offered: The *A* Format, introduced in 1973 by Ampex; a format similar to — but not compatible with — *A,* introduced by Sony; and the *B* Format, introduced in 1975 by Bosch. None of the three were not compatible, and following pressure from station engineers, a forth format — accepted by the major VTR suppliers — was developed. The *C* Format was first shown by Sony at the 1976 NAB in Chicago. By the end of the decade, the *C* Format had been accepted by SMPTE and ANSI as a national standard. The Bosch B format, because of its differences with the Ampex and Sony machines, was defined by SMPTE as its own standard.

The U Format was introduced in 1971 with little interest or fanfare. Intended initially as a consumer or industrial format, broadcasters paid little attention to it until the arrival of small, lightweight ENG cameras. At that point, a portable machine was needed. The *U* Format, with improvements to bring it up to broadcast quality, filled the bill.

Broadcasters began experimenting with teletext during the seventies. Experiments began in the U.K. in 1972, and migrated across the Atlantic to the U.S. By 1978, local stations were studying the possible applications of teletext.

Digital technology began to make its presence felt with the introduction of products containing microprocessors. Digital video products began to appear also, most notably the timebase corrector, introduced by Consolidated Video Systems in 1972. In 1978 a digital VTR was demonstrated, although it would be many years before the technology would mature into an actual product.

The Decade of the Eighties

If the pace of technology was rapid during the 1970s, it was been frantic during the next. The '80s was the decade of computers, digital audio and video processing and effects, new (and often confusing) videotape formats, satellite distribution, satellite news gathering, fiber optics and high definition television.

It is hard to over-estimate the impact of digital technology on the broadcast industry. Hardware and software borrowed from the computer industry changed the work that stations did, and the way that it was done. It was hard to imagine producing a commercial without digital video effects — flying characters, shimmering logos, marble backgrounds, page turns, posterized images, and all of the other visual sizzle used countless times during each broadcast day.

The first half of the decade was concerned primarily with generating the desired effects. Product price was important, but the real challenge was just making a machine produce what you wanted, at whatever price. After 1985, however, concern shifted from generating effects at any cost to producing new and dazzling effects at prices that open the market to more than just the top 5 to 10% of the post production houses and the major television networks.

Cost reduction with performance improvement is the byproduct of feverish development in the computer industry. First there was the 8086 microprocessor, then the '286, then the '386, and then the '486. With each improvement in microprocessor technology, and equally dramatic improvements in random access and hard disk memory, the features and performance of new systems improved, while at the same time the cost (usually) dropped.

Less visible during the decade to viewers, but equally important to broadcasters, was the video format fever that began in 1981. In that year, Sony introduced the Beta format for professional use and Matsushita (and others, including RCA) introduced the M format. These two 1/2-inch formats were aimed at essentially the same markets, ENG and EFP. The battle was on.

While the M format made little market penetration, it signaled the shape of things to come for the users of video recording equipment. The days when you could tell the type of format with a ruler were long gone. The industry had gotten a taste of this problem with the non-compatible 1-inch formats introduced during the 1970s. Users at the networks and local stations objected to the incompatibility of formats and forged, under the direction of SMPTE, a solution. Thus was born type *C*. Users hoping for a similar solution to the problems posed by 1/2-inch video formats were sadly disappointed during the decade of the '80s.

The M format was superseded in 1985 with the introduction by Panasonic of M-II. That move was followed a year later by a dramatic announcement by NBC that it would begin a program to convert its entire technical operation to M-II. That announcement guaranteed M-II would survive in the marketplace.

Other formats surfaced, including two digital recording formats, D-1 and D-2. D-1 represents the model of standardization. It is a true international standard to which equipment manufacturers in a number of countries subscribe. D-1 is also expensive. The machines are expensive and the digital component input/output ports present significant interface problems for an NTSC world. Enter D-2, the *composite* digital format. When first shown in prototype form in 1986 by Ampex (the ACR-225), many members of the broadcast and post production communities objected, saying that the D-1 standardization effort had been undermined. Time proved this not to be the case, as both formats began to find their own particular applications.

High definition TV both excited and frightened the professional video industry during the '80s. First demonstrated in the U.S. in 1981, the 1125/60 HDTV system developed by NHK in Japan went on to become an ANSI approved national standard. However, European countries launched — for a variety of reasons, some political — their own HDTV program, Eureka 95. Meanwhile here in the U.S., broadcasters and the FCC were grappling with the immense task of sorting out the 20 or so proposed improved definition, extended definition, enhanced definition and advanced definition TV systems for terrestrial television. It was clear that any hope for a worldwide standard on the production of high definition television had vanished, let alone a worldwide transmission standard.

While television spent the decade worrying about videotape formats and HDTV, AM radio was reeling from the effects of what probably could be considered the worst broadcast-related decision from the FCC since it picked the CBS whirling disc color system in 1950. Back then, however, the commission had the good sense to reverse itself. This time, we were not so lucky.

The "marketplace" decision on AM stereo left the industry arguing over the relative merits of the 5 proposed systems. Eventually, players dropped out one by one, until only Leonard Kahn (who had been working on stereo AM since the 1950s) and Motorola were left. The battle continued through the end of the decade. The big losers in this fight were the AM stations that desperately needed improved receivers in the field (which AM stereo would provide), and a new image in the eyes of young listeners.

While the commission kicked AM the pants with its "marketplace" decision, it patted FM on the back with docket 80-90. The ruling, which required FM stations to upgrade their facilities to certain minimum levels or face re-classification at a lower level, did more to spur a refurbishment of the FM band than anything since stereo. FM stations took their new-found wealth and invested it in new studio and transmitting plants.

The RF scoreboard for the 1980s is nothing short of amazing. Substantial progress was made across the board to improve transmitter reliability, performance and efficiency. The later attribute will pay long term dividends for the entire broadcast industry. UHF stations finally began to see light at the end of the efficiency tunnel. The tremendous efficiency penalties faced by UHF operations were removed by improved devices, including the Klystrode and the *multi-stage depressed collector* (MSDC) klystron.

AM broadcasters also shared in the efficiency gains, with all solid state, high efficiency transmitters up to and including 50kW. Increased efficiency translates to significant savings for stations, making facility updating an attractive option. FM radio and VHF-TV transmitters also improved during the decade, although not as dramatically as AM or UHF. The biggest change for FM and VHF was the use of solid state drivers for high power (20kW and above) units, and sophisticated fault diagnosis equipment built into the rigs.

All in all, the decade of the '80s was a period of dramatic growth and change. It was, in fact, about as much fun as the industry could stand.

CATEGORIES OF BROADCAST MEDIA

Basically there are three categories of broadcast media:

- Radio
- Television
- Internet

RADIO

Radio emerged as one of the most potent media of mass communication since it made possible the transmission and reception of signals by means of electronic wave and without the use of connecting wires. Within a century of its invention radio has grown enormously going out of Marconi's workshop to a permanent fixture in almost all the homes the world over.

Eventually the industry came to recognize radio as a way of stimulating sales. By 1930, a magazine, Billboard was reporting that "sheet music and record dealers now consider !radio a boon to their business, rather than a detriment." The magazine's initial radio coverage, a one-eighth-page section called Radio Entertainers that first appeared in 1928.

By 1930, the full-page Radio Entertainers section joined the front-cover list of Billboard's regularly covered entertainment businesses, which also included burlesque, skating rinks, rodeos, and, of course, popular songs. In those days, the magazine known as The Billboard was billed as "The Theatrical Digest And Show World Review." About that same time, stations' regular on-air personalities began to make news in Billboard, not just the visiting entertainers The radio business at that time was divided into independent and network-affiliated stations, and most programs aired in 15-minute blocks. Unlike today's focused, niche programming, a typical station's programming in 1932 was 62.9% music, 21.3% educational, 11.8% literature, 2.5% religion, and 1.5% "novelties," according to a study released that year.

Following the Japanese attack on Pearl Harbor and the start of U.S. involvement in World War II, Billboard's radio coverage focused on the medium's role in the war effort. That role was a vital one, since radio provided the country not only with news, but with public-service messages, entertainment, and much-needed morale boosting. In the war's first year, a typical NBC station aired 5,300 government announcements, 4,500 War Bond announcements, and 2,700 war-effort programs, for a total of

990 hours of war-related programming over and above news reports.

Many forms of presentations emerged and met extinction within a short life span of radio spreading over the last fifty years. By 1975, the once-popular nostalgia format was fading, drama radio had been dead for more than a decade, and the disco format was "being studied based on the records played in the growing number of discotheques throughout. Since its development in 1895, the radio has long since been revolutionizing the world. It has become so common that it is very improbable that one could ever pass a day without coming into contact with radio in some shape or fashion. In the beginning, radios were the only form of entertainment other than family outings and live shows such as those seen on Broadway. However, it seems like radio has outlived its passion for the programs and evening news and now concentrates almost completely on music.

Radio Broadcasting in India

In India, radio broadcasting was introduced by amateur clubs in Calcutta, Bombay, Madras and Lahore. The first among them was the Madras Club which came into existence on May, 16, 1924. It started broadcasting on July 31. At the early stage financial difficulties came in the way and forced the club to close down Broadcasting on a regular basis was resumed from 1927 when a private concern known as the Indian Broadcasting Company came into existence. The early years of the broadcasting were full of difficulties as it happens in all major ventures.

Earlier the set up run by the Government was called ISBS. It was given its present name All India Radio later. The change took effect from June 1936. The radio not only revolutionized the world but also created a new form of entertainment and education that will more than likely carry on for many centuries to come. Perhaps this invention was able to travel through space, collect tremendous amounts of data from the universe, and spell out for us the reality of new frontiers waiting to be explored. Truly the radio will live on forever.

With the advent of community broadcasting, a whole new exciting world awaits listeners in far-flung areas where radio listening revolves around community centres. The proposed community radio serves to bring small groups together through their own participation to reflect their day-to-day concerns. The community will participate by creating contents of the programmes for its own people. This narrow broad casting does not require big transmitters. Community radio of the future will strive to bring people together through interaction. Like teleconferencing, the listeners will be able to talk to each other through the radio network using small wireless sets. This will help in business activities of the particular district or a village where the artisan will know his prospective buyer for his wares. At present, however, programmes will be created for the listeners in the community and reflect what is relevant for their needs and aspirations. The community in these areas is well-knit.

There is always a collective response to all radio programmes as the listeners generally assemble at one place where they listen to radio programmes, discuss and react. This turns into public service broadcast because it is here that the aspirations of the people can be fulfilled. To achieve this, the programmes have to be drawn up with a foresight keeping in mind the priorities of varied areas so that people can easily identify themselves with the programmes. Out of the existing network of All India Radio, the Frequency Modulation, commonly known as the FM, technique of the radio wave has a distinct advantage. The Medium Wave and Short Wave suffer from the disadvantage of deteriorating sound quality with the increase in distance. The FM provides stereo quality and is ideal for short-range broadcasts.

In the far-flung rural areas where the availability of power supply is unreliable, the FM is ideally suited for community broadcast for dissemination of information, education and entertainment. The Working Group on the 10th Plan has recommended future expansion of radio, primarily in the FM mode. To supplement the broadcasting by All India Radio, the Government, in July 1999, approved private participation in FM broadcasting. After offering licenses to private FM broadcasting in 40 cities through 110 channels for commercial broadcasting, the Government has decided to offer private licenses to the established educational institutions and organizations having their own campus and residential schools

AIR has a large number of FM transmitters covering more than 21 per cent of area and about 31 per cent population of the country. Private licensees for FM broadcasting have been offered in 40 cities for 110 channels for setting up 10 KW radio transmitters, except in four metro cities where the capacity could be between 10 to 20 KW. These private channels are already operating in Delhi, Mumbai, Kolkata, Chennai, Bangalore, Indore, Ahemedabad, Pune and Lucknow. Next in the line are Patna, Bhuvaneswar, Cuttack, Jabalpur, Coimbatore, Tirunelveli and Vishakhapatnam. The number of channels will provide plurality of choice to the listeners leading to improvement in the quality of programmes.

To start with, programmes on the community radio service will focus on issues relating to education, health, environment, agriculture and rural and community development. The Government expects these programmes to be popular if done innovatively done to sustain the listeners' interest. This service is expected to provide a platform for students and teachers to give expression to their creative talent in producing programmes and in socio-cultural cohesion of the masses at the local level. The licensees will not be allowed to broadcast any news, current affairs programmes, election and political broadcasts. They will also not be allowed to air any advertisement of sponsored programmes.

The Government is aware of the need to safeguard the radio stations from being misused for desirable propaganda against national interest and safety and security of the country. Therefore, in the first phase, the Government has given licenses to only the selected and established educational institutions in the country for community broadcasts. For the sake of credibility, the licensees will ensure that nothing is included in the program that goes against good taste and decency. The code of conduct rules out anything obscene, defamatory and innuendos. The licensees will also ensure that there is nothing that amounts to contempt of court or by casting aspersions on the integrity of the President or the judiciary. The program code will almost be the same as for All India Radio. It would strive to promote national integration, religious harmony, scientific temper and Indian culture. The applicant will be permitted only one licence valid for three years and the licence will provide service on free-to-air basis. No channel will be permitted for commercial purposes.

The Government will have the right to inspect broadcast facilities and reserve the right to take over the entire services or network or revoke or suspend the licence in the interest of national security. The licensee will ensure that all foreign personnel likely to be appointed as employees or consultants obtain security clearance from the Government. The licensee will be expected to furnish a bank guarantee to ensure timely performance of the licensee agreement and failure to start the services within the stipulated period can result in cancellation of licence and forfeiture of the bank guarantee. The people are likely to immensely benefit from community radio because of its inter-active nature and low costs of broadcasting. (PIB Features)

On 2 May 1996, All India Radio got connected on the information superhighway, by mounting an experimental on - line information service on the Internet. AIR daily news update, commentary on topics from current affairs and the significant highlights from the country's newspapers are fed regularly once a day in text mode. The system and home page design for this pilot service has been executed by the Research Department of AIR. The address for the site is : http:/air.kode.net. This AIR service on the Net has received global appreciation and in the first ten days itself, over 7.5 lakh hits were reported. Most of the users are non - resident Indians and diplomats / officials all over the world. The experience and insightful feedback gathered from this experimental program will be useful for setting up a regular information service of AIR on the Net.

The following are the characteristics of radio :

Easy accessibility

Radio is accessible to the majority of our countryman in comparison to the other media. Low cost transistors within the easy reach even the economically weak people are available in the market. It can therefore, be used as means of imparting education.

Wide Coverage

Today we cover a major portion of our territory by radio broadcasts as broadcast facility is available through out the world. As such, the radio can extend learning at a distance as it can easily and quickly reach the isolated rural audiences. The AIR has many years of experience of combining the radio with correspondence and non-formal education.

Low capital investment and operating cost

Radio technology is comparatively cheap in terms of installation and production of radio broadcast, it is quite economical and needs less production facilities compared to other electronic media.

Easy learner-reception

Radio broadcast can be listened to even while one is doing manual work. Distance learners can listen to programmes from where ever they desire to.

Effective thought promotion

Radio taps the thinking process of the learners as listening is invariably accompanied by simultaneous information processing. It can also stimulate the listener imagination with a tactful used of music or techniques of pause.

Motivative supportive facilities

Broadcasting can make education interesting and enjoyable, when it is used imaginatively. The feeling and motivation of learners can be stimulated and directed by music and other sound effect.

Easy production

Production of creative radio programs is simpler compared to TV or video program production. No complicated mechanism, nor any sophisticated instruments are need for such productions. It requires less manpower compared to the production of a TV/ video program..

Effective recreation/Transmission of reality

A powerful audio version brings a scene into sharp focus and also establishes movement effectively. A live broadcast can make listeners share the experience of a scene of reality taking place, say some hundred mile away. It can also make listeners partake of an experience of a scene of the past that took place, say some hundred years ago.

Feasible mode of learner enrichment

The most common function of media in education is enrichment. This function is easy to materialize with the help of radio and relatively with little expense.

Direct instruction

The use of radio for direct instruction has been tried. This, however, demands intensive and systematic use of the radio. Under such scheme syllabus based programmes are broadcast for definite target groups.

Alongside the non-broadcast use of audio in the form of taped lessons, radio broadcasting is equally popular means of serving the need of education. The reach of radio now extends to all nooks and corners of the world. In India, school broadcasting first started in 1938 followed by Tanzania in 1954 and Kenya in

1963. The first radio programmes were broadcast successfully in England in 1920. School broadcasting as a part of educational broadcasting began in 1924. At present, there is a huge network of local stations operating in almost all the countries of the world.

School Broadcast

Even before the AIR came into existence there was occasional broadcast for schools from Bombay and Calcutta. It was only in 1937 that organized school broadcasting in Calcutta. Funds were allotted to schools to buy radio sets. Out of enthusiasm, the AIR authorities embarked on school programmes from Delhi, Calcutta, Madras and Bombay without waiting for schools to acquire radio sets. In the beginning, the school programmes were not strictly governed by the curriculum, With the passage of time an acquisition of more experience. The AIR tried to make its radio broadcast more curriculum oriented but in the absence of common syllabi and time table in school, even within the same states, it could not success in making its broadcast fully curriculum oriented.

The AIR is assisted by various agencies in planning their educational programs, particularly the programmes for the young-the primary and the secondary level students.

University Broadcasts

Radio programmes on subjects of academic interests have been broadcast from the AIR stations from the very beginning of organized broadcasting. In 1965, an attempt was made to assess the impact of these broadcasts on students and it was found that there was little interest among students. It was believed that the desire to expand higher education as widely as possible among the different strata of the society, could be fulfilled through the use of educational radio broadcasts. Consequently two types of programmes, general and enrichment came into existence. While general programmes include topics of general interest the enrichment programmes support correspondence education offered by universities in a respective jurisdiction.

Responsibilities for planning of the courses rests with the educators while their broadcast is arranged by the radio stations in consultation with the universities.

Language Learning

In 1979-80 the AIR conceived of and implemented an experiment to use radio broadcast for language teaching. The experiment was conducted in collaboration with the Department of Education, Government of Rajasthan. Under this experiment an attempt was made to teach Hindi as first language to school going children. The experiment was named 'the Radio Pilot Project' and it aimed to cover 500 primary schools of Jaipur and Ajmer districts. The Project was found useful for the children and research studies have revealed the contribution of the Project to the improvement of the vocabulary of the children.

Future Trends in Educational Radio

The future of radio apparently looks bleak with the developments in educational television and the other sophisticated media of communication like Internet. Still it is popular among the rural masses and the economically weak sections of the society. It is hoped that radio will enjoy long life to serve the educational and developmental purposes of the society since to cater to the educational and entertainment needs, we cannot switch over to the other sophisticated gadgets overnight.

TELEVISION

Television was first started in the United States of America in 1920 on experimental basis. These experiments used a mechanical scanning method with the help of a disc that did not scan a picture rapidly. Picture tube, which was invented in 1923 brought some advantage in the method. By 1930 NBC had set up its TV station in New York. Simultaneously BBC started offering regular TV programmes.

The breakout of second World War reduced the speed of improvement in TV technology but by 1940s and early 1950s, television had become a feature of life in the most developed countries. In 1948, there were as many as 48 TV stations in the United States covering 23 cities through receiving sets which number about half a million. Within the next one decade the number jumped to 533 stations covering 55 million receivers. The other advanced countries mainly Canada, Germany and Japan did not leg behind in the new venture.

In fact, television in India was started as an educational project of UNESCO. Its distinct advantage is the vastness of the geographical area it covers by the telecast. The main disadvantage was the enormous expenditure which has now been reduced considerable with the introduction of the new communication technology. It is a tool for visualization of the events and a visual demonstration of rare and complex materials improve presentation of aspects of physical sciences, medicine, geography and the elements of drama and history.

According to the Ministry of Information and Broadcasting, the following are the objectives of public television in India;

(a) To act as a catalyst for social change

(b) To promote national integration

(c) To stimulate a scientific temper among the people

(d) To disseminate the message of family planning as a means of population control

(e) To stimulate greater agriculture production by providing essential information and knowledge,

(f) To promote and help preservation of environmental and ecological balance

(g) To highlight the need of social welfare measures including welfare of women, children and the less privileged

(h) To promote interest in games and sports

(i) To stimulate appreciation of our artistic and cultural heritage.

In the advanced countries, educational television has been developed well. Many institutions offering education with the audiovisual modes have come into existence. The British Open University makes wide use of TV-time to beam its various faculty programs. The United States' public television programmes for schools serve teachers and students in the classroom and at home besides National University Consortium consisting of several colleges.

The followings are the characteristics of television :

Social Equality in Education

Television promotes the goal of social equality in education catering to the masses of rural background and those living in slums of urban areas. Television increases the effectiveness of instruction and cuts down dropout rates.

Higher quality of Instruction

Television programmes are well planned/ organized and better presented than the usual classroom instruction.

Reduce dependency on teacher

The students learn from television with their own efforts. They need minimum help from the teacher in case television is pressed into service.

Flexibility

Rapid and continuing change in curricula and instructional methods are made possible through educational television. Courses can be constantly modified not only to update them but to incorporate the constantly changing needs of the society and the expansion of knowledge. This is not possible with some of the advanced electronic media like the videodisk.

Use of the best available teacher

Educational television make educational opportunity equal through out the country. The students in rural and deprived areas of the country, where educational resources are not available, get the same quality of education as their counterparts in the urban centers. The best teacher is equally available for every student. Thus television bridges the gap between the poor and the rich, the privileged and the under privileged, the rural and the urban.

Cost Effectiveness

If television is utilized on a large scale, then it proves cost-effective. It can provide education through out the country at a minimum cost without lowering the quality of instruction. The initial expenditure of course, will be high.

In-Service Training

Educational television can be used for in-service training of educators in non-school hours.

Logistically Simple

In operating an effective distance education system, educational television is logically very simple. The problems of planning, implementing and operating distance learning can be overcome by some extent by teaching through television.

Combination of Audi and Video Components

Television has the advantage of audio as well as video. That is why it has a greater appeal than the audio and the print media.

Stimulation

Through educational television, we can control the stimulation to get desired response.

Mass Education

Educational Television can cater to the explosive increase in student numbers.

Growth of Educational Television in India

The Government of India set up the Verghees Committee in 1978 which strongly recommended granting broadcasting franchise to the educational institutions empowering national level institutions in higher education to use low-power radio or television transmission solely for the propagation of quality education to large masses of students and others.

The Delhi Centre of TV took the decision of telecasting curriculum-based lessons on selected subjects, particularly on science with an objective of improving standard in the teaching of science at the secondary level. The disadvantage of shortage of teachers in science subjects was also overcome by the visual medium thus offered by television. The evaluation of results of the educational broadcast also suggested its usefulness as 'an aid to the teaching of science subjects'. According to a NCERT (National Council of Educational Research and Training) survey on the utilization of educational television in schools under the Delhi Administration, only 30% of the 500 schools provided with receivers in the secondary classes for which 16 lessons were telecast every week, hardly switched on the program. Some of the reasons are poor maintenance of receivers, shoddy viewing conditions in the classroom, indifference among teachers and students. Television Centres in the other parts of the country transmit educational programmes in English, Hindi and the other regional languages.

Television is regarded as the most powerful medium of mass communication. It is widely used for the instruction of students at all levels: primary, secondary and university. Now most of the TV channels are being run privately. The Government of India is also very much concerned about the utilization of the potential of television in education. Doordarshan more telecast time for education through its various national, regional and ETV service than ever before.

There are many factors responsible for steady growth of television as a medium of instruction. One of the most significant among them is the replacement of celluloid by video which contributed to at least a 10 times reduction in the price of the medium. The cost of TV sets, VCRs, VCPs, cassettes, cameras, editing and the post-production equipment is going down because of the technological advancements. Ten years back, a film of 30 minutes duration on video involved an expenditure of around one lakh on its production. The approximate cost today is Rs. 30,000/. Further the programmes have a higher degree of resolution. The number of viewers has gone up considerably because of the access to the medium and its popularity. Various surveys suggest a shift in the learning behavior of students and increasingly more dependence on the audio visual media.

In 1984, the University Grants Commission introduced the Countrywide Classroom. The work was coordinated at the Mass Communication Research Centre of Jamia Millia Islamia in New Delhi. Over the time, it has registered growth in terms of the resources available and the number of viewers through out the country. The broadcast is available in Hindi also in addition to English language.

UGCs INSAT'/TV Project popularly known as the Countrywide Classroom was launched at the Mass Communication Research Centre, Jamia Millia Islamia, New Delhi. It heralded an era for the educational communication in the country. A number of Educational Media Research Centres/ Audio Visual Research Centres were established to augment the process of production of educational software.

In 1984 only 20% indigenous programmes were telecast on Doordarshan whereas by 1992 this ratio was just reversed and 80% of the productions were produced within the country. Now a separate TV channel of educational communication is working in the country like the other advanced nations and the ratio of indigenously produces educational software is very high comparing with the last decade.

In this direction an exclusive 24 hours Educational TV, Gyandarshan, has been implemented by Doordarshan. Gyandarshan channel was shifted from INSAT-2B to INSAT-3C once the latter became operational in February 2002.

Transmission (analogue + digital) using the same transponder was introduced in March 2002. Indira Gandhi National Open University (IGNOU) is planning to replace analogue transmission by five more digital channels by March 2003. All the six digital channels will be earmarked for specific aspects of educational/ developmental programmes in technical education, agriculture, vocational, secondary education and distance education.

Curriculum-based programmes are produced with active involvement of State educational administrators and teachers. Satellite based enrichment programmes for school children are produced by the State Institutes of Educational Technology (SIET): Marathi at Pune, Gujarati at Ahmedabad, Oriya at Bhubaneshwar and Telugu at Hyderabad which are relayed by all transmitters in the concerned states. Hindi programmes are produced at State Institutes of Educational Technology at Delhi, Lucknow and Patna. Education Media Research Centres and Audio Visual Research Centres at different places produce programmes for university students. These enrichment programmes provide quality education within the reach of students in small towns and villages

The University Grants Commission appointed a Curriculum Development Committee to design common curricula for all the universities. It was a positive sign for the media production agencies. Earlier they had problem in deciding the contents of a program since the syllabi of nearly all the institutions were different. Now, producers are. able to identify the themes of the programmes that have the widest application.

Educational Media Production Agencies

A number of educational media production agencies have been established for production of software. These agencies include, Doordarshan, Inter University Consortium for Educational Communication; mass Communication Research Centre/Educational Media Centres/Audio Visual Research Centre, Central Institute of Educational Technology/State

Institutes of Educational Technology/District Institute of Educational Technology, Indian Institutes of Technology, Technical Teachers Training Institutes, Agriculture Universities, Indira Gandhi National Open University/Electronic' Media Production Centre, Central Institute of Indian languages and other Govt. and private; agencies.

From the decade of 1980's onwards, a number of educational media organizations have come into existence. They include government as well as private agencies. Some of the popular media organizations are the following:

(a) Central Institute of Educational Technology (CIET)

CIET at the National Council of Educational Research and Training, New Delhi is a premier media organization of the country, mainly entrusted with the work of producing educational software for radio and television programmes. It is involved in the teaching and learning enhancement of the schoolteachers and students through its various activities.

The CIET stated in 1942 as an adjunct to the Department of Education of the Government of India. After independence it formed the nucleus of the Audio Visual Section of the Ministry of Education in 1948. With the birth of National Institute of Audio Visual Education in 1959, it became a part of the Institute. In 1961, when the Institute was merged with NCERT, it was renamed as the Department of Teaching.

CIET organizes workshops and training programmes for the staff of SIETs and DIETs in management of library collections and documentation. One such seminar was organized in collaboration with UNESCO in 1986 and its theme was Documentation Systems for Educational Media. Later on in 1992, another workshop was organized on management of media collections in CIET. SIET and DIET libraries

(b) Consortium for Educational Communication (CEC)

CEC was established in 1993 to undertake the challenging

activities relating to the Countrywide Classroom of the University Grants Commission. CEC has the responsibility for coordination with the media centers, the University Grants Commission and television as well as for overall system management related to the broadcast of educational programmes.

CEC is the custodian of all the master tapes produced by the Media Centers and has a computerized Media Tape Library with up-to-date storage and retrieval facilities. It also has facilities for program production and dobbing of English programmes in other Indian languages through a digital audio workstation.

E-mail and Internet facilities have been provided to the Library. For which sufficient computer hardware support is available. One of the most significant feature is that the Library uses a software for its operations which has specifically been designed for the tape libraries with assistance from the Development and Educational Communication Unit of the Space Application Centre, Ahmedabad.

(c) Electronic Media Production Centre (EMPC)

EMPC is situated at the Sanchar Kendra of the Indira Gandhi National Open University (IGNOU) New Delhi. It is equipped with the state of the art technology. EMPC is the Centre from which the Gyan Darshan-Educational TV Channel of Doordarshan telecast its programmes.

EMPC produces audio an video courseware of IGNOU programmes, disseminate educational programmes through both broadcast and non-broadcast modes, coordinates with the broadcasting and distribution agencies, adapts and integrates new communication technologies for distance learning: develops quality courseware in media studies and provides hands on experimental training to educational institutions/agencies, conducts researches to strengthen the content utilization and delivery aspects of distance learning: develops and offers audio/ video library resources designs and coordinate pilot projects in the application of communication technology to improve and strengthen distance learning and also undertakes marketing and sale of EMPC/IGNOU products and facilities.

(d) Commonwealth Educational Media Centre for the Asia (CEMCA)

CEMCA was founded in 1987 by the Commonwealth Heads of Government at their meeting in Vancouur, Canada. The Commonwealth of Learning (COL) has a mandate to the development of knowledge resources and technology for learning through out Commonwealth countries. CEMCA is hosted by the Indira Gandhi National Open University in India and it covers the Asian Commonwealth region comprising of Bangladesh. Brunei, India, Malaysia, The Maldives, Pakistan, Singapore and Sri Lanka.

(a) Media databases

CEMCA Media Database contains information about audio and video programmes developed by the educational institutions in the region. The database can be searched through title-keyword, subjects, producer, institution and many other options. The database is constantly updated and is made available off line to participating institutions twice through CD ROM services.

(b) Educational Media Links

This facility links all the educational media organizations of the Commonwealth countries such as radio, TV, online information networks etc.

(c) Archives

CEMCA operates as a regional service to COL. Workshop on multimedia courseware and development on media management are on the anvil. It also covers educational materials on application of television production techniques of teleteaching.

(d) Promotion of Research

CEMCA promotes research on use of information and communication technologies through appropriate funding, training and capacity building of researchers. Research proposals are also invited from interested scholars and researches withir the scope of CEMCA's mandate through out the year of consideration. Currently, thrust areas of research at CEMCA include:

(1) Use of multimedia by distance learners
(2) Learning from multimedia
(3) Use of ICT for development and training
(4) Internet and World Wide Web
(5) ITC for people with disabilities
(6) Digital divide
(7) Gender issues in technology use in education.

The ultimate aim of CEMCA is to promote cooperation and collaboration among educational and broadcasting organizations in the Commonwealth in the use of electronic media by promoting the development of human resources through the application of distance education techniques and technologies in response to the development needs of the member countries. The deployment of modern communication and information technologies can be a major instrument for widening access to learning, enhancing the quality of education and providing cost-effective education to a large segment of the population for their social and economic betterment. The creation of a common database on educational media resources is the major function of CEMCA.

Video and audio signals can be sent round the globe by broadcasting on Internet. Each individual's Internet connection can virtually be used manifold. An individual cannot only receive what is available internationally but can contribute to the resources whatever he or she wishes to upload for the benefit of the mankind. This will facilitate an exponential growth in the bulk of the media resources, consequently, standardisation of methods of entry and retrieval will become mandatory. We have already achieved success in case of the textual information in this direction The Common Communication Format recommended by UNESCO for data entry and retrieval will certainly lead to serious thinking in the matter and the efforts in listing all the available educational media resources drawn from all over the world will soon become a reality for the common man.

Resource Sharing

The Educational Television (ETV) has grown faster during the last one decade. The setting up of the Mass Communication Research Centre (MCRC) at the Jamia Millia Islamia in New Delhi in 1985 with the assistance of the Canadian International Development Agency is regarded as a milestone in the history of ETV in India. The year is significant because two other national agencies namely the Central Institute of Educational Technology (CIET) and the Indira Gandhi National Open University (IGNOU) were also established in the same year.

India has two well established networks for the ETV production and distribution. The Countrywide Classroom (CWCR) of the University Grants Commission had its modest beginning as INSAT TV Project at MCRC and the first program under the project went on air on 15th of August 1984. Initially the programmes were aimed at the postgraduate students as sufficient infrastructure was not available to cope with the production needs for the undergraduates. Gratified with the success of the project, the Government of India decided to establish media centres in all the regions of the country. As a result, the Educational Media Research Centres (EMRCs) and the Audio Visual Research Centres (AVRCs) were established. The programmes produced by all these agencies are being telecast by the Consortium for Educational Communication (CEC) in the Countrywide Classroom.

In 1984 hardly 20% home-made programmes were telecast in the CWCR and the dependence on the foreign countries mainly

USA, Russia, England, Germany and Australia was 80%. Within a decade the Consortium for Educational Communication has created a sound base of around 3,500 programmes excluding the non-broadcast titles. There is another significant change as far as the viewer ship is concerned. The decision to telecast CWCR programmes in Hindi yielded better results as till today the majority of college and university students in North India do not properly understand the programmes in English. A survey published in the *University News* 15 August 1994 issue has revealed these findings.

The Development and Educational Communication Unit (DECU) of the Indian Space Research Organization (ISRO), Ahmedabad has come out with a software package for automation and networking of the libraries of CWCR. Their software has been improved over the years by incorporating changes as a result of the practical difficulties in its use as experienced by the various media centres of CWCR. The software has already been distributed to all the EMRCs and AVRCs with a suggestion to mount the record of productions in the prescribed format. The staff of media centres has been trained in advance for its use. It is possible to improve the software further in order to use it for networking of all CWCR libraries providing the E-Mail facility with the Consortium for Educational Communication as a central agency. But despite all the abovementioned efforts the software is hardly being used by any media centre except MCRC so far.

Networking and resource sharing is possible only after the availability of data, a suitable software package and also the telecommunication link to transmit the information both in the form of text as well as audio visual media in case of the ETV libraries. So far there has not been a single notable effort in centrally listing all the available ETV productions so that a comprehensive record may be available. The first major attempt in compilation of the union catalogue was made by the Electronic Trade and Technology Ltd., New Delhi. They have been basically a supplier of electronic hardware items who occasionally undertook the production as well as the distribution of ETV programmes.

Now the work of distribution has been undertaken by Educational International, New Delhi. In addition to the programmes of CWCR, CIET, SIETs, they are negotiating with IITs, IIMs, IGNOU and many other producing agencies for distribution of their ETV productions. The advantage attached with WEL is that they have a long history of book supply and understand the educational needs of the academic community. Perhaps this is the reason why the sale of their programmes has increased enormously.

Resource sharing among ETV libraries will be useful in many respects. It will not only make possible the compilation of a union catalogue of all the media centres but will also facilitate the finalization of the topics of the forthcoming productions. By sharing the stock shots, which are very rare some- times, the cost of production can be minimized considerably. There are instances when complete video productions have been raised by using the stock footage only and without even touching a camera. Since many of the educational disciplines are closely related and contain the same fragments of subjects it will be possible to use such common shots in all the related programmes.

INTERNET

Internet is the next paradigm shift in human life after the printing press. It has provided a powerful medium of communication for individuals of different tastes. And education is no exception. Virtual universities are being established all over the world and the beginning has already been made in India with about all major cities organizing such institutional support to the students. One can enroll with such universities for the desired academic course without being physically present.

With increasing convergence between computer and communication technologies and the spread of telecommunication networks, present day open universities are expected to gradually transform themselves as virtual universities where all functions of the university will take place electronically over the digital links and networks,

The origin of Internet is traced to the beginning of computer communication project called ARPANET which was established in 1969. This computer network was transformed into the Internet in 1989 when the total users worldwide began to explode. It became more famous by its communication services like e-mail which is more quick and economic unlike the postal services. The early 1990s saw a very rapid rate of Internet adoption including the World Wide Web, specially after the development of MOSAIC, a software technology that made the Internet much more user-friendly.

Growth of Internet

Internet became more popular by its feature of the World Wide Web in 1991 Tim Berners-Lee, a young scientist working in European Particle Physics Laboratory (CERN) produced Internet's first browser. According to him, "the dream behind the Web is of a common information space in which we communicate by sharing information. "By its application, someone could scan every document or photo or video on the net". It gave an opportunity to share the resources by individuals and organizations on the basis of mutual understanding. In the past ten years, it has been so popular that the number of Internet users jumped from 600,000 to 140 million and it is expected to grow further to 350 millions within the next three years.

Internet has emerged as the most powerful medium for storage and retrieval of information. It works round the clock and connects every nook and corner of the globe. With an unprecedented growth in the quantum of knowledge worldwide and the easy accessibility, Internet has become an unavoidable necessity for every institution of higher learning and research. Internet is continuously growing internationally. Within a short span of ten years, its services have been spread among all the nations of the world. In 1991 it was within the reach of 73 countries but within four years of its existence Internet reached 148 countries. The number of Internet users is also increasing tremendously as they are almost doubled after every two years. In the meanwhile Internet widened its scope. Now it is used for storage, manipulation and dissemination of textual data as well as the multimedia.

With the increasing dependant on micro literature for research in the universities and the availability of improved technology for information handling, the traditional library practices of classification and cataloguing are proving to be less relevant. As the information needs of users even in the academic institutions are satisfied with some alternate means. The growing use of Internet by medical and engineering institutions is a clear indication of what is in store for the libraries of the future? PUBMED, a service of the National Library of Medicine provides access to over 11 millions of citations back to the mid 1960s and additional life science journals. It includes links to many similar websites providing full text articles and other related resources. The service is available free of cost. Journals are the most pertinent sources of information for research in the universities. They are available in plenty on Internet. Moreover a large number of them is free of cost and if priced they cost less compared to their print counterpart. After the print media, journals could not figure in any other format except the digital media. The audiovisuals remained short lived and barring a few political ones no worth mentioning journal could surface in the audiovisual media.

Advantages of Internet

Universal Availability of Information

Internet has democratized the process of higher education in the true sense librating it from the clutches of the few knowledgeable and powerful without whom research was a distant dream for the students. It has affected almost every sphere of human activities. In the field of education, the work of traditional gurus has been taken over by Internet now, which provides information on the latest advancements and researches taking place in the various disciplines of study. It also supports further activities of collecting data, analyzing and synthesizing it. Moreover it presents the events in international perspective hence the research work is supposed to be unique whereas the chances for repetition were higher in the past when things were perceived in the limited geographical limits.

Resource Sharing Medium

Internet has not only facilitated resources sharing across the boundaries of the countries but also freed libraries from many complicated and inconvenient practices such as the inter library lending where the documents were required to be dispatched physically. It involved risk of loss. Only the trusted institutions could render the service on the basis of mutual understanding. The idea was always good but it could never work satisfactorily.

Internet services are easily available and affordable as the cost of connectivity and computer hardware and software has come down considerably during the last few years. Moreover, there has been standardization in the ever-changing configuration of systems. The software has been made more user friendly for computer as well as netsurfing. Now, the services are also being offered through cable TV and in case this facility widens there will be no need to purchase the computer hardware and software at all.

Largest Storehouse of Information

Now, Internet has emerged as the most powerful medium for storage and retrieval of information. It works round the clock and connects every nook and corner of the globe. With an unprecedented growth in the quantum of knowledge worldwide and the easy accessibility, Internet has become an unavoidable necessity for every institution of higher learning and research.

There has been an unprecedented growth in the quantum of information on Internet. World's two famous search engines, namely google.com and yahoo.com allow access to 4.2 billions and 3.1 billions of home pages. The other search engines have websites in addition to it.

Internet in India

Internet is the newest of the information technologies that have made a very recent entry in India. The exact date of inception of Internet in the country is not known. However, it is safe to assume that the beginning was made less than a decade ago. It made a very slow beginning mainly because of the costs were initially prohibitive and the plans and policies for its growth were either inadequate or silent and definitely not very facilitative. The necessary infrastructure was not at a very advanced stage and was certainly not geared to its use on a large scale. The picture in the last five years or so is showing a major shift both policy-wise as well as infrastructure-wise. Internet has now started growing at a very fast rate.

India was one of the few countries to enact the Information Technology Act 2000 to enable Digital signatures and e-commerce. Setting up of gateways for Internet, laying of fibers & cables was freely permitted to the ISPs. Tax incentives were showered on the industry, infrastructure status given & mergers and acquisitions facilitated. Unfortunately the result is not in line with expectations of what has happened elsewhere in the world. The net users still stagnated at 5 million, less than India's 7 million mobile phones and less than 12% of the 42 million telephone connections in India. What went wrong in India which did not go wrong in the other countries?

The estimated number of Internet subscribers varies from 500,000 to a little over 600,000. It is estimated that there are about 30 million Internet users in the country. It is still largely a metro or an urban phenomenon. However, it is spreading into small towns very fast and it has also made inroads in the rural areas. Indians, by and large, have adopted this technology very fast. This holds true both user-wise as well as business-wise. As it will be seen in the later part of the article, even illiterate persons have started to avail of the services of the Internet facilities. A large number of Indians know English well and this facilitates the use of the technology. In addition, several Indian language based websites are created which make the use of Internet even more user-friendly and popular.

According to the Indian Government's Planning Commission, the number of Internet connections in the country will grow from more than 3 million now to 23 million during its 10th Five-Year Plan, which is scheduled to end in 2007. Other private agencies have looked at India's Internet subscriber numbers as well.

A recent study by the Gartner Group has suggested that the country has topped the list of Internet users in the Asia Pacific region for 2001. India has an estimated 3.1 million regular Internet surfers, although the number of registered users would hover at just about 1 million. The study conducted by India's Manufacturers Association of Information Technology (MAIT) has revealed that the number of Internet subscribers has increased to 1.12 million during the 2000 - 2001 period from just 651,000 in the previous year; the home segment registered a whopping compounded annual growth rate (CAGR) of 215 percent. "The number of active Internet subscribers increased to 1.12 million by March 2001, leading to 67 percent penetration among PC-owning business establishments and 54 percent penetration in PC-owning homes,".

IDC India predicts that the number of Internet users will grow eight-fold to 37.5 million by end-2005, representing a CAGR of 53 percent for the period 2000 - 2003; the research firm had estimated that there were 4.47 million unique Internet users in India in 2000. India is expected to be next only to China in the Asia Pacific region in terms of total number of Internet users by end-2005. IDC also forecasts that India's home and small business segments will drive the growth in the Internet user base for the next five years. For the period 2000 - 2005, the Internet user base in the home segment is expected to witness a CAGR of 87 percent, while that of the small business segment is expected to grow by a CAGR of 72 percent. Despite the differences in actual prediction figures, all agencies have agreed on one point India is expected to see the highest growth rate in the region's Internet market in the next five years. Seeking to promote the spread of the Internet, the Planning Commission said that telecom operators must get the required bandwidth and the last-mile connection to achieve that aim.

The use of cable network and DSL technologies may be actively promoted to provide higher bandwidth to Internet users. "For dial-up Internet users, telephone call charges are a major element of cost, with the higher local call charges and multi-metering of local calls discouraging its usage. Call charges for Internet use need to be brought down substantially," according to the Planning Commission's report. Creation of a separate Ministry of Information Technologies and sound proactive policy decisions have helped the growth of IT sector in the country. Internet is one of those technologies to benefit from it. Initially only government agencies like VSNL and Department of Telecommunications were permitted to be Internet Service Providers (ISPs). This sector has now been opened up to private entrepreneurs and there are already about 300 Internet service providers in the country. The exact number of Indian web sites is difficult to determine. But it definitely runs into hundreds. India has slowly started entering into the e-commerce area.

Some estimations of the profile of the Indian Internet users are available through studies of NASSCOM, IMRB etc. 80 per cent of the users are males, they belong to the 19-34 year age group. The average time spent is 10 hours per week and nearly 90 per cent of the use is for email purpose. The estimated advertising spent per user comes to Rs.140/- (about 4 dollars) and less than 5 per cent of the users buy anything on the net.

The use of Internet is dependent on the following factors:

(1) cost of the computer

(2) cost of subscription and telephone; and

(3) efficiency of the telephone lines.

The cost of the personal computers has been coming down very substantially. It is possible to obtain a good configuration PC for about 700 to 800 dollars. The rate of growth of the PCs has been very fast. In 1999, the estimated number of PCs was 3.2 million and growing fast. The growth can really now be described as exponential. It is important to look at the other necessary link of Internet, the telephone. The estimated number of telephones is 20 million. In India the telephone user is required to pay even for in-city calls. A call is for a duration of 3 minutes. So in an hour of continuous usage of telephone, it amounts to making 20 calls.

Use of the telephone for an hour will cost approximately Rs. 30/-. Apart from the cost, a major problem really lies with the state of technology of the telephones. It largely uses a very archaic technology especially while covering "the last mile", i.e. from the telephone exchange to the subscribers. The bandwidth of the line is very low and that slows down Internet especially the download of graphics, sound or even the text material. This would mean that it takes much longer for a transaction to be completed or for downloading of a file or for accessing information and so on. All this adds to the cost. Apart from the expenditure for the phone call, the subscriber has to pay a fixed yearly amount to the ISP. The exact amount is dependent upon the number of hours per year that one subscribes to. These costs have been coming down steadily because of the increased competition. But still it is on the higher side. In a year if one books 500 hours of Internet use, it would cost the subscriber about 135 dollars. For using 500 hours of subscription, one has to pay equivalent to 10,000 telephone calls which comes to another 225 dollars and thus total cost of the subscriber is 360 dollars per year. Given the overall spending capacity of the Indians and taking into account several other priorities Internet subscription will remain by and large a preserve of the rich and the upper middle classes.

However, one must hasten to add the fact that the per capita use of the technology in India is always much higher than the actual subscribers. This has happened in several other technologies in the past. When the number of television sets were fewer, it was observed that a large number of persons of the neighbourhood would come and watch program. Several neighbours and friends use a telephone. Even the newspaper is often borrowed and read by more than one family. Similar thing happens about the Internet. Large number of what have come to be known as cybercafé kiosks has come up. A cybercafé would charge approximately Rs. 30/- hour of use of the Internet. A large number of users avail of this facility. The Internet is also very much an institutional arrangement in India. That means in an office one account will be used by a much greater number of persons as happened in the case of television.

Internet in Education

Internet has been put to very innovative uses in India. These examples clearly indicate that the Internet need not remain a toy for the rich or yet another additional source of information for a few elite members of the society. Many people probably know the use of Internet for education. Its use for better governance and development is probably not that well known. India has played a pioneering role in this regard. Two examples from India illustrate this point very succinctly.

An example comes from a very small village Tirunelveli in the southern state of Tamil Nadu. The 'Special Issue 2000' of a widely read magazine 'India Today' carried an interesting story on this. A local resident once said, 'this is a town that sleeps even during the day'. For totally unknown and inexplicable reasons this local person opened a cybercafé in January 1999. It created no excitement whatsoever. Free demos and free seminars did not create any excitement. But before long excitement came indirectly through a feature film called *Kathalar Thinam* (Love's Day). The film is about a couple who falls in love in a chat room. The villagers are great movie fans and they became curious about this strange world cyber cafes and chats and visitors started trickling in the cyber café. By August 1999 15 Internet cafes came up.

Thereafter the use was not restricted to entertainment only. There was a huge rush to the cybercafes when the higher secondary school results were put on the net. It is being used, apart from educational purposes, for transacting business, email, sending gifts, exchanging greetings etc. Two new local portals, Tirunelveli.com and Nellaionline.com and the website set up by the local municipal corporation, have helped in creating a proximity to migrants from the village who may be spread all over the world.

It is definitely very early days to know the impact of the Internet. But the seeds are clearly seen. It has opened up a vast reservoir of information and knowledge. It opens up enormous possibilities for education, development and better governance. It can be put to a variety of innovative uses as the two examples cited above clearly point out. It also opens enormous possibilities for new communication research studies. Development and Educational Communication Unit (DECU) Ahmedabad, India has already plans for many studies in this area. It is an interesting area to look forward to.

Info-Thela

Recently, the Indian Institute of Technology, Kanpur has undertaken a project to popularize Internet among the rural masses. A project named Info-Thela has been started just like the mobile PCO service. For this purpose, a pedestal rickshaw fitted witn a computer and having the provision of Internet connectivity through wireless system is taken out to the rural areas to make them aware of the potential of information technology, specially Internet. The Info-Thela is also fitted with PCO and pathological lab instruments also to provide additional services. The rural masses can get information relating to the harvest and also can get themselves medically examined through Info-Thela.

5

Communication Technologies

The word communication has been derives from the Latin word 'communico' which means to communicate. The word is used for exchange of information. Communication needs language as well the channel for communication between two or more than two points. The early man communicated messages by primitive means such as by smoke, drum beating, lighting etc, but as the technology advanced, the means to communicate were also improved. In the 16th century, the postal service developed. In India, horse riders were employed for communication of messages by 1930. Later on telegraph, telephone, wireless, and then the communication technology of today mainly Internet made the system of communication much easier and faster. The following are the communication system of the present time:

RADIO COMMUNICATION

Radio emerged as one of the most potent media of communication since it made possible the transmission and reception of signals by means of electronic wave and without the use of connecting wires. Within a century of its invention, radio has grown enormously going out of Marconi's workshop to a permanent fixture in almost all the homes the world over.

Eventually the industry came to recognize radio as a way of stimulating sales. By 1930, a magazine, Billboard was reporting that "sheet music and record dealers now consider !radio a boon to their business, rather than a detriment." The magazine's initial radio coverage, a one-eighth-page section called Radio Entertainers that first appeared in 1928.

Many forms of presentations emerged and met extinction within a short life span of radio spreading over the last fifty years. By 1975, the once-popular nostalgia format was fading, drama radio had been dead for more than a decade, and the disco format was "being studied based on the records played in the growing number of discotheques throughout. Since its development in 1895, the radio has long since been revolutionizing the world. It has become so common that it is very improbable that one could ever pass a day without coming into contact with radio in some shape or fashion. In the beginning, radios were the only form of entertainment other than family outings and live shows such as those seen on Broadway. However, it seems like radio has outlived its passion for the programs and evening news and now concentrates almost completely on music.

The radio not only revolutionized the world but also created a new form of entertainment and education that will more than likely carry on for many centuries to come. Perhaps this invention will soon be able to travel through space, collect tremendous amounts of data from the universe, and spell out for us the reality of new frontiers waiting to be explored. Truly the radio will live on forever. Photography coupled with sound heralded a new era in field of communication of ideas. It followed the invention and application of a variety of technologies for recording and presentation of information. It began with the art of sight and sound which later transformed into tape slide shows. But with further improvements in synchronization of sound with the moving images, the present day cinematography took its birth.

TELEVISION

Television is used to telecast picture and sound simultaneously. It is an ideal medium of communication for the general use. Television signals are received across the geographical boundaries of the countries. Live telecast makes this medium more popular and interesting.

COAXIAL CABLE

Coaxial cable consists of a single strand of copper running down the axis of the cable. This strand is separated from the outer shielding by an insulator made of foam or other dielectrics. A conductive shield covers the cable. Usually an outer insulating cover is applied to the overall cable—this has nothing to do with the carrying capacity of the cable. Because of the construction of the cable, obviously coaxial in nature, very high frequencies can be carried without leaking out. In fact, dozens of TV channels, each 6 MHz wide, can be carried on a single cable.

MICROWAVE TRANSMISSION

Microwaves uses space as transmission medium. As the microwave beams travel in a straight line, it is advantageous to place microwave towers on hills or mountains to minimize interference from land mass. Usually towers are placed between 25 to 30 miles from each other in order to maintain visibility. Microwave transmission may carry 600 to 1800 voice channels. Advantage of microwave transmission include lower cost than coaxial cable where right-of-way must be maintained and higher cost is involved when the cable is laid over long distances. But the signals are subject to fading caused by absorption and scattering from moisture and precipitation in the air The rain can also cause severe transmission problems.

OPTICAL FIBERS

Fiber optics communicates data in digital form and is a very reliable channel for communication of huge quantity of data. A single glass fiber is thinner than the size of a human hair and it can transmit all the characters in dozens of books of the same size across the country in a single second. Such a quantity of information will normally take about 21 hours to send over a copper telephone line. Fiber Optic technology is a cutting edge method of transmitting information over great distances (150 km without using a repeater) using pulses of light.

Fiber optic technology sends data without electricity through a conductor. Instead of electrical signals, modulated light is used to quickly transmit data over great distances through an insulated glass Fiber-type material.

Fiber optics is currently the best long distance communications method because it provides much faster data transfer speeds when compared to traditional interconnection media such as copper wire. The signal cannot be disrupted by outside sources like electricity, rain, humidity, or other things that tend to damage conventional copper wire signals. Fiber Optic Cables are ideal for volatile environments because there is no fear of damage should they break like there is with traditional copper wiring.

Optical Fiber is lightweight compared to copper cabling because it is a thin glass strand and has huge bandwidth because information travels along the Fiber at the speed of light. Thousands of fibers can be fit in the same amount of space as required for one cable. The developments in fiber optics suggest that the future cost of broadband transmission capability will be within the reach of small organizations and individuals.

The technology in which communication signals in the form of modulated light beams are transmitted over a glass fiber transmission medium. Fiber optics technology offers high bandwidth, small space needs and protection from electromagnetic interference, eavesdropping and radioactivity.

In recent years it has become apparent that fiber-optics are steadily replacing copper wire as an appropriate means of communication signal transmission. They span the long distances between local phone systems as well as providing the backbone for many network systems. Other system users include cable television services, university campuses, office buildings, industrial plants, and electric utility companies. This is an overview of fiber-optic technology, telecommunication applications, fiber-optic advantages and disadvantages, and fiber-optic economics.

Fiber Optics Technology

A fiber-optic system is similar to the copper wire system that fiber-optics is replacing. The difference is that fiber-optics use light pulses to transmit information down fiber lines instead of using electronic pulses to transmit information down copper lines. Looking at the components in a fiber-optic chain will give a better understanding of how the system works in conjunction with wire based systems.

At one end of the system is a transmitter. This is the place of origin for information coming on to fiber-optic lines. The transmitter accepts coded electronic pulse information coming from copper wire. It then processes and translates that information into equivalently coded light pulses. A light-emitting diode (LED) or an injection-laser diode (ILD) can be used for generating the light pulses. Using a lens, the light pulses are funneled into the fiber-optic medium where they transmit themselves down the line.

Light pulses move easily down the fiber-optic line because of a principle known as total internal reflection. "This principle of total internal reflection states that when the angle of incidence exceeds a critical value, light cannot get out of the glass; instead, the light bounces back in. When this principle is applied to the construction of the fiber-optic strand, it is possible to transmit information down fiber lines in the form of light pulses.

Application of Fiber Optics

The use of fiber-optics was generally not available until 1970 when Corning Glass Works was able to produce a fiber with a loss of 20 dB/km. It was recognized that optical fiber would be feasible for telecommunication transmission only if glass could be developed so pure that attenuation would be 20dB/km or less1% of the light would remain after traveling 1 km. Today's optical fiber attenuation ranges from 0.5dB/km to 1000dB/km depending on the optical fiber used. Attenuation limits are based on intended application.

The applications of optical fiber communications have increased at a rapid rate, since the first commercial installation of a fiber-optic system in 1977. Telephone companies began early on, replacing their old copper wire systems with optical fiber lines. Today's telephone companies use optical fiber throughout their system as the backbone architecture and as the long-distance connection between city phone systems.

Cable television companies have also began integrating fiber-optics into their cable systems. The trunk lines that connect central offices have generally been replaced with optical fiber. Some providers have begun experimenting with fiber to the curb using a fiber/coaxial hybrid. Such a hybrid allows for the integration of fiber and coaxial at a neighborhood location. This location, called a node, would provide the optical receiver that converts the light impulses back to electronic signals. The signals could then be fed to individual homes via coaxial cable.

Advantages and Disadvantages of Fiber Optics

There are several advantages that have been established with the development and implementation of fiber-optic cable systems. Compared to copper, optical fiber is relatively small in size and light in weight. This characteristic has made it desirable as intra-floor conduits and wiring duct space has become increasing plugged with expanded copper cable installation .

Optical fiber is also desirable because of it's electromagnetic immunity. Since fiber-optics use light to transmit a signal, it is not subject to electromagnetic interference, radio frequency interference, or voltage surges. This may be an important consideration when laying cables near electronic hardware such as computers or industrial equipment. As well, since it does not use electrical impulses, it does not produce electric sparks which can be an obvious fire hazard.

Advances in optical fiber technology has lead to decreases in signal loss, or attenuation. As an electric pulse or a light pulse travels down it's respective cable line, it will eventually lose signal energy due to imperfections in the transmission medium. To keep the signal going, it must be boosted every so often along the medium line. A signal regenerator is used to boost the electronic pulse in a copper cable. An optical repeater is used to boost the light pulse in a fiber-optic cable. The advantage of optical fiber is that it performs better with respect to attenuation. Fiber-optic cable needs fewer boosting devices, along the same length of line, than copper cable.

. A characteristic feature of optical fiber that has yet to be fully realized is it's potentially wide bandwidth. Bandwidth refers to the amount of information that a fiber can carry. The greater the bandwidth, the greater the carrying capacity of the optical fiber. It is said that currently, the fastest fibre circuits used in trunk connections between cities and countries carry information at up to 2.5 gigabits per second, enough to carry 40,000 telephone conversations or 250 television channels. Experts predict larger bandwidths than this as light frequency separation becomes available. Private communication systems are already using much higher bandwidths.

A disadvantage of the fiber-optic system is it's incompatibility with the electronic hardware systems that make up today's world. This inability to interconnect easily requires that current communication hardware systems be somewhat retrofitted to the fiber-optic networks. Much of the speed that is gained through optical fiber transmission can be inhibited at the conversion points of a fiber-optic chain. When a portion of the chain experiences heavy use, information becomes jammed in a bottleneck at the points where conversion to, or from, electronic signals is taking place. Bottlenecks like this should become less frequent as microprocessors become more efficient and fiber-optics reach closer to a direct electronic hardware interface.

Fiber Optic Economics

One of the initial economic factors to consider when converting to fiber-optics is the cost of replacing wire systems with fiber. Increased demand for optical fiber has brought the prices down within competitive range of copper. Cable sales are expected to increase. However, since transmitters, converters, optical repeaters, and a variety of connecting hardware will be needed, the initial cost of changing over to fiber can be expensive. Increased demand, advances in the technology, and competition has brought the prices down somewhat.

Short term and long term gains should be considered when updating a communications system. In the short term it is often less expensive to continue using copper cabling for covering expanded communication needs. By simply adding more wire to an existing system, expanded needs can be covered. This avoids the expense of adding the transmitters and receivers needed for integrating optical fiber. Long term needs, however, may require more expansion in the future.

In the long term it may be more cost effective to invest in conversion to fiber-optics. This cost effectiveness is due to the relative ease of upgrading fiber optics to higher speeds and performance. It has already been seen in the industry as communication providers are wiring customers with optical fiber bandwidth that exceed consumer bandwidth needs. This is in anticipation of future bandwidth needs. It is generally accepted that customers will need increased bandwidth as the information highway grows. Replacing copper with fiber today would avoid continued investment in a soon to be outdated copper system. Recent changes in the laws regulating the telecommunications industry have helped to promote and spur the use of fiber optics. The passage of the Telecommunications Act of 1996 has helped this effort by allowing television and telephone companies to enter each others markets. Fiber optics will play a pivotal role in this race since the bandwidth needed for providing an all-in-one service with television, telephone, interactive multimedia, and internet access is not available in much of the wiring of America.

SATELLITE TRANSMISSION

Satellite transmission has turned the entire world into a

global village. Satellites relay or transmit information such as TV, phone, weather, military intelligence, and data. Communications satellites provide a worldwide link. In 1960, Echo 1 was launched becoming the first communications satellite. The primitive Echo 1 was an inflatable metallic sphere with instruments that bounced radio signals back to earth. Two years later, Telstar 1 became the first active communications satellite. These satellites orbit the earth at a relatively low altitude. This made them difficult to track and not very suitable for communication. Active satellites receive, amplify, and retransmit signals to different locations. Telstar 1 was responsible for the relay of the first live television broadcast across the Atlantic Ocean.

Weather forecasting has undergone a revolution because of the availability of pictures from geostationary meteorological satellites—pictures we see every day on television. All of these are important aspects of the space age, but satellite communications has probably had more effect than any of the rest on the average person. Satellite communications is also the only truly commercial space technology. By the time EARLY BIRD was launched, communications earth stations already existed in the United Kingdom, France, Germany, Italy, Brazil, and Japan. Further negotiations in 1963 and 1964 resulted in a new international organization, which would ultimately assume ownership of the satellites and responsibility for management of the global system. On August 20, 1964, agreements were signed which created the International Telecommunications Satellite Organization. By the end of 1965, EARLY BIRD had provided 150 telephone "half- circuits" and 80 hours of television service.

In 1965, when EARLY BIRD was launched, the satellite provided almost 10 times the capacity of the submarine telephone cables for almost 1/10th the price. Satellites are still competitive with cable for point-to-point communications, but the future advantage may lie with fiber-optic cable. Satellites still maintain two advantages over cable; they are more reliable and they can be used point-to-multi-point (broadcasting). Cellular telephone systems have risen as challenges to all other types of telephony. It is possible to place a cellular system in a developing country at a very reasonable price. Long-distance calls require some other technology, but this can be either satellites or fiber-optic cable. Cellular telephony has brought us a new technological system, the personal communications system (PCS). In the fully developed PCS, the individual would carry his telephone with him. This telephone could be used for voice or data and would be usable anywhere. Several companies have committed themselves to providing a version of this system using satellites in low earth orbits (LEO).

The inherent "broadcast" nature of satellite communications has made direct-broadcast a recurrent theme—yet one never brought to fruition. Each year from 10-20 communications satellites are launched making the process of communication of information more easy and effective day by day.

The confluence of satellite and multimedia resulted in making the communication technology available at an unimaginably lower cost to the betterment of the common man although it originated in labs for scientific researchers. Now, Internet services are primarily based on these technologies.

DATA TRANSMISSION

Analog Communication

In analog communication, there is a continuous up and down pattern. For example one wave constitute one cycle, which is measured in the units called Hertz (cycle per second) The term cycle and Hertz may be used interchangeably. Thus it is customary to describe channel as transmitting a certain number of cycles per second.

Digital Transmission

In digital transmission, wave patterns are translated into

discrete bits and are separated by intervals. Bit are the smallest units of information in data processing. They may be compared to light bulb, which is either on or off. When the bulb is on information is being transmitted; when it is off there is a blank or interval. The telephone network originally intended to carry only the human voice, operates mostly in the analog mode, although all digital transmission is available as well. Digital transmission has the advantage of being entirely compatible with computer and terminal originated messages.

Frequency and Bandwidth

The information may be available in the form of sound, picture or digital data. It must be converted to electric signals for the purpose of transmission. Such signal must be modulated in some way to fit them into the carrying medium. The amount of information that can be sent over a given channel in a given time is dependant on the bandwidth. The bandwidth available increases with increasing carrier frequency.

Frequency is the rate at which wave or cycle alternates between high and low or on and off. One cycle per second is called Hertz (HZ). The concept of bandwidth can be explained with the help of the traffic network. If there is a two way street consisting of signal lanes, one in each direction only one line of vehicle can travel in each direction. On super highway, however there may be three or four lanes in each direction and cars can travel on them in parallel each at its own rate of speed. In the same way the width of the electronic path determines how many cycles or bits can travel along this given path at a given time; the more the bandwidth available the more bits may be transmitted.

COMMUNICATION CHANNELS

Communication channel consists of two points which allow communication links. A telephone is the simple example of communication channel. Other channels include coaxial cables. Fiber optics, satellite, a beam, microwave and others. Transmission may take place in a number of different modes as simplex, half duplex and full duplex. Libraries generally use the later two modes of transmission.

Synchronous Communication

Synchronous communication is the communication taking place at the same time. Synchronous, or real-time, communication has yet to emerge as a popular technology in online education, but the likely merging of Web and audio/video delivery formats over time may, if successful and affordable, effectively virtualize education on a global scale.

Text-based Synchronous Communication

Chat rooms either reside on a server or can be imported into Web sites as applets. Real-time interactive environments like MUDs (multiple-user dungeons) and MOOs (multiple object orientations) are Unix-based programs that reside on servers. In both kinds of synchronous communication, users connect with the help of chat-client software and log in to virtual "rooms" where they communicate with each other by typing onscreen. Because MOOs and chat rooms frequently attract many users, it is advisable to access them using a high-end computer (Pentium-class PC or Macintosh PowerPC) and a fast connection to the Internet (T1 or better). The computer should also be running Netscape or Internet Explorer 4+ and should be Java enabled. MOOs and chat rooms often have their own sound effects to denote communicative gestures (such as laughter and surprise); to use or hear them, the computer must be equipped with a sound card and speakers.

Audio/Video-based Synchronous Communication

Because this technology is usually delivered over digital subscriber lines rather than through the Web, it is beyond the scope of this project. Digital subscriber lines, also known as DSL, deliver voice and data simultaneously at speeds 30 times faster than 56K modems. Implementing DSL involves making business and telecommunication decisions that require expertise in media production as well as computer networks. This is an expensive technology and as of this date has not gained widespread use beyond the corporate learning environment. Popular corporate packages currently include Interwise Millennium and Centra.

Asynchronous Communication

Most PC serial devices such as mice, keyboards and modems are asynchronous. Asynchronous communication requires nothing more than a transmitter, a receiver and a wire. It is thus the simplest of serial communication protocols, and the least expensive to implement. As the name implies, asynchronous communication is performed between two (or more) devices which operate on independent clocks. Therefore, even if the two clocks agree for a time, there is no guarantee that they will continue to agree over extended periods, and thus there is no guarantee that when point A begins transmitting, point B will begin receiving, or that Point B will continue to sample at the rate Point A transmits. See the figure below for an illustration of what happens when transmission clocks differ significantly.

Most PC serial devices such as mice, keyboards and modems are asynchronous. Asynchronous communication requires nothing more than a transmitter, a receiver and a wire. It is thus the simplest of serial communication protocols, and the least expensive to implement. As the name implies, asynchronous communication is performed between two (or more) devices which operate on independent clocks. Therefore, even if the two clocks agree for a time, there is no guarantee that they will continue to agree over extended periods, and thus there is no guarantee that when point A begins transmitting, point B will begin receiving, or that Point B will continue to sample at the rate Point A transmits.

In asynchronous communication, data is preceded with a start bit which indicates to the receiver that a word (a chunk of data broken up into individual bits) is about to begin. To avoid confusion with other bits, the start bit is twice the size of any other bit in the transmission. The end of a word is followed by a stop bit, which tells the receiver that the word has come to an end, that it should begin looking for the next start bit, and that any bits it receives before getting the start bit should be ignored. To insure data integrity, a parity bit is often added between the last bit of data and the stop bit. The parity bit makes sure that the data received is composed of the same number of bits in the same order in which they were sent. See the diagram in Figure 11 for a portrayal of how asynchronous communication works.

Modem — (Modulator, Demodulator) A device that connects a computer to a phone line. A telephone for a computer. A modem allows a computer to talk to other computers through the phone system. Basically, modems do for computers what a telephone does for humans. Modems are devices which function like translators, changing the digital signals coming out of the terminal to analog so that it van travel along a voice-grade terminal.

The need to communicate between distant computers led to the use of the existing phone network for data transmission. Most phone lines were designed to transmit analog information - voices, while the computers and their devices work in digital form - pulses. So, in order to use an analog medium, a converter between the two systems is needed. This converter is the MODEM which performs MODulation and DEModulation of transmitted data. It accepts serial binary pulses from a device, modulates some property (amplitude, frequency, or phase) of an analog signal in order to send the signal in an analog medium, and performs the opposite process, enabling the analog information to arrive as digital pulses at the computer or device on the other side of connection.

Modems, in the beginning, were used mainly to communicate between DATA TERMINALS and a HOST COMPUTER. Later, the use of modems was extended to communicate between END COMPUTERS. This required more speed and the data rates increased from 300 bps in early days to 28.8 Kbps today. Today, transmission involves data compression techniques which increase the rates, error detection and error correction for more reliability. In order to enable modems of various types and different manufacture to communicate, interface standards were developed by some standard organizations

Today's modems are used for different functions. They act as textual and voice mail systems, facsimiles, and are connected or integrated into cellular phones and in notebook computers enabling sending data from anywhere. The future might lead to new applications. Modem speeds are not expected to be increased much over today's 28.8 kbps. Further dramatic speed increases will require digital phone technology such as ISDN and fiber optic lines. New applications might be implemented such as simultaneous voice and data. Videophones are an example of this.

SWITCHING MECHANISM

Switching mechanisms are devices to send messages in many directions without the delay in transmission. Provision is made for an alternate path in case the routine channel is engaged. Switching is carried out by computer in most cases. Computers also serve to collect messages for transmission over higher capacity lines. The lines used in the telephone network are wires, coaxial cables, microwave and satellite links. The different techniques of switching mechanism are described below:

Circuit Switching

In circuit switching system a communication path is actually established before the message is accepted for transmission. For voice communication system circuit switching is the norm where by a path through connected circuit is established. This method is suitable to telephone traffic for not very efficient or economic for data which is transmitted at different bit rates in a varying amounts.

Message Switching

According to this method the system accepts all messages, store them in a computer or transmits them as and when channel a become available.

Packet Switching

The method used to move data around on the *Internet*. In packet switching, all the data coming out of a machine is broken up into chunks, each chunk has the address of where it came from and where it is going. This enables chunks of data from many different sources to co-mingle on the same lines, and be sorted and directed along different routes by special machines along the way. This way many people can use the same lines at the same time. You might think of several caravans of trucks all using the same road system to carry materials.

FAX

Fax is the transmission of photographs, drawings, maps, and written or printed words by electric signals. Light waves reflected from an image are converted into electric signals, transmitted by wire or radio to a distant receiver, and reconstituted on paper or film into a copy of the original. Facsimile is used by news services to send news and photos to newspapers and television stations, by banks, airlines, and railroads to transmit the content of documents, and by many other businesses as an aid in data handling and record keeping. Facsimile systems involve optical scanning, signal encoding, modulation, signal transmission, demodulation, decoding, and copy making.

Scanning

Scanning is done in a manner similar to that used in television. An original, a photo for example, is illuminated and systematically examined in small adjacent areas called pixels (picture elements). Light reflected from each pixel is converted into electric current by an electronic device, a photocell, photodiode, or charge-coupled device (CCD).

A single such device may be used to cover one pixel after another in a row, row after row from top to bottom until the entire image has been translated into electric impulses. This is rectilinear scanning. Scanning may also be done a row at a time by a battery of devices; this is array scanning. In multispot scanning, a vertical array of photodevices moves across the image, examining the pixels column by column. As the array passes down the copy, it produces a set of current pulses from each photodevice. The separate currents, however produced, are then transmitted successively over a single circuit to the distant receiver.

Facsimile & SSTV History

Facsimile (Fax) a method of encoding data, transmitting it over the telephone lines or radio broadcast, and receiving hard (text) copy, line drawings, or photographs.

Fax Machine

Alexander Bain invented a machine capable of receiving signals from a telegraph wire and translating them into images on paper.

Facsimile (Fax)

Invented in 1842 by Alexander Bain, a Scottish clockmaker, who used clock mechanisms to transfer an image from one sheet of electrically conductive paper to another.

Early Telegraph Facsimile

Bain's fax transmitter was designed to scan a two-dimensional surface (Bain proposed metal type as the surface) by means of a stylus mounted on a pendulum.

Analog Telephone Facsimile - Digital Facsimile

Between 1920 and 1923 the American Telephone & Telegraph Company (AT&T) worked on telephone facsimile technology, and in 1924 the telephotography machine was used to send pictures from political conventions in Cleveland, Ohio, and Chicago to New York City for publication in newspapers.

Background

Demon Internet have introduced a service that allows faxes to be delivered to an email addressee. With the service, a fax number is allocated to the user who can publish it just like any other telephone number. Fax messages arrive in an email format and are forwarded over the Internet. The user can pick them up as email from anywhere around the world.

How does it work?

Customers of the service are allocated a unique fax number on registration and select an email address for the delivery of incoming fax messages. The service allows customers to receive faxes on their desktop, via email, that have been sent manually via an ordinary fax machine.

Benefits of using fax to email

1. Faxes are received straight to the desktop and can conveniently be read as email
2. Captured in electronic format and can be forwarded easily
3. Faxes can be received and stored 24 hours a day, 7 days a week
4. The personal fax number ensures privacy and confidentiality of sensitive faxes
5. Can be printed straight to the printer, which retains its original quality
6. No special equipment is required by the user
7. Received faxes are accompanied by a status page giving transmission information.

Features

1. Unique fax number

A unique number is allocated to the customer on registration. Once a fax is sent to this number, it is delivered as an email to the recipient.

2. Inbox email account

This allows users to specify an email address as the destination for faxed documents to be delivered to. This allows the user to mix fax and email deliveries on a one to one basis. These can then be downloaded, forwarded, stored and printed as emails.

COMMUNICATION NETWORKS

Computers have acquired the capability to communicate. The advancement in technology have ushered an era of not only the computing power but also but of access to information services at least in those countries which have been extensive and reliable computer networks. The transmission over telephone not only of voice but most recently of text and illustrations through telefascimile laid the foundation for this age in which communication is taken for granted in developed countries.

The Oxford English Dictionary defines that a 'network is an interconnected chain or system of immaterial things'. It is also defines as two or more libraries and/or other organizations engaged in a common pattern of information exchange through communication for some functional purposes. Organizations may be in different jurisdictions but agree to one another on the same basis s each service its own constituents.

UNISIST II working document defines information networks "a set of interrelated information systems associated with communicated facilities which are operating through more or less formal agreements and institutional arrangements in order to jointly implement information handling operation with the view to pooling their resources and to offer netter service to their users.

The Major Types of Networks

The following type of communication networks are in operation

Local Area Networks (LANs).

- Wide Area Networks (WANs), and
- Metropolitan Area Networks).

Local Area Networks

Local Area Networks extend the usefulness of one computer by connecting it to others. Often a computer on a network is connected to other networks as well, and has essentially unlimited access to resources and services around the world. At the local level, the network may be any of several popular types. Local area networks have very low error rates and propagation delay that is negligible for most purposes. Transmission in most local area networks is by broadcast — every station on the network receives every transmission. Thus, there are no routing decisions to make. Every packet (message unit) follows the same path, so reordering does not occur. These characteristics make LANs suitable for applications that depend on timely results, for example interactive processing involving files or other resources located on several different systems or time-critical response to a monitoring device. The broadcast mode of operation is suitable for applications requiring message exchange among a number of stations, like checking individual calendars to schedule a meeting or searching for a processor able to share in a demanding computational task.

A combination of technology and the performance expectations of LANs limits the distances they can cover. A small LAN might connect a few computers in an office, or in a home; a large LAN could extend over an office park or university campus, connecting computers and other devices in a number of buildings. Common speeds are 10Mbps (mega bits per second) or 16 Mbps.

All local area networks have the same components: communications medium, an interface between the computer and the medium, and software to drive the interface to send and receive transmissions. The software coexists in the computer with other hardware drivers, such as those for printers and modems;

and with other software such as compilers and databases, text editors and spreadsheets.

Wide Area Networks

Unlike local area networks, wide area networks consist of specific point-to-point links. Messages pass from one network station to another through a communications subnet. The communications subnet consists of nodes whose function is to pass the message from its origin to its intended destination quickly and accurately.

Wide area networks are characterized by significant propagation delay in message transmission and by high incidence of lost or damaged transmissions. Message units, called packets, are passed from one intermediate node to another until they arrive at the destination. Effective routing techniques are important to network performance. Packets from a single message may travel by different routes and arrive at the destination out of order. Typical transmission speeds range from 56 Kbps to 1.54 Mbps.

Since a wide area network is composed of point-to-point connections, connectivity is an important design consideration. Routing is easy: each station only has to know which direction to go to reach the destination. The obvious weakness is vulnerability: in case a single node (other than the ends of the chain) fail to function correctly, communication is lost across the faulty node.

Again, routing is easy: every node connects directly to every other node. Vulnerability to failure is minimized, since no node is dependent on any other. The problem here is cost. From graph theory, we know that a complete graph with n vertices has edges, where is the combination of n things taken two at a time. Fully connecting five nodes might be extravagant; fully connecting a hundred nodes (links) is probably unreasonable. Networks of many thousand nodes clearly require another approach.

No single node loss would cut off any operating node from

the others. On the other hand, loss of two nodes could interrupt communication among the remaining nodes, depending on which two nodes failed. Routing is no longer obvious in this network. Since there is a direct link from node A to node B, it is likely that is the best route for communications between those nodes. To get from A to E, however, a transmission could go by way of B or C. Many factors could enter the decision. One path might support higher transmission rates. Security concerns may dictate the better choice. Different costs may be involved. Even these issues would not be difficult if the best choice were always the same. Transient conditions such as heavy congestion complicate the decision process. Processes running in the nodes respond to instructions from the host computers regarding routing; but they also monitor the behavior of the network and learn what paths are best.

Often the station connected to the subnet is a gateway to a local area network. Thus, the user with access to the resources of a local network can reach out to a larger network for still more resources. Local area networks (or Metropolitan Area Networks) connected to other networks combine to form very complex patterns with characteristics similar to point-to-point wide area networks. Similar problems concerning routing decisions, dealing with failures, temporary conditions, etc. arise. A further complication concerns the differences among the types of local area networks: the required format for transmissions, maximum lengths, conventions for acknowledging successful delivery of a packet, etc. The stations that join two or more local area networks and address these issues are called routers .

Transparent access to very remote files and printers is not impossible, but is rare. Although the most common application of a wide area network is explicit communication (electronic mail and file transfer) another popular use is to login to a remote computer that offers a particular service. Thus, for instance, the NSFnet gives access to supercomputers to researchers working at sites far removed from such a resource. Travelers also use wide area networks to login to their own computers while away from the home or office.

Metropolitan Area Networks

The term Metropolitan Area Networks is often applied to the new high-speed network technologies to distinguish them from wide area and local area networks. These technologies have pushed the carrying capacity of the communication links into the gigabits range. They can be used over larger areas than LANs, and are often used to connect LANs together to form a greatly extended LAN environment.

Another important potential for these networks is the ability to carry information in forms that require many more bits than conventional text or simple graphics. An ordinary computer monitor screen displaying 25 lines of 80 characters contains only 2000 characters. At 8 bits per character, only 16,000 bits are needed to fill the screen. At 10Mbps, the standard speed of LANs, only 1.6msec would be needed to fill the screen. However, when that same screen displays high resolution, bit-mapped images at 1024 by 768 bits, 786,432 bits are required to fill the screen. At 10Mbps the screen is refreshed every 78.6 seconds. If the display includes color (256 color images are common), the time required to deliver the information for a full-screen display (at 10Mbps) grows to 20.13 seconds — hardly suitable for smooth motion video. Clearly, the standard LAN speeds are not adequate. High speed networks, approaching gigabits per second, are needed to provide the ability to deliver the full potential of multi-media displays to the user from a source on a different machine and to connect LANs together and deliver timely access to resources.

Open System Interconnection (OSI)

Communication between two different systems is a difficult process since there are many different protocols for LANs and WANs. The International Standards Organization (ISO) has attempted to solve this problem by the introduction of Open Control Interconnection (OSI). OSI defines a set of procedures and standards grouped into seven layers for the exchange of information between terminals and computers. Some countries have also developed their own standards in order to meet their individual requirements

Integrated Services Digital Network (ISDN)

ISDN's name refers to the combining of voice and data services over the same wires (so computers can connect directly to the telephone network without first converting their signals to an analog audio signal, as modems do). This integration brings with it a host of new capabilities combining voice, data, fax, and sophisticated switching. ISDN uses the existing local telephone wiring, it's equally available to home and business customers. Most important for Internet users, however, is that ISDN provides a huge improvement in access speed.

A given pair of wires connecting two parties for communication can carry electrical signals in one of two forms: analog or digital. An analog signal changes gradually through an infinite number of values, while a digital signal changes instantly (in theory) between just two values. The human voice and a musical instrument are examples of analog signals — both produce complex variations in frequency and amplitude. A light switch typifies a digital signal — it can be either on or off.

An analog signal's infinite number of variations makes it impossible to reproduce exactly. An analog signal will go only so far in copper wire; to go further the signal must be regenerated electronically with a device called a *repeater*. The repeater converts the weak input signal to a stronger output signal, unavoidably distorting it in the process. Each regeneration degrades the signal a bit more (in the same way that photocopies of photocopies get worse at each iteration). In a large telephone network, the "copy of a copy" problem becomes very expensive to solve, requiring sophisticated equipment and costly cabling.

Digital signals, on the other hand, are easy to regenerate precisely. Because there are only two possible states for the signal, even a heavily degraded signal can be regenerated into an exact copy of the original. What's more, the cost (and complexity) of equipment to regenerate digital signals is trivial compared with that for analog. Not surprisingly, telephone companies recognized this cost advantage a long time ago and have since converted all long distance transmission to digital signaling. When a subscriber makes a long-distance call, the central office (CO) converts the analog signal to digital using a technique called sampling (see "Analog-to-Digital Conversion Diagram"), in which the state of the analog signal is captured about 8,000 times per second. Each state is converted to an 8-bit binary number, and the resulting string of binary numbers becomes a digital data stream at 64 Kbps. This digital stream is routed along the long-distance network, being regenerated as needed. Each regeneration produces an exact copy of the original digital data stream, so no information is lost. When the destination CO receives the digital data stream, it reverses the sampling process and transmits the resulting analog signal to the receiving subscriber. (On a side note, many local telephone companies are converting to digital switching, even for local calls).

ISDN cuts out the middleman by eliminating the need for voice digitizers in the CO. ISDN carries through the 64 Kbps digital signal from the CO right to the subscriber, and the subscriber can use it for voice or data as required. Advances in electronics make it practical to do voice digitizing right in the subscriber's phone, and direct digital attachment of computers eliminates the need for modems.

COMMUNICATION STANDARDS AND PROTOCOLS

Standards

Communication between two devices might work only when the interface is defined and agreed. For modems, the standards define techniques used for modulation, for error correction for data compression, and other attributes. There are some standard organizations for the development of interface standards. The ITU - International Telecommunications Union an agency of the United Nations (Geneva, Switzerland), ISO - International Standards Organization, and CCITT - International Telegraph and Telephone Consultative Committee a group of ITU.

Protocols

Protocols are rules governing the initiation and maintenance of data flows. They are implemented in different ways for different types of equipment and networks. Information professionals are most likely to encounter these when setting up their software and hardware for on line searching. The two major components relating to WAN are the protocol and the media. The media are the actual pathways that the protocol travels in. The network protocol defines the format in which data are sent through the media.

6
Distance Learning

The beginning of the present day open universities can be traced back to the beginning of distance education, which was mainly developed with industrialization when the quest for learning increased and the alternate ways of acquiring knowledge were adopted. In distant mode of education, learners were not required to be physically present in the classroom. This phenomenon boosted ones desire of self-education while in employment. The improved methods of communication and transportation made the task easier since they enabled the learners to get delivery of educational materials at a place of their choice.

"Distance Learning", "Distance Education", "Home-study Programs", "Just-in-time Learning", "Anytime/anywhere Learning", "Open University", "University without classrooms", "Alternative Education", "Open Education" or "Virtual Education", are some of the different names given to systems of instruction where physical presence is not necessary. We could define it as a system of education where students and teachers are separate by time and distance, aimed principally at experienced people with a desire to investigate who don't require permanent contact with professors or classmates.

During the last two decades, technology has mobilized the way we communicate, revolutionized our style of work and also our manner of study. In the field of teaching it is already common to talk about open universities, distance systems, virtual classrooms and online universities. Educational institutions worldwide offer courses and university careers through distance education systems. As a result, there is no longer any excuse for those who live far from big cities or those who cannot coordinate their schedule with the program of a traditional university.

The educational technology supported by the telecommunication devices has revolutionized the field of education and research. Never before has there been the possibility for millions of people to earn a degree without neglecting their families and jobs. Mature adults are those who will benefit most from this system, breaking barriers and eliminating the obstacles of regular class attendance. Living and working far from the campus, commuting to or from work during rush-hour traffic, spending hours in the classroom listening sometimes to subjects that are not of specific interest, competing with students much younger than yourself, and daily trying to organize an agenda overbooked with commitments are some of the obstacles that hinder a continual training.

Universities have also adapted their educative processes to the circumstances and needs of the adult student. Universities are developing more flexible programs with more emphasis on the needs of the pupils than their own interests. We may infer, after evaluating the changes in the educational field, that people who are hindered in pursuing training by traditional methods, either because of place of residence or schedule complications, are now more taken into account. This method allows students to administer their time with academic backing via techniques developed for this purpose.

This system has been in effect for more than 100 years, but today there are new tools that enrich distance education. The major development of this educational means began together with new technologies, especially with the popularity of the internet. Almost everyone has access to a computer, can communicate by electronic mail, know the advantages of Internet, have VCRs, access to bibliographies, and many have satellite or cable TV. We see there are numerous options to take classes by audio o video, interactive classes, videoconferences, or simply send us your work by e-mail or fax.

Virtual universities, online tutoring, and multi-media classrooms are concepts of this 21st century. It's incredible to know that one can obtain a masters degree for example, without ever having entered a classroom. On the site of The Virtual College of New York University's School of Continuing and Professional Studies the welcome page states: "The virtual college exists because we recognize that in this fast-paced world, you don't have time to go and sit in a traditional class and prefer the convenience of studying in your home or at the office."

This tendency is growing in all the world, and Latin America is no exception. Internet use for students and professors is on the rise. At the beginning or the year 2000, some 13 million people were pursuing university majors in the United States at a distance, according to Donald Perrin, editor of *Education at a Distance.*

HISTORY OF DISTANCE LEARNING

This method has been in existence for almost two centuries and has been used in the United States for more than one hundred years. It was after the Second World War that its use increased dramatically in England, Australia and the United States. In the mid 70s it was enhanced by communication and computer developments. In the 80s the increase of distance students was notable. Its only logical, since competitive global trends have propelled the technological and internet revolutions and have pushed everyone to acquire new degrees. This is why today thousands of European, American and Australian Universities offer a wide range of options. Following is the chronology of distance education :

1840 Isaac Pitman begins to teach by correspondence.

1850 The University of London offers distance courses and major fields of study to its inhabitants in far away colonies like India and Australia.

1856 In Europe, Toussaint and Langenscheidt begin language courses by correspondence.

1858 The University of London establishes its external program.

1873 The Society to Encourage Studies at Home is founded.

1883 The Chautauqua Institute in New York is authorized to function by correspondence.

1890 The Colliery Engineer School of Pennsylvania gives distance courses in mining.

1891 The University of Queensland of Australia offers very complete programs at a distance.

1892 The Pennsylvania State College begins its correspondence courses in agriculture

1901 The Moody Bible Institute commences alternative courses.

1906 The University of Wisconsin establishes a distance extension.

1915 The National University Continuing Education Association is founded.

1916 The University of South Africa appears.

1922 The Pennsylvania State College begins its radio courses, as does Columbia University.

1925 The State University of Iowa does the same.

1926 The National Home Study Council is founded.

1934 The State University of Iowa begins filmed courses.

1950 The Ford Foundation begins educational programs by television.

The Ford Foundation begins educational programs by television.

1964 The Nova University is founded.

1965 The University of Wisconsin gives courses based on telephone communication.

1968 Stanford University creates a television network.

1969 The Open University of London begins.

1970 The Walden University and the University of The State of

New York open their distance courses via the Regents External Degree Program.

1971 The British Open University acquires great prestige.

1974 California State University offers a Masters in Arts.

1976 Pacific Western University and the University of Phoenix appear.

1979 A correspondence program is offered by the California College for Health Sciences.

1982 The National University Teleconferencing Network is founded.

1983 IBM creates a satellite education network.

1984 The National Technology University offers videotapes and satellite courses, and the Electronic University Network courses with software for DOS and Commodore64 computers.

1901 The Moody Bible Institute commences alternative courses.

1906 The University of Wisconsin establishes a distance extension.

1915 The National University Continuing Education Association is founded.

1916 The University of South Africa appears.

1922 The Pennsylvania State College begins its radio courses, as does Columbia University.

1926 The National Home Study Council is founded.

1934 The State University of Iowa begins filmed courses.

1950 The Ford Foundation begins educational programs by television.

1964 The Nova University is founded.

1965 The University of Wisconsin gives courses based on telephone communication.

1968 Stanford University creates a television network.

1969 The Open University of London begins.

1970 The Walden University and the University of The State of New York open their distance courses via the Regents External Degree Program.

1971 The British Open University acquires great prestige.

1974 California State University offers a Masters in Arts.

1976 Pacific Western University and the University of Phoenix appear.

1979 A corresponde nce program is offered by the California College for Health Sciences.

1982 The National University Teleconferencing Network is founded.

1983 IBM creates a satellite education network.

1985 Indira Gandhi National Open University is established in New Delhi.

1985 Connected Education with online programs is founded.

1987 The Mind Extension University and Colorado State University take off.

1989 The University of Phoenix starts its online programs.

1992 The Electronic University Network develops virtual programs.

1993 The University of Nebraska begins online programs.

1994 Some universities unite to offer distance education.

1995 Regent University and Stanford University begin new programs.

1996 Duke University begins distance programs with short residences.

1997 California Virtual University, Johns Hopkins University and the Graduate School of America offer different varieties of study.

1998 New programs developed in the British Open University.

2000 New universities arise, the Jones International University, Touro University, Capella University, etc.

THE ADVANTAGES OF DISTANCE LEARNING

The advantages are obvious, students may maintain their live style, their normal daily pace and fulfill `their family, social and work obligations as they continue their education. Studies of distance learners show that the student is more self disciplined, independent, motivated and investigative than the one who simply sits in the classroom and listens. On the other hand, the tuition is usually less.

Distance learning is not limited just to the simple comprehension of a textbook or listening to a teacher, the background of a student is recognized by awarding credits for experience and previous studies, and in many cases the programs are tailor-made for students. With Traditional education all the students are, in effect, the same. Quite the opposite, distance education realizes that no two people are equal in knowledge, experience, and of course their goals and objectives are different.

We have often heard it said: "I'm sorry, we wanted to promote you on the job, but you don't have a degree." How many times have we read in the want ads: "University graduate wanted, preferably with post-graduate studies." That "piece of paper", the Diploma, becomes a necessity. The increased competition raises the demands at the time of job searching. The last two decades of the 20th Century changed the rules of the game under the influence of the globalization process. Today, the only one responsible for a professional career, training development and systematic education is an individual. This is the key for personal success. With the growing global trend, companies have entered a new level of competence, which has impacted in greater demands of organizations at the moment of choosing personnel because the only way to maintain the competitive edge is to have well-educated people. The weakness in the person-company link that has produced in recent years basically affects people with lesser capabilities. The scene is a cruel one, and it becomes worse when one does not have that "piece of paper".

Those who are economically active have changed their "attitudes" about work – taking more initiative with entrepreneur criteria and a global vision, more involved in trouble-shooting company problems and demonstrating a "can-do" attitude – and its necessity of "degrees". Today it is not enough to be a professional, languages and postgraduate diplomas are sought (the need to know computer tools goes without saying).

To be at the front of this change distance learning minimizes the usual difficulties of traditional education, making it possible to obtain the formation, training and diplomas that will improve your personal possibilities for success.

OPEN UNIVERSITY OF THE UNITED KINGDOM

The Open University admitted its first students in 1971. It is the UK's largest university, with over 200,000 students and customers. The OU represents 22% of all part-time higher education students in the UK.

The university is ranked amongst the top UK universities for the quality of its teaching. Of the 23 subjects assessed by the Quality Assurance Agency, 17 have been placed in the top 'Excellent' category. Courses are available throughout Europe and, usually by means of partnership agreements with other institutions, in many other parts of the world. About 26,000 learners are studying OU courses outside the UK. The OU's undergraduate level courses do not require any entry qualifications. Over a third of people starting these courses have qualifications below conventional university entry requirements. Despite this, around 70% of OU students successfully complete their courses each year. Two thirds of students are aged between 25 and 44, but students can enter at the age of 18. Nearly all OU students are part-time and about 70% of undergraduate students remain in full-time employment throughout their studies. More than 150,000 OU students are on-line.

OU courses are considered to be among the world's best distance education materials and are regularly awarded for their innovation. In recent years, 'Computing, An Object-Oriented Approach' won a British Computer Society award for IT, 'Discovering Science' received a British Environment and Media Award for its innovative use of CD Rom, and 'Geology' was named as one of Europe's best new multimedia products when it won the knowledge and discovery category at the prestigious EuroPrix awards. Nineteen subject areas within the OU have been recognized as producing research work with evidence of international quality and a further seven subjects show evidence of national excellence.

CRTVU, China

China is the largest country of the world population wise. In order to educate the masses, its higher learning system has its own characteristics. The national multimedia distance learning institution of China is called the Central Radio and Television University (CRTVU). If we take into account the number of students and their geographical distribution, this University appears to be the largest distance teaching institution of the world. The chief aim of the University was to overcome the shortage of technical and management personnel and qualified teachers in the country.

The success of the institution points to the feasibility of using the media of television and radio to train more people for the modernization of the country in a shorter time and on a larger scale than conventional system.

Television and radio are chosen as the master medium for communication by CRTVU yet the courses of CRTVY follow a multimedia approach. Most of these courses consist of radio and television broadcast supplemented by printed teaching material. The input of these non-print media varies according to the subject area . For example, the proportion of TV programs for science and engineering courses is greater than that of the other media. For social science courses radio is the chief medium.

TV- programs are transmitted by the Central China

Television (CCTV) nationally through the microwave network. The transmission time for these program is 33 hours per week. The transmission of radio program is the responsibility of provincial radio stations.

Likewise, courses offered by provincial universities are produced and transmitted jointly by them and provincial radio/ TE stations. These stations have to decide how much time they should use for these programs. TV classes also organize courses taught by part time tutor who sometimes also use audio or video tapes produced by CRTVU.

Printed textbooks are compiled and offered by the CRTVU. These textbooks are not written or developed by the CRTVU. They are selected from the available textbooks prepared mostly by the conventional universities. The CRTVU is engaged in preparing supplementary teaching materials and distance teaching materials for radio and television presentation.

INDIRA GANDHI NATIONAL OPEN UNIVERSITY (IGNOU)

The distance education system has been gaining widespread popularity over the years. By widening access to higher education, the distance mode provides an opportunity to all those who are unable to pursue higher education through the traditional system. In India, the number of students enrolled in higher education have increased from about 0.2 million to about 6 million within the last fifty years. This 6 million figure represents only 6% of the total young population of the country posing a serious challenge for the planners of higher education.

Indira Gandhi National Open University was established in 1985 to democratize higher education. The aim was to provide cost-effective, quality education to large sections of our population including those living in remote and farflung areas. A mere fifteen years since its inception IGNOU has carved a niche for itself among the premier educational institutions in the country. The University has been a pioneer in Distance Education and the recipient of the Centre of Excellence in Distance Education award conferred by the Commonwealth of Learning in 1993.

Open Universities today are the prime avenues for imparting education through the distance mode. All the systems amenable to self-learning and learner friendly are incorporated in the system for serving the isolated distance learners.

The distance/open learning system aims to:

* provide an opportunity for education to all aspirants including those in service, women, adults, handicapped from remote place etc.
* allow self-paced learning
* provide innovative and flexible education
* provide learning materials that are self explanatory, user-friendly and appropriate for the target group.
* Provide opportunity for a number of diverse courses-professional, technical, vocational and general.
* Cater to the needs of certification, education, knowledge, skill up gradation etc.
* Provide regular counseling and other appropriate learning support through networks of study centers and last but not least to
* Incorporate new technologies, satellite communications, networking, internet, e-mail etc for easy access to learners.

State-of-the-art telecommunication systems have further helped in reaching out to the hitherto unreached sections of the society. Quality and equity have been the guiding principles behind all the endeavours.

The University's Act states that, the University shall:

* impart education and knowledge through various means suited to the Open and Distance Education Mode.
* provide not only higher education to large sections of the

population, but particularly disadvantaged segments of society.

* encourage, coordinate and assist Open Universities and Distance Education systems while determining standards in such systems in the country.
* provide national integration and strengthen the natural and human resources of the country through the medium of

IGNOU has two main functions:

(i) It offers various academic programmes that lead to Certificates, Diplomas and Degrees. It develops and produces courses for delivery through open learning and distance education mode. IGNOU is also actively involved in research, training and extension education activities.

(ii) In its capacity as an Apex Body, it co-ordinates and monitors distance education system throughout the country. IGNOU has also constituted the Distance Education Council and has provided expertise and assistance to other Open and Distance Learning Institutions in the country.

IGNOU stands significantly apart from other universities because of:

* national jurisdiction
* flexible admission rules
* individualized study : flexibility, in terms of place, pace and duration of study
* use of latest educational and communication technologies
* student support services
* cost-effective programmes
* modular programmes
* resource sharing, collaboration and networking between other Open Universities

Indira Gandhi National Open University, the National

Resource Centre for Open and Distance Learning with international recognition and presence is committed provide seamless access to sustainable and learner-centric quality education, skill up gradation and training to all by using innovative technologies and methodologies and ensuring convergence of existing systems for massive human resource required for promoting integrated national development and global understanding.

The distance education system offered by IGNOU adopts various modern communication technologies in narrowest mode: audio-video cassettes, radio broadcasts, interactive radio counselling, satellite based interactive technology etc. A Sanchar Kendra was set up at IGNOU with Japanese collaboration in 1996. It has marked great milestone and emerged as a National Resource Centre in the area of educational communication helping realize the true potential of modern communication technologies in reaching out education to the unreached segments of the society.

The Sanchar Kendra has also been entrusted with the prestigious and unique honour of transmitting Gyan Darshan-The exclusive Educational Television Channel of the country. A Joint collaborative venture of MHRD/CEC, NCERT/CIET and various transmission of the Channel was commissioned on the Independence Day in 2000. It started from 4 hours daily broadcast but has now increased telecast time enormously. Followed by this success the Interactive Radio Counselling offered in collaboration with AIR which began with just one centre at Bhopal a year ago witnessed a phenomenal growth to cover about 69 Primary AIR stations centres and the network is still growing and is expected to cover all the stations of AIR in the year 2000 only.

Now, IGNOU has about 10,00,000 students with extremely varied profiles, spread throughout the length and breadth of the country. The University has an efficient and effective networking of 48 Regional Centres (22 are IGNOU Regional Centres, 8 are IGNOU North-East Regional Centres, 5 are Army Command

Centres, 8 are IAF Command Centres, 4 are Navy Command Centres and 1 are Assam Rifles Command Centre) and over 1094 Study Centres, all over India. As an Open University, IGNOU has come a long way since 1985, having crossed national boundaries providing higher education as well as assisting other developing countries in this regard.

The solution for education and research facilities for the masses now lies in the opting for the distance mode of learning through establishment of the open university special for a country like India with ever growing population.

HIGHER EDUCATION SCENARIO

In India, the Inter-University Board (later known as the Association of Indian Universities) was established in 1925 to promote university activities, by sharing information and cooperation in the field of education, culture, sports and allied areas. The first attempt to formulate a national system of education in India came in 1944, with the Report of the Central Advisory Board of Education on Post War Educational Development in India, also known as the Sargeant Report. It recommended the formation of a University Grants Committee, which was formed in 1945 to oversee the work of the three Central Universities of Aligarh, Banaras and Delhi. In 1947, the Committee was entrusted with the responsibility of dealing with all the then existing Universities.

Soon after Independence, the University Education Commission was set up in 1948 under the Chairmanship of Dr. S Radhakrishnan "to report on Indian university education and suggest improvements and extensions that might be desirable to suit the present and future needs and aspirations of the country". It recommended that the University Grants Committee be reconstituted on the general model of the University Grants Commission of the United Kingdom with a full-time Chairman and other members to be appointed from amongst educationists of repute.

In 1952, the Union Government decided that all cases pertaining to the allocation of grants-in-aid from public funds to the Central Universities and other Universities and Institutions of higher learning might be referred to the University Grants Commission. Consequently, the University Grants Commission (UGC) was formally inaugurated by late Shri Maulana Abul Kalam Azad, the then Minister of Education, Natural Resources and Scientific Research on 28 December 1953.

The UGC, however, was formally established only in November 1956 as a statutory body of the Government of India through an Act of Parliament for the coordination, determination and maintenance of standards of university education in India. In order to ensure effective region-wise coverage throughout the country, the UGC has decentralized its operations by setting up six regional centres at Pune, Hyderabad, Kolkata, Bhopal, Guwahati and Bangalore. The head office of the UGC is located in New Delhi.

The UGC has the unique distinction of being the only grant-giving agency in the country which has been vested with two responsibilities: that of providing funds and that of coordination, determination and maintenance of standards in institutions of higher education.

The UGC's mandate includes:

- Promoting and coordinating university education.
- Determining and maintaining standards of teaching, examination and research in universities.
- Framing regulations on minimum standards of education.
- Monitoring developments in the field of collegiate and university education; disbursing grants to the universities and colleges.
- Serving as a vital link between the Union and state governments and institutions of higher learning.
- Advising the Central and state governments on the

measures necessary for improvement of university education.

In order to execute its responsibilities, the UGC receives both Plan and non-Plan grants from the Central government. It allocates and disburses full maintenance and development grants to all Central Universities, colleges affiliated to the Delhi University and Banaras Hindu University and some institutions that have been accorded the status of 'Deemed to be University'. State universities, colleges and other institutions of higher education receive support only from the Plan grant for development schemes. In addition, the UGC also provides financial assistance to universities and colleges under various schemes/programmes for promoting quality, excellence, teaching and research.

India is a diverse country with a composite culture. Its one billion plus population consists of people from different religions, geographical areas and varying social and economic backgrounds. They face wide disparities arising out of regional imbalances, as well as exclusion from the mainstream on account of social, economic, gender or physical handicaps and discrimination. The higher education system has to grapple with these issues in addition to problems of unplanned growth of institutions and student enrolment. One of the greatest challenges to the system is to make higher education more accessible, more relevant and, at the same time, more affordable.

The UGC gives special development grants to colleges and universities located in geographically and educationally backward areas so that they can get the much-needed academic and physical infrastructure facilities. The following functions are bound to boost the services being provided by the government of India in higher education through distance education.

Digitization of Learning Resources

Ones the educational resources are available digitally, they may be made available through to the masses through the various delivery system at a very low cost. In its endeavour to encourage sharing of resources electronically, the UGC is establishing 16 mirror sites across the country with 2 mbps Internet lines which would be evenly distributed geographically. These will contain current and previous volumes of research journals in all disciplines and will provide free access to teachers and research workers.

Lifelong Learning

The necessity to provide chances of learning to those persons who could not afford to get them educated due to financial problem or age factors led to the advancement in lifelong learning projects. The UGC acknowledges the leading role played by universities and colleges in bringing about social change through outreach activities. It has been using adult and continuing education as an effective tool for lifelong learning and outreach activities under its Non Formal Education programmes.

Adult and Continuing Education Program

The UGC assists in the nationwide program of eradication of illiteracy by pursuing various adult education programmes in the university centres/departments of Adult Education by involving the teachers and students. These programmes focus, among other things, on literacy, post-literacy, continuing education, science for people, environment education, legal literacy and technology transfer.

Population and Development Education

To promote population and development education programmes, 17 Population Education Resource Centres (PERCs) have been set up in select universities in collaboration with the United Nations Population Fund (UNFPA). These Centres provide technical support to various activities related to curriculum development, teaching and learning material.

Relevant and Professional Education

India is teeming with a multitude of graduate and

postgraduate students who, because of the tack of skill-oriented education, are unable to find jobs in the market. The relevance of education has, therefore, assumed importance, with employers seeking professionally qualified graduates with a sound knowledge of their core discipline and expertise in the concerned skill.

To meet this challenge, the UGC has been advocating the adoption of an open and flexible approach at the undergraduate level. Such an approach would allow students to either simultaneously acquire a degree as well as a diploma in skill-oriented disciplines or acquire a dual degree with the addition of one more year after completing graduation. The UGC is also pursuing schemes to make the youth aware of the importance of positive health, value education and human rights and duties education, besides promoting the study of traditional languages and research on some prominent Indian thinkers.

The following innovative schemes are being taken up by UGC for promoting relevant education:

Vocational Education: The UGC has initiated a major scheme of vocational education at the undergraduate level designed to equip graduates with necessary add-on skills for gainful employment.

Curriculum Revision: As part of the UGC's efforts to support teaching- learning innovations in various subjects, a model curriculum is prepared from time to time by a panel of fe experts at the undergraduate and postgraduate levels for suitable adoption by the universities. During 2001, the UGC prepared a model curriculum in 32 subjects with the help of Curriculum Development Committees. Universities use the UGC Model Curriculum for upgrading their curriculum. CDC Reports

Bilateral Exchange

As Indian higher education has the potential of being accepted in other countries, there is a need to make special efforts to export it. Under this program, several Indian universities have established campuses abroad. These include Birla Institute of Technology and Science (BITS) Pilani, Biria Institute of Technology (BIT) Ranchi and Manipal Academy of Higher Studies (MAHE).

The UGC has been conducting bilateral cultural exchange programmes under which Indian and foreign scholars visit universities in each other's countries.

Foreign universities are keen to commence operations in India in coordination with Indian universities. This will promote a free flow of students between nations.

Innovative Programmes

Addressing the need to promote teaching and research in several new frontline areas that have emerged in various disciplines, the UGC is providing financial assistance to select universities/institutions under its Innovative Program Scheme. The Commission is supporting postgraduate level programmes in the following emerging areas/disciplines:

Environment/Energy

Electronics

Futurology

Remote Sensing

Nano-Technology

Computer Software Application

Bio-informatics and Bio-Technology

Atmospheric Science & Meteorology

University Faculty and Venture Business

Quality and Excellence

The phenomenal increase in the number of students clamouring for higher education and the lack of infrastructural facilities in institutions of higher learning have led to quality and excellence taking a backseat. The information, communication and technology (ICT) revolution has necessitated a change on the part of institutions towards developing modern methods of teaching, learning and evaluation.

The UGC has devised steps to promote quality and excellence in higher education in a focused manner. It has been promoting a large number of reforms in classroom teaching, laboratory practices, fieldwork, evaluation methods and other related aspects, which have a bearing on the quality of education.

World over the higher education is passing through interesting phase. The development of higher education in 21st Century, features among the highest national priorities throughout the world. It is changing radically, by becoming organically flexible in diversity of programmes, in its structure, in its curricula, in its delivery systems and it is adopting itself to clever use of information and communication technologies.

Indian Higher Education has seen an unprecedented growth in last 50 years and it is one of the biggest higher education systems in the world today. Our higher education system is certainly facing several constraints but on the whole it has played a significant role in developing a sound education foundation. The Indian economy has shown steady growth in recent years. The Indian graduates, in all subjects and disciplines, have given a new image to India both internally and also at a global level. The Indian graduates are now accepted at global level as value-added-skilled human power at premier level. Thus India is now recognized as a nation with a potential to give "knowledge creators" to strengthen both our internal as well as world economy.

This does not mean that all is well with our Indian Higher Education system. We continue to face issues like increasing demand, relevant education, quality and excellence, governance and resource crunch. These issues continue to encircle our higher education system mainly because of extreme unwillingness of all the players in higher education to change with time and adopt new ways and methods to address various issues that emerge over a period of time. The access to higher education, even after

50 years of independence, is still an important issue. Today there are 8.8 million students in formal and non-formal system. The formal system is sharing 80% of the burden and the non-formal is sharing 20%. The combined access parameter (formal + non-formal) is 6.9 and it is 5.75 for formal system alone. This is far away from the access parameter, which hovers between 30-55 in developed countries. In the Xth Plan we intend to reach combined access parameter of 10. We may then have to cater the need of around 14 million students by the end of 2007-08. How can one meet such an enhanced demand? We may have to go for a strategy where the existing physical and academic structure is used more effectively, probably round the clock, and also by combining both conventional and distance education modes in an open seamless structure.

However, it is not only the challenge of number. We are facing a bigger challenge of giving quality education. Every nation in the world is struggling to meet diametrically opposite demands of education that of quality and enhancement in number of students. Quality and quantity, both, ask for better academic and physical infrastructure and also greater financial resources. This is where the importance of UGC Information Network comes in the picture. The entire infrastructure, which is established with the help of ERNET, would be fully supported by the UGC and students and teachers would have free access to the network for coming five years.

Making higher education relevant has always remained an open issue for last five decades. If one critically analyses the scenario it becomes very clear that the real issue is with bulk of student population, around 83% in the formal education, which is pursuing traditional disciplines like Arts, Pure Sciences, Humanities and Social Sciences, Law and Commerce. We have to make education more relevant for these students. The opportunity has emerged to address this question more cleverly in this 21st Century.

The emergence of new economic environment demands

for graduates, particularly in the traditional disciplines, who are sound in their fundamentals but enriched with appropriate utility oriented skills. This is where, our strategy in the Xth Plan, where universities would be encouraged to make three years structure more open and flexible so as to allow students to pursue both degree and utility oriented certificate and diploma programmes together, would make a significant difference. The relevance achieves a greater significant at postgraduate level. Just like at undergraduate level, master's degree with sound foundation is a necessity. This means no compromise should be made in respect of intensifying of teaching in core subjects at master's level. But what is needed, to serve the nation better and also for retaining our global identity, is an acceptance of credit based modular structure at postgraduate level.

Two major activities have been initiated recently; one is Internet and Intranet connectivity for colleges and Universities through establishment of UGC Infonet. And the other activity, which would bring India at the centrestage of South Asia is establishment of Inter University Centre for International Studies at Hyderabad. This Inter University Centre is going to emerge through convergence of academic and physical infrastructure available at IACIS, Hyderabad for addressing contemporary issues in the field of humanities and social sciences, education, culture, peace, economics and commerce, trade, health, environment, internal and international security and many other similar issues that need to be addressed in the present time scale of futuristic approach. This Centre would provide a dynamic and vibrant platforms for discussions and deliberations for experts in various disciplines and fields at a global level. This would be first of its kind Inter University Centre in humanities and social sciences where SAARC, South and Central Asian Countries could play a very important and pro-active role, in collaboration with exports across the world, to visualize the future of mankind as it is seen by the 1/3rd of the humanities in the world.

BOOSTING THE DISTANCE LEARNING

Intranet and Internet

In the Xth Plan UGC plan to set up two independent research councils in the discipline of Sciences and Technology as well as Humanities and Social Sciences. It would provide substantial amount of money for supporting research at an individual, group and also at departmental level. The UGC Infonet would provide through 16 mirror sites, spread across the country, access to research materials and research journals in e-format through repository of digital database. In fact, the subscription of research journals is becoming more expensive and this step of UGC would provide indirect subsidy to each of the university as they would be saving around 50-60 lakhs rupees per year. The saved money can be used for purchase of textbooks which are so much needed for giving knowledge access to the students.

To provide Intranet and Internet connectivity to universities and colleges across the country, the UGC is establishing its own network, ' UGC InfoNet', which is expected to give an impetus to higher education in the country. The Commission plans to bring about a virtual enhancement of the academic infrastructure through the InfoNet. The connectivity will be achieved by using radio links, very small aperture satellite terminals (VSAT), optical fibre links and digital subscriber telephone lines. This would provide unlimited free access to the world of Internet to students, researchers, teachers and employees of universities and colleges.

e-Education Content Development

Many universities the world over have taken advantage of the ICT revolution to prepare multi- media courseware in teaching and learning, which can be easily accessed through the Internet. The UGC is identifying suitable university departments with the requisite expertise to help in developing multimedia courseware for various disciplines and also to create a courseware repository. Subject experts familiar with multi-media would finalise the contents for the courseware. This is being done at three levels:

(a) Search, analysis and integration of available multi-media material suitable for class room teaching.

(b) Development of short duration multi-media segments for enriching teaching.

(c) Full multi-media e-content development for a teaching course and entire program.

This would ultimately lead to a web-based interactive e-content development, which will ensure an effective blending of subject expertise available in colleges and universities and software expertise available in industry. The UGC plans to enter into a Memorandum of Understanding with the National Association of Software and Service Companies (NASSCOM) and other apex organisations in the infotech sector on this issue.

The UGC is promoting a novel concept of building research facilities through Inter University Centres (lUCs) on a large scale for the benefit of researchers working in different universities. These lUCs provide the right research environment and encourage research students and faculty to undertake major research activities.

Media and Educational Technology

The UGC has taken the initiative to utilise the time slot given for higher education by televising the TV programme in higher education and entitled "Countrywide Classroom" which has taken higher education to remote areas of the country. The Commission is at present supporting Educational Media Research Centres (EMRCs) at various Universities and Central Institute of English and Foreign Languages (Hyderabad). Audio-Visual Research Centres (AVRCs) at various universities, are being supported for training of personnel and production of software. In order to make distance learning more effective and bring best teachers in the country within the reach of all sections of students including semi- urban and rural students, the Commission undertook a project to produce non-broadcasting video lectures for under-graduate students. During the year, negotiations were finalized for telecasting the serial Race to Save the Planet. Negotiations were also under way to sell similar programmes to the Commonwealth of Learning. The Consortium for Educational Communications (CEC), an autonomous Organisation under UGC provides programmes for transmission through the enrichment channel of Doordarshan. The Commission has also established Consortium for Export of Educational material as a project mode of CEC.

Adult, Continuing and Extension Education Programes

The Commission is providing assistance to universities for the implementation of Total Literacy (TLC) through their departments of Adult, Continuing and Extension Education. Such assistance is also provided for population education and planning forums.

An action plan was also drawn up for prevention and control of AIDS with the help of the university and college community through the introduction of self-study courses, dissemination of information with the help of PERCs and medical experts, provision of community services through NSS and NCC, publicity through countrywide classroom programmes, preparation of course material, and by providing additional grants to universities and colleges for purchase of books on AIDS, population education, environmental and drug abuse.

Distance Education/Correspondence Courses

Assistance is provided to universities to the tune of Rs. 10 lakhs as seed money for the first five years for introducing distance education programmes/correspondence courses. Further assistance to the tune of Rs.5 to Rs.7.50 lakhs is provided after five years for running undergraduate and post-graduate courses respectively. Guidelines were circulated advising universities to upgrade their existing Correspondence Course Institutes (CCIs) into Distance Education Mode. A Distance Education Council, set up by IGNOU on the recommendations of the UGC, is responsible for determining and maintaining standards in the field of distance education.

It is expected now that in the time to come, distance learning in India will be popularized more and more and the means for such mode of learning will easily become available for the common man.

7
Learning Technology

According to the Random House Dictionary of English Language, 'learning' is 'knowledge acquired by systematic study in any field or fields of scholarly application". Learning may also be defined as the process of gaining knowledge, skills or experience. Meaningful learning is that which equips the learner to apply his/her newly acquired abilities in authentic and novel situations.

We all acquire knowledge through out our lives. Learning is a continuous process. People learn for a variety of reasons. The most basic of which is survival, this is why we learn what's good to eat and what isn't and who we can trust. A further reason is societal pressure. In most developed countries the law requires that children receive full time education for a decade or so. Family and peer pressure can also be a powerful motivator. The realization that increased knowledge and skills lead to a higher status and better-paid job also drives us to learn. And many choose to learn purely out of interest and/or enjoyment.

We live in the information age where a large quantity of information is available freely. Education may play the following role in the present time:

- Often, learners are unaware of what it is that they need to learn. Education can guide the learner through the mass of available knowledge towards that which is most appropriate to their particular needs.
- Whilst children are born naturally curious about their world they might not have the natural desire to acquire the basic literacy, numeracy and other skills essential to modern

citizenship. Education can "sell" the advantages of mastering these basics as well as providing a taster of the broad range of fields of human endeavour with a view to enabling the individual to identify those he/she wishes to pursue further.

- Education can provide feedback on the learner's progress. It can identify strengths and weaknesses, provide more detailed explanation in the case of difficulty, and provide remedial pathways where appropriate.
- Reputable educational institutions can provide learners with certification as proof they have attained a certain level of competence in a given discipline.

In the traditional model students sat in rows of chairs facing a teacher standing before a blackboard. The teacher would speak and the students made notes, occasionally asking questions. Students would complete exercises to test their comprehension and practice their ability to apply the subject matter. The teacher would monitor progress and offer guidance before demonstrating the correct solution and method.

Students might be given assignments to complete outside class, which drew upon what they should have learned. At the end of the session students sat a timed examination and were expected to recall appropriate parts of the material in response to the exam questions. Students would often "cram" for exams - memorizing large amounts of relevant facts and figures immediately prior to the exam, only to forget most of them just as quickly as soon as the paper had been completed.

The traditional educational model could be described as a behaviourist approach to learning, although its methods were in used long before the development of behaviourist theory. This style of education was well suited to industrial age society where individuals had rigidly defined roles in which carrying out certain actions under certain circumstances would generally yield the desired results.

LEARNING IN THE INFORMATION AGE

The information age has replaced the relative predictability of the industrial age with an increased degree of uncertainty that will require greater levels of flexibility and adaptability in order to survive and thrive. Workers will be more involved in the planning and decision-making processes. Individuals will need to develop the discernment required to make sense of the mass of facts, figures claims and counter-claims that surround them.

Education will need to change from being a process of conditioning to one of empowerment. Learning will need to change from being a homogeneous commodity to a customized experience tailored to the needs and characteristics of the individual. Learning will no longer end in the teens or early-twenties. Instead it will continue throughout life as individuals need to continually update knowledge and skills to keep pace with ever-changing technical and social conditions.

In order to meet the learning requirements of the information age learning opportunity providers should adopt a more constructivist approach to learning, creating conditions in which learners may learn by actively engaging with realistic scenarios and exchanging views and experiences with peers and mentors.

HISTORY OF LEARNING

Throughout the ages, new innovations and improvements in the existing techniques of learning have taken place all around the world. These inventions being popularized were adopted for the benefit of mankind. The process still continued and some new technologies are awaited. To reflect the growth of learning technology, a timeline has been designed which is as given below:

History of learning is essentially linked with the growth of human civilization and the availability of improved technology for recording and reproduction of the acquired know how. A Learning technologies timeline was created by University of Illinois students enrolled in courses on New Literacies, Literacy in the Information Age, Learning Technologies, or Computer Assisted Instruction. An earlier version of the site was known as the Educational Technology Timeline. The timeline covers all major achievements in the field of learning which took place all over the world. It also includes the projected learning technologies of the future.

Year	*Events*
40,000 BCE	Writing develops as a means of communication when people try to convey messages to others by cave paintings.
4000 BCE	The Ancient Egyptians develop the first known paper-like substance.
1400 BCE	First writing in China, on bones.
1000 BCE	Phoenician alphabet established .
650 BCE	Ashurbanipal's Royal Library at Nineveh comprising cuneiform tablets is developed as the world's largest collection for reference and research.
387 BCE ·	The Academy, the first university, is established in the city of Athens.
331 BCE	One of the Earliest Major Medical Schools Make.
196 BCE	The Rosetta Stone represents a simple but very effective technology, which revolutionized the knowledge about Egypt after its discovery in.
105	The invention of paper.
600	"Arabic" Numerals developed in India
751	Spread of Papermaking.
860	Cyrillic Alphabet is Invented.
1000	Beowulf—manuscript written, Invention of the reading stone and Musical notation
1453	The printing of the Bible with moveable type by Gutenberg transforms

1564	Graphite is discovered.
1755	The first English dictionary
1775	Continental Congress establishes a postal system
1795	Nicholas-Jacques Conte of France discovers the process of mixing graphite with clay
1800	Blackboard chalk becomes common in the classroom as class size increases.
1801	Chalkboards arise in U.S. Military schools
1816	Rene T.H. Laennec invents the stethoscope so he can listen to the sound of a female patient's heart without placing his head directly upon her chest
1827	The first photograph
1831	Michael Faraday makes one of his greatest discoveries - electromagnetic induction
1872	QWERTY: Christopher Sholes develops a machine to print the alphabet Efficiency is not always the goal!! — QWERTY is developed by Christopher
1876	Telephone invented
1895	Marconi makes first wireless transmission Dr. Miller Reese Hutchison invents the first hearing aid The Invention of the Radiotelegraph
1901	Marconi sends a radio signal across the Atlantic
1903	The Great Train Robbery, the first motion picture with a plot, makes its debut.
1905	John Ambrose Fleming develops the Fleming valve
1906	Lee de Forest develops the audion tube First "broadcast" radio signal with the human voice)
1927	First electronic television transmission
1928	The first edition of the Oxford-English Dictionary is completed)

1945	ENIAC Begins its first set of computations
1946	The Library School teaches about audio-visual materials and equipment
1947	The first transistor was created in 1947 by Brattain and Bardeen Mass production of calculators begins
1951	First Color Television Broadcast
1957	USSR launches Sputnik, first artificial earth satellite
1961	First stereo FM radio broadcasts
1962	Xerox puts out the first photographic copy machine
1966	The Educational Resources Information Center (ERIC) is established as a national information system
1970	Through the invention of the continuous wave helium-neon laser and enhancements to optical fiber, researchers develop 20dB/km fiber optics cable that is tested successfully in The Arpanet goes online
1978	HyperStudio, a multimedia authoring tool that allows people to communicate ideas on diskette, CD-ROM or Internet.
1979	A rising star. Wordstar becomes the 1st successful selling word processor.
1985	Aldus PageMaker is released for the Macintosh and desktop publishing is born
1987	Apple begins shipping Hypercard, a programming system and multimedia authoring tool
1989	The World-Wide Web begins at the Conseil European pour la Recherche Nucleaire Tim Berners-Lee invents World Wide Web The Introduction of CD-Recordable Format Invention of first digital camera. No more dealing with loading films! (Tina Chen)

1990	PowerPoint for Windows launched the first search engineWhiteboards begin to erase the chalkboard from schools
1994	Netscape offers a beta version of its Navigator browser on the Internet The first American Indian tribal web site goes online, May 3
1995	Classroom Connect offers educational WebQuests for classrooms all over the world
1997	Electronic ink is first developed at MIT Media Lab
1998	Launching of one of the world's first user-generated, science-based, interactive soap-opera Merriam-Webster publishes Spanish-English dictionary. High Definition Television
1999	The Advanced Cluster Computing Consortium introduces a super computer built with off the shelf parts Electronic course management and online courses come to the elementary schoolIBM introduces a prototype of the world's smallest computer with "full screen" capability
2000	NEATscape version 5.0 is released. Under the "decrypting wizard" button anyone can use any computer to read their native language Technology developed for superior quality, large size electronic maps
2002	Apple releases its third generation iMac in teal with a built-in microphone. Students take it to class, and it records the lecture so that the student can organize the lecture to meet his/her learning style. Big brother in high schools
2003	PaperGraderXPress, a wand-like, wireless device, which reads and analyzes any type of student composition, typed or hand-written A new PLATO satellite system, in which students have small handheld devices which they carry with them to

and from school The New York Times ceases printing on newsprint All public television stations must convert to digital The future is digital

2004 Thanks to advances in Cross-Language Information Retrieval (CLIR) techniques, multilingual text searches and displays are now widely available to international users of Internet resources. Virtual reality training now a requirement for all healthcare professionals

The Future Projections

Based on the direction of historical development and the future prospects, the following assumptions have been made for the shape of learning technology in the time to come. It covers a period of forty years in distant future:

2005

Books will be published in a dual format: Opti-books, which can be read as print books, but also have a CD-ROM embedded in the back. The first three- dimensional online university is established. Classroom chalkboard becomes electronic touchpad multi-task system.

2010

The e-Trapper will be introduced as the "all-in-one school tool". The Internet is accessed entirely through wireless, handheld, pocket computers. The first widespread use of electronic textbooks in US schools. Children's Interactive Easy Reader Series debuts in book format. 625 million homes to own DVD players. A large amount of communication will take place using wireless instant messaging. Fiber optics will become the backbone of type of communication. Old ink textbook will come to an end. Sandisk and Lexar release new Secure Digital EX cards

2015

Trieger Industries announces the arrival of TalkTech, a revolutionary, voice-activated technical assistant that can troubleshoot any technology related problem. Using BK3 Technology at speeds of 2.0 megs/second, consumers will purchase and rent digital films and music solely through the web. Smart space technology is now everywhere.

2020

Lamplighter School students use Logo to program a robotic teacher's aide. AT&T introduces Desktop Learning. The Individual Student Computer Automated Desk is introduced. Virtual reality is the phase of the Internet. Students learn history via virtual reality. VowerLife first used in classroom.

2040

Students use the Power Pencil, which stores the information that is written with it.

The invention of the Composition Room. First total ear transplant on a human to restore complete hearing in deaf infant; human classroom teachers are assisted by robots to aid students in their work; virtual reality trips in history; the idea of a classroom has a new global boundary

LEARNING TECHNOLOGY

Learning Technology is defined as 'the application of technology for the enhancement of teaching, learning and assessment. Learning Technology includes computer-based learning and multimedia materials and the use of networks and communications systems to support learning'. Learning Technology clearly embraces a wide range of applications of the available technologies.

An essential component in a Learning Technology is the ease with which the learner can interact with the contents. This is often referred to as the HCI, or Human-Computer Interface.

Over the last decade there have been many changes made within the Higher Education System, for example, the creation of new universities, the growth in the number of students gaining a university place and the increased availability of learning technologies. These changes, in combination with various internally and externally directed academic audits and quality assessment exercises, have resulted in many academic staff re-evaluating the instructional methods utilized within their courses and how these relate to the quality of their students' learning. High unemployment has also resulted in many perspective employers being able to redefine the range of skills, such as good communication and team working skills, which should now accompany the body of knowledge required from a university graduate.

As a consequence, universities are now tending to provide a broader range of instructional methods but at the same time students are also expected to undertake more independent learning. Many students starting university do not always possess the pre-requisite skills to cope with the challenge of the new and changing learning environment. An environment where they are expected to study without being told specifically what or when to study. Ultimately, their success or failure within university courses can be determined by their ability to adopt the most appropriate strategy within a particular learning situation. This might, for example involve working within a group to prepare an oral presentation on a given subject or studying for a multiple choice question test. Each requires a different set of skills. With many courses having their intended outcomes as being the development of higher level cognitive skills, such as the ability to think creatively or to be able to analyze or synthesize new information etc. course designers are now considering ways in which students can be encouraged to adopt a more active approach to their learning in order to undertake learning of a higher quality. This can involve not only considering the way in which the course is designed but also the level of study skills support provided for the students.

World Wide Web is the future environment of educational technology. Distance learning will use little else, and students based locally to their institutions will use it from home, leading to most students learning, at least in part, in a quasi distance learning environment. Software currently in use for viewing material on world wide web includes Netscape and Mosaic, both of which are free. Virtually any software can be used to create material for world wide web and, although sophisticated page design requires some (but not a lot of) expertise, a basic web page can be constructed by a beginner virtually instantly using some of the free facilitating software available on the WWW. It is currently possible to present text, graphics (still and video), and sound, and it will not be long before the viewer software will be able to present documents prepared for other environments (e.g. Powerpoint slide-shows) in screen windows at the click of a link.

The educational potential of world wide web is vast. It can, for example, be used;

* to deliver course material
* to provide revision resources
* to provide an environment for assessment (a web version of Question Mark is available, for example), and
* to develop IT-awareness

It can also be used for another form of student knowledge engineering — *student knowledge identification and dissemination* — with a focus on knowledge discovery, collation, and presentation, rather than knowledge clarification and understanding.

Students like this environment. They enjoy the challenge of discovering the unknown, of the discovery that people other than their tutor have made material available on the topic in which they are interested, and they enjoy the freedom it gives to control their own educational discovery process. They do not enjoy the slow speed at which it can operate. Therefore today's academic adopters and integrators of Web technology into their courses may need to make local copies of as much of the material they intend to use as possible. The Web is also, incidentally, ideally suited to obtaining a wide variety of project submissions from very simple assignment definitions.

THE POTENTIAL OF LEARNING TECHNOLOGY

The following are the areas where technology may enhance education:

- Technology may provide powerful solutions for the delivery of high-quality learning suited to the needs of the age. In addition to shaping the desirable outcomes of the learning process the information age offers potential enhancements to the ways in which learning may take place.
- Technology provides near instantaneous access to vast quantities of information and learning materials at near zero cost to anyone with Internet access. Educationalists may provide a pathway through the mass of available content by means of selective, quality-assured directories and search engines, effectively forming subject-specific "digital libraries".
- Technology may relieve the "loneliness of the long distance learner" by providing asynchronous communication channels bridging both temporal and geographic distance. A major function of learning environments is the ability they offer learners to communicate with both peers and tutors irrespective of physical locality or time zone. There is enormous learning potential in the exchange and discussion of ideas.
- Technology offers the potential of delivering a personalized learning experience to individual learners. People have different strengths and weaknesses and learn in different ways. In a classroom setting the same experience is delivered to every student. In technology mediated learning a unique learning experience may be presented to every learner based upon individual characteristics and performance in previous lessons.

– Technology can provide models and simulations that actively involve the learner to a greater degree than was ever possible in classroom-based learning. The learner is able to receive feedback on his/her interactions with the system and is thus able to learn by doing within the safety of

LEARNING WITH NEW MEDIA

Exploiting the power of new media and techniques to support all three types of learning. The complexity of transformational-change projects makes learning difficult, whether in conditioning staff emotionally to accept change, conveying the new context of redesigned processes to those employees that have to assume new roles, or developing a new way of working. It has been observed that a few organisations have tried to support the learning process with the help of new and innovative methods, tools and technologies. Visualization and simulation have beenidentified as promising techniques that help to ease, enable and facilitate the learning process:

* Facilitating learning with the help of visualization. The common saying, 'a picture tells a thousand words', builds on the recognition that the vast majority of people are visually oriented rather than auditive. This can be exploited, especially in complex cases. A striking example is the effort of a US-based consumer-products company currently redesigning its distribution process. It took a completely new and creative approach both to stimulate ideas and discussion about how to change the old complex process (with the purpose of 'unfreezing'), and to educate and inform its staff about the new redesigned process. A set of large posters was created with the help of outside professionals with the visualization expertise to tell a whole story in one picture. The set of posters visualizes the complete process and marketplace context of the company, the 'big picture', in a self-explanatory way. It employs

depictions of working situations, icons and descriptive terms with which the staff are familiar. These pictures are designed to support education and training and, as they will be displayed on every floor, to communicate and reinforce the message in a pervasive way. The effort and intense thinking that goes into making the learning a permanent process is remarkable. The use of video clips or multimedia-based material builds on the same recognition of visualization that has been applied in other projects.

* Enabling learning with the help of simulation. Helping individuals to adopt new behaviours, play new roles, and acquire new knowledge and skills is done more easily if one can demonstrate 'live' the new environment, how the new process works and who the new customers are. An emerging, powerful technique for simulating the future is the Business Reengineering Laboratory. A comprehensive description of a lab will be given in the third section of this report. A particularly unique characteristic of a lab is that it enables full simulation of the new process including supporting information systems and tools. Because the simulation of the new way of working is realistic but not yet operational, it allows learning to occur in a totally different and much richer way than simple classroom education.

SUPPORTING SELF-CONTROLLED LEARNING

The new way of working is often based on caseworkers or teams who have to cope with a much broader scope of tasks and duties. Often, what these individuals will have to learn to accomplish their mission successfully is simply not foreseeable. It is 'on the job' (real or simulated) where they will find out whether they need more knowledge or new interpersonal competencies. In the new work context, the employees will be best placed to determine what they have to learn and the best way of learning it. One supporting means to monitor learning progress is measurement. Without effective and easily available measures of the performance of the work process, and preferably of the individual's or team's contribution, it is difficult to develop self-controlled learning.

E-LEARNING?

E-learning is defined as Education via the Internet, network, or standalone computer. Network-enabled transfer of skills and knowledge. E-learning refers to using electronic applications and processes to learn. E-learning applications and processes include Web-based learning, computer-based learning, virtual classrooms, and digital collaboration. Content is delivered via the Internet, intranet/extranet, audio or video tape, satellite TV, and CD-ROM.

E-learning is the modern method of learning with the help of electronic media. It is the learning technology, which allows anyone to learn anywhere and usually at any time, as long as one has a properly configured computer. E-learning is also defined as the use of technology to enable people to learn anytime and anywhere. e-Learning can include training, the delivery of just-in-time information and guidance from experts Cell phones allow to communicate any time and usually anywhere, as long as you have a properly configured phone.

Benefits of E-learning

E-learning has definite benefits over traditional classroom training. While the most obvious are the flexibility and the cost savings from not having to travel or spend excess time away from work, there are also others that might not be so obvious. For example:

1. **It's less expensive** to produce e-training is virtually free once you reach the break-even point. Synchronous programs will have continued costs associated with the instructor managing the class, but will still be lower than traditional courses.

2. **It's self-paced** - Most e-learning programs can be taken when needed. The "books" that you set up create a module-based design allowing the learner to go through smaller chunks of training that can be used and absorbed for a while before moving on.
3. **It moves faster** - According to an article "Training and Development Magazine," e-learning courses progress up to 50 percent faster than traditional courses. This is partly because the individualized approach allows learners to skip material they already know and understand and move onto the issues they need training on.
4. **It provides a consistent message** - E-learning eliminates the problems associated with different instructors teaching slightly different material on the same subject. For company-based training, this is often critical.
5. **It can work from any location and any time** - E-learners can go through training sessions from anywhere, usually at anytime. This Just-In-Time (JIT) benefit can make learning possible for people who never would have been able to work it into their schedules prior to the development of e-learning.
6. **It can be updated easily and quickly** - Online e-learning sessions are especially easy to keep up-to-date because the updated materials are simply uploaded to a server. CD-ROM-based programs may be slightly more expensive to update and distribute, but still come out cheaper than reprinting manuals and retraining instructors.
7. **It can lead to increased retention** and a stronger grasp on the subject - This is because of the many elements that are combined in e-learning to reinforce the message, such as video, audio, quizzes, interaction, etc. There is also the ability to revisit or replay sections of the training that might not have been clear the first time around. Try that in a crowded auditorium!

8. It can be **easily managed** for large groups of students. Managers can review a student's scores and identify any areas that need additional training.

Learning Resources

Learning Resource supports the learning process by providing quality materials, services and support to all students, faculty, and staff. The audiovisual catalogue containing multimedia titles can be searched from any computer with Internet access. All staff and students may book interactive videodiscs and CD-ROMs, along with traditional videotapes and supporting materials.

These resources are of the following categories:

- CD-ROM-based
- Network-based
- Intranet-based
- Internet-based

E-learning can include the following formats:

- text
- video
- audio
- animation
- virtual environments.

It can be a very rich learning experience that can even surpass the level of training experience in a crowded classroom. It is self-paced, hands-on learning.

E-learning can suffer from many of the same pitfalls as classroom training such as:

- boring slides
- monotonous speech
- little opportunity for interaction.

The beauty of e-learning, however, is that the educational

software allow the creation of very effective learning environments that can engulf anyone in the material.

E-learning can incorporate many elements that make learning new material, a new process or a new program more fun. Making learning more fun or interesting is what makes it more effective. If you aren't pulled into the material, you really aren't learning as well as you could be. This is what makes e-learning so great for so many types of learning. Obviously, every type of training can't be turned into e-training, but many can with excellent results.

The keys to successful e-learning include:

Varying the types of content

Images, sounds and text work together to build memory in several areas of the brain and result in better retention of the material.

Creating interaction that engages the attention

Games, quizzes and even just required manipulation of something on the screen creates more interest, which in turn builds better retention.

Providing immediate feedback

E-learning courses can build in immediate feedback to correct misunderstood material. The more immediate the feedback the better, because each step of learning builds upon the previous step. If no feedback is given, then the next step may be building upon an incorrect interpretation.

Encouraging interaction with other e-learners and an e-instructor Chat rooms, discussion boards, instant messaging and e-mail all offer effective interaction for e-learners, and do a good job of taking the place of classroom discussion. Building an online community significantly influences the success of online programs.

E-Learning Elements

The following are the e-learning elements which are needed to be incorporated in a training program:

Self-paced

E-learning courses offer user-controlled elements that just aren't feasible in regular training classes. For example, differentiating the sound of an irregular *heart* beat from that of a regular heart beat by clicking on icons on the screen allows the learner to listen at their own pace and replay the sound as often as they like. This self-paced element is one of the things that makes e-learning so effective.

Interactive

Another element that e-learning offers is interactivity. This type of interactivity can be in the form of simply clicking on appropriate responses to questions, clicking to animate an object or start a process, or dragging and dropping items to practice a skill.

Interactive games based on the training message are also very effective at improving learning. Now, you may be thinking of "Doom" or "Tomb Raider," but gaming in a training setting doesn't have to be quite that elaborate — although it certainly can be!

Think about games where you go through a series of tasks, learning about the environment, and use tools you've discovered along the way. Those same techniques can be incorporated into many types of learning programs. Games can take you through an adventure in almost any type of scenario. Being able to explore, try, succeed or fail makes good training.

This type of game scenario could be easily created by using photos or graphics, and applying hot spots that link to video clips. Once the video clip has played, a multiple-choice quiz box could pop up that asks the user what he or she should do next. The options for answers could be linked to individual video clips that play out that scenario. Once the scene has played, the results of the choice (i.e. whether it was the right decision or the wrong decision) could then be revealed as either a talking head video, an audio response or simply a text box. This scene could be as simple or as intricate as you want to make it.

Motivating

Being motivated to learn is half the battle. Knowing the course you are taking is going to have some "fun" elements like video, audio, animation and the "gaming" scenarios we mentioned above creates more interest and curiosity in learning. This, too, leads to better retention and faster learning.

Other motivating factors with e-learning are the conveniences that it offers, such as being able to go through the course any time and anywhere (almost). It is much easier to work training into a busy schedule when you don't have to take two days off to travel and then sit in a classroom.

Other e-learning elements

Besides the bigger issues like interaction, control of the pace, and motivation, e-learning can readily put to use the information that researchers have been studying for the past 30 or more years. These studies have identified things that can greatly affect memory and recall. Some of the key research found significant improvements in recall when:

* using colors and specific color combinations
* combining images with words
* combining sounds (or voice or music) with images
* using multiple types of media
* using layouts that flow with the natural movement of the eye

MEDIA COMPONENTS

Various categories of the available media are integrated to create an e-learning environment. This can be done, for example, by presenting information in one form (e.g. text on the screen stating a fact), then including an audio or video clip of something related that fact, then using the information to help the student create his or her own visualization of the fact. This last step could come in the form of a quiz that asks questions forcing the student to use reasoning to combine the two facts in order to come up with the correct answer. Or, it could be turned into a game that takes the student through a process which draws into play the two related bits of information.

Incorporating text

Text is not necessarily seen as multimedia, but it is an important element in e-learning. The problem with many e-learning programs is that the developers have simply taken their existing text-based teaching and put it on the computer screen. The interactivity of the program consists of reading text and then clicking on an arrow to proceed to the next page. You have to use some text, but you can do it responsibly. Keep it to no more than six lines per screen and intersperse it with other elements. Also, don't overdo your text animations.

Technology allows to have text appear and disappear, or simply move to another location on the screen, within pre-set time increments or upon a click or rollover of the mouse. Using this type of animation may make more sense in many training instances. For example, you might have an audio clip that ends with a question posed to the student. If the student doesn't respond within a set amount of time, text could pop up that gives a hint or instructs the student to do something else.

Incorporating audio

The power of audio may often be overlooked, but the combination of written and spoken words does have a big impact on recall and retention. Audio represents the missing back or the information that is not covered by the other forms of presentation. Audio, just like other media files, requires good bandwidth if you're producing a Web-based program. When using audio, one has to be sure that it is enhancing the message. The audio clips should add value to the other elements on the screen, not detract from them.

Incorporating video

Video as a learning tool is very effective in online education. It is used for the following:

* Use video stories to put the subject into its context of use.
* Use video clips followed by questions to encourage active participation from trainees and build on existing knowledge.
* Ensure that these clips have the information required to answer the questions.
* Limit the length of talking head video clips and use them to elaborate on specific points.

Students could go through portions of learning material, then begin a video story that they control through selecting actions that create a scenario. Their choices would be graded based on the correct actions. By relating to characters on the screen and being able to control their "destinies," students can learn from mistakes that would be too costly to make in the real world. By putting that portion of the training on the Web, updating the files is easier than recreating and distributing new CD-ROMs.

Incorporating animation

Animated graphic elements are highly effective when used in training. They are fun to watch, and can get a message across that words or audio cannot. Animation is another element, however, that has to be used appropriately. While animations don't typically require the bandwidth that video does, they still can slow down a Web-based program.

Technology now provides some tools to aid in creating animations and even some video. SmartCap is a tool that can be used in software or other computer-screen-type training. It can capture a series of screen movements and export those movements to a video. One can animate almost any graphic image or text to put on the page. This can include buttons that play specific sounds when clicked, or even that change to another image when the mouse moves over them. This is known as a rollover. One can probably see this type of effect on Web pages. Rollovers can actually do more than just alter an image — they can bring in another path or choice for the student. The possibilities for animations and interactivity are only limited by imagination.

Incorporating quizzes and tests

Interspersing the course with quizzes that pop up after material has been presented offers good feedback and reinforcement for learning. In most learning situations, the more immediate the feedback, the better — it's the building effect of learning.

Inserting questions and quizzes amounts to selecting "Question" from the "Insert" menu and then deciding what type of question you want it to be. Inserting multiple choice, multiple-multiple choice, true-or-false, matching or fill-in-the-blank questions is simple, and feedback can be given immediately after the question is answered. The feedback can be in the form of an audio response or text response. The answers to these questions can be tracked and used to compute the student's final score and grade for the course.

Methods of E-Learning

People learn in many different ways and at different times. To support these different learning needs, one needs different e-learning delivery methods. The following are the methods of E-learning:

Synchronous e-Learning

* Virtual Classroom
* Audio and Video Conferencing
* Chat
* Shared Whiteboard

* Application Sharing
* Instant Messaging
* Asynchronous e-Learning
* Self-paced Courses
* Discussion Groups

Synchronous Learning

Synchronous e-Learning lets teachers conduct classes over the Internet. The synchronous technologies also allow people to interact with peers and experts.

Virtual Classroom

A virtual classroom duplicates the capabilities found in a real classroom. A virtual classroom provides.

* **A place to meet**: Students and teachers use their computers to go to a virtual meeting place instead of a classroom.
* **Take attendance:** A list of students is recorded.
* **Lecture:** Teachers can choose from a variety of synchronous technologies including:
* Slide presentation
* Audio and video conferencing
* Application sharing
* Shared whiteboard
* **Interaction with students:** Students can indicate when they want to speak by virtually raising their hand. Teachers can let students speak through audio and video conferencing. Teachers and students can use instant messaging and chat.
* **Quizzes:** Teachers can present questions to students.
* **Breakout Sessions:** Students can work together in groups.

Most companies that sell virtual classroom software provide all of these capabilities in a single package.

Audio and Video Conferencing

Audio conferencing can be implemented in two ways:

* Computers connected to the Internet. Common names for this kind of implementation are IP Audio Conferencing or Voice-over-IP.

* Phone conferences. People dial the same number to participate in an audio conference.

Video conferencing can also be implemented in two ways:

* Computers connected to the Internet. The computers need digital cameras.

* Special video conferencing devices that connect over the Internet or over phone lines.

Chat

Chat allows several people to communicate with each other. Each participant uses a computer to type their comments. The other participants can see the name of the person and their comments.

Shared Whiteboard

A shared whiteboard lets a group of people communicate by typing comments, drawing, highlighting and pointing. The whiteboard shown on the right is provided by Microsoft's NetMeeting. NetMeeting is free conferencing program that works well with a small group of participants. NetMeeting also provides video conferencing, audio conferencing and application sharing.

Application Sharing

You can demonstrate how to use software applications to remote learners with application sharing. A teacher can also let the learner take control of the application to practice performing tasks.

Instant Messaging

Instant messaging is similar to chat. One person communicates to another through typing. Instant messaging also provides some additional features. With instant messaging, you can keep a list of list of people that you might like to chat with. The list will indicate if they are online, offline, available for chat or busy. These features make instant messaging an excellent tool for learning from peers.

Asynchronous Learning

Asynchronous e-Learning lets people learn at anytime.

Self-Paced Courses

Self-paced courses can be delivered in many ways including:

* Internet
* Intranet or Local Area Networks
* CD-ROM or DVD
* Wireless

The obvious advantage of a self-paced course is convenience. People can get the training they need at any time. This can include just-in-time training where a person gets exactly the training that they need to perform a task. Self-paced courses are created with e-learning authoring tools.

Many people need external motivation to take and complete a course of study. Since self-paced courses can be offered without a teacher and without a required completion time there may be many learners who will not enroll or complete the course work. One must be sure that there are professional and/or personal incentives for learners to take and complete self-paced courses. Some people need help understanding the learning material presented in a course. Since self-paced courses can be offered without teachers, those people may fail to learn. One will need to provide experts who can answer their questions.

Self-paced courses usually have these features:

* **Multimedia:** A mix of text, graphics, animation, audio and video to enhance the learning process

* **Interactivity:** An instructional strategy that helps a learner practice what they have learned
* **Bookmarking:** Lets the learner stop the course at any time and restart it from the same point
* **Tracking:** Report the learner's performance within a course to a Learning Management System (LMS)

Some self-paced courses have these advanced features:

* **Simulation:** Providing practice with a mock-up of a real system
* **Online Experts:** Provide access to experts through chat or online discussion
* **Multiple Bookmarks:** Designate one or more pages of the course to access while on the job
* **Search:** Search through a course to find information required to complete a task
* **Notes and Highlights:** Mark one or more parts of a course that contain the most important information

Discussion Groups

A discussion group is a collection of conversations that occur over time. Other names for discussion groups are message boards, bulletin boards and discussion forums. A discussion group might start out as a question from an individual. Some time later, another individual responds to that question. Others can respond to the question (creating a thread) or they can start their own conversation (forming another thread). A threaded discussion might also start with a teacher asking an open-ended question that leads to a class discussion. Discussion groups can be used to support a group of people taking the same class or can be used to support people performing similar tasks.

Threaded discussions allow experts to provide guidance to more people than they could with individual communications. They can do this because their answers are recorded for others to see and because they can answer the same type of question just once. Learners may be able to get answers to questions immediately even though no expert is available.

It is evident from the above discussion that the learning technologies will play greater role in education in the time to come. Some countries have adopted it for most of their activities. The developing countries like India are expected to gain momentum in this direction as a result of its advancing technologies.

8

Internet as a Reference Tool

Internet has revolutionized the world of information. It is one of the two technological innovations that have greatly influenced the development of communication strategies and practices in both the general and the business communities of the world. The first innovation was the invention of the printing press by Johann Gutenberg around 1450 in Mainz, Germany. Gutenberg's invention served to democratize the possession and transmission of texts, for it made the production of books much easier and, thereby, much cheaper than did the manuscript method it replaced. A little over four hundred years after Gutenberg began printing books with his press, Alexander Graham Bell invented the first telephone for practical use.

In the twentieth century, the invention and development of radio and television, like the invention of the telephone in the nineteenth century, have further led to the democratization of communication in both the social and business spheres. Like printing, radio and television have generally been confined to unidirectional communication. The users of these communicative channels have almost entirely been receivers rather than transmitters of information.

The invention of the computer and the development of the Internet have recently begun to alter the historical unidirectionality of mass communication. By creating pages for the World Wide Web, E-mail messages for Mailing List subscribers, and articles for UseNet news groups, most people can now for the first time economically publish their ideas for world consumption. If for no other reason than this one, college students would be well advised to learn how to use these latest technological innovations, innovations so powerful that they could perhaps be characterized as potentially the most revolutionary since Gutenberg's invention.

Equally important is the growing centrality of the Internet to the myriad functions of the world's business communities. Indeed, most of the major newspapers (and many of the major news magazines) have themselves, being well aware of the revolutionary promise of the Internet, begun to publish special Internet editions. Even more importantly, most of the major businesses organizations of the world have created, or are in the process of creating, websites that supply information about their products.

Students of the process of communication in general and of business communication specifically are also increasingly becoming aware of the revolutionary nature of another Internet application specially, electronic mail. While in 1860 the postal system could deliver a business letter in eight days and today under the best of circumstances a similar letter between the same two cities in two or three days can be delivered almost the same time through a posted E-mail. The implications for businesses daily facing competitive pressures are obvious.

WHAT IS INTERNET?

The Internet is a global network of computer networks. Thousands of networks are linked together, forming a worldwide network. This network makes it possible for millions of people to communicate, to share information about common interests and to work on the same documents in multi-media format. This network is also a new way to do business electronically through the World Wide Web or Web, which is an enormous collection of web sites facility that brought the sudden popularity to the Internet. Many people think of the Internet as the WWW. It is a web of multi-media hypertext documents linked around the world.

The most popular feature of the Internet is the Web sites or electronic documents (files) that are stored on computers (servers) all over the world. The documents are written in a special programming language called HTML (hyper text markup language), which are read using a web browser such as Microsoft's Internet Explorer or Netscape's Navigator. A web site can have formatted text, images, animation, sound, music, movies, and more. With more and more sophisticated and easy-to-use Web browsers, an Internet user can access many documents with a mouse click.

Internet has become user-friendly for computer-illiterate people to use. Originally, the Internet was created for government use, to make military communications more secure. It was started so that technical data could be transferred more easily. Since then, however, the Internet has expanded to much more than that.

The Internet is composed of Local Area Networks (LAN), Metropolitan Area Networks (MAN), and Wide Area Networks (WAN). This is a way of breaking down the huge web of networks into smaller groups to organize them better. The Internet is not really owned or run by a single person or organization; rather, it is a collection of networks all over the world that is comprised of many organizations and companies. One of the main reasons why the Internet has become so popular is because nobody really rules over it and so users have a lot of freedom in what they do. There is one group, however, which tries to organize the Internet to make it more usable. This is the Internet Society, based in Washington, DC. The purpose of this group is to sponsor agencies that "bring order from chaos in such a huge Undertaking .(*http://www.mozcom.com/user/ig/history.html*)

The Internet is a packet-orientated network which means that the data someone transfers is divided in packets. This principle is not new, It was already used in the 1960s. The networks are linked by special computers, the so-called Routers. A Router checks where the packet goes and decides in which direction to send it but not every Router is linked with every other Router, they just decide on the direction your data takes. So if the Routers know where the data is going, there must be some address. There is an address, namely the IP - protocol. The data transferred with IP is divided in packets. This is handled by another protocol, the TCP. It was soon discovered that the IP - addresses that are, in fact, just numbers are easy to handle for computers, but not for us humans. So the Domain Name System was introduced in 1984. This was a brief description of how the Internet functions.

After the Internet was born in 1969 during the cold war when the United States Department of Defence created the ARPANET or Advanced Research Projects Agency Network, a network that provided research agencies access to software they could not afford it has grown and is used for many purposes. E-mail is one of the most prominent components of the Internet because it is a quick and easy way to communicate with other people. For the next decade, the Internet was used mainly to support e-mail and discussion groups, as well as the transferring of government files.

Internet is continuously growing internationally. Within the last one decade, its services have spread among all nations of the word. In 1991, it was within the reach of 73 countries only but by 1995 it reached 148 countries. The number of Internet users is also growing tremendously. It almost doubles after every two years. The scope of Internet is also widening as it is being used for publishing of ideas apart from being an effective tool for storage aid retrieval of information.

USES OF THE INTERNET

There are basically three uses of Internet:

- Communication
- Research
- Publishing

COMMUNICATION

E-mail

The primary Internet communication tool is electronic mail. E-mail is nothing more than sending and/or receiving messages through computer. It combines the immediacy of the telephone with the word processing power of the computer. E-mail is being increasingly used for business, to keep in touch with friends and relatives, and to work on a project with someone at a place of choice.

E-mail is an extremely low-cost form of communication. Unlike telephone or standard postal services, there are no volume or long distance surcharges for sending e-mail. One can send one e-mail message across the city or 10,000 messages to the other side of the world for the same fee.

If you are hooked up to the Internet through an Internet Service Provider (ISP) or Commercial On-Line Service, e-mail is part of the service. Alternatively, one can get a stand-alone e-mail account that allows to send and receive messages without ever seeing the rest of the Internet. For people who do not have their own account, or who will want to access their e-mail remotely, Web e-mail accounts are also available. These accounts are hosted entirely on a Web site and your mail is protected by a login name and password. Many of these accounts are free. Anytime one can access to the World Wide Web will have access to e-mail. Web e-mail accounts are particularly appealing to people who anticipate moving frequently because their address would stay the same even as they changed ISPs. Some people prefer the relative anonymity of Web e-mail or wish to avoid the unsolicited bulk e-mail, or spam, that may result if users participate in a newsgroup that is subsequently "harvested" for addresses by bulk e-mail companies. With the advent of pre-paid usage cards, Web e-mail accounts may become more popular yet. To a lesser extent, the Internet is also used for communicating in chat rooms, newsgroups, list serves and through telephony.

Internet Telephony

Internet telephony (IPT) is the transport of telephone calls over the Internet. IPT could use traditional telephony devices, multimedia PCs or dedicated terminals to take part in the calls. The calls could entirely or partially be transmitted over the Internet.

Phone, fax and video calls (IP telephony) can now be placed over the Internet (or any IP network) using market available client software or hardware. In most instances, users will only need to make a one-time purchase of client software or hardware to begin placing unlimited long distance calls for the cost of an Internet connection. The quality of the calls will not match that of calls placed over the traditional phone network. However with additional hardware and software purchases, higher quality communications can be achieved.

Briefly, an Internet telephony application compresses and digitizes your analog voice signals and sends them as individual packets across an IP network (a digital network) to the recipient Internet telephony application. The recipient application then decompresses the voice transmissions as a result you have Internet voice communications.

Generally, one needs at least a 75 MHz system, with a sound card, microphone, speakers, a connection to the Internet and the software or hardware application that will enable you to place and receive calls over the Internet. Most of the Internet telephony applications will only allow to communicate with other users of the same application, so the call's recipient must be using the same Internet telephone application.

RESEARCH

For researchers. Internet is the library of the present and future. A growing number of people are using the Internet for research. Business people are assessing new markets, students and writers are looking for information and concerned parents are searching for the latest facts on nutrition. The Internet is the ultimate technology of the time to come. The following Internet Information Sources are useful in research.

Newsgroups

Special interest Usenet newsgroups are excellent places to locate expertise in a given field. Newsgroups act as electronic bulletin boards through which people exchange information, ask technical questions, offer solutions, gather leads and forge new contacts. One can log into a newsgroup, check any or all of the messages that have been posted, add your own message if desired, or simply leave. Anyone on the Net can participate, and it's free. With ten of thousands of newsgroups in existence, it is difficult to imagine a subject matter that is not covered.

List Serves

List serves, or mailing lists, are useful tools for gathering information. They are similar to newsgroups in that individuals post messages to a centralized location, and everyone on the list gets the message. The biggest difference between newsgroups and list serves is that newsgroups require active monitoring, whereas list serves are passively monitored. If you subscribe to a list serve, every message posted to that list by other users will wind up in the e-mail in-box. List serves are good for individuals who do not have the time to actively monitor a range of newsgroups, but who still want to remain current on a specific topic.

Information Services

Other types of information-gathering services are available on the Internet, including commercial information services and research companies. Also, thousands of libraries are connected to the Internet, permitting even casual users to access their catalogues and request loans through inter-library programs.

In addition to those information services, the number of on-line journals, newspapers and trade magazines increases each month. Much of the information in these publications is free, although some are accessible only to paid subscribers.

Educational Internet sites

One of the best ways to locate meaningful information is through any of the public and private sector organizations that have established an Internet presence. Government departments and agencies, private corporations, law firms, retailers, trade associations and educational institutions publish a tremendously rich and diverse collection of information. And as more organizations develop their own Internet sites, the value of the Net as a research tool will only increase.

PUBLISHING

In 1995, the World Wide Web emerged as the most popular part of the Internet. The multi-media Web allows for the display of still images, moving video, audio and text in any combination, and its growth is phenomenal.

A site on the WWW is open 24 hours a day, seven days a week. Sites can be as simple as a one-screen greeting designed by a hobbyist, or as complicated as an interactive catalogue designed for a major corporation. Anyone can design and maintain a site for whatever legal purpose they wish. How many Web sites are there? No one knows – but best estimates put the number of sites added to the World Wide Web every day in the thousands. The information on World Wide Web sites is not restricted to technology issues.

Home Paging

The concept of homepage grew along with the World Web, also known as the Web, WWW or W3. The term has multiple meanings. The sense in which it is used today is not the same as used in the past. Earlier, being represented by many terms, a homepage now refers to the first page of a website or the page which is approached first by a searcher while connected with a website. It is also the page, which is referred to in the website repeatedly as the search within the website generally starts afresh from the homepage.

A homepage establishes the identity of an individual or organization on the net and is like putting up a flag for someone in the cyberspace. It is the Guttenberg's press of our time with extended facility for low cost publishing. Anyone cab publish any kind of information including text, graphics, sound and video or a combination of all on the web through the homepage. It opens the doors of the millions of Internet users all over the world to receive ideas floated by someone. A homepage can be a full service front and for an organization. Here we restrict to discuss a home page about the universities only.

A homepage is needed for global recognition of an individual or organization. Universities stand for teaching, research and extension and what distinguishes them from college is the facility for research. Higher the intended level of research in an academic institution, more is the need for a good information system that is effectively provided by homepage across the geographical boundaries of the institutions. The basic requirements for creation of a homepage are computer, Internet connection, Web space, contents creation and file transfer.

SEARCHING ON THE INTERNET

A Web page may have hypertext links to other documents. That is, a word, group of words, or an image can be an anchor referencing another page somewhere on the Internet. Using this feature, someone can go from one page to another with a click on the mouse button.

Most pages have links to other pages of the same topic or interest. Once you have found a page of your interest, you can easily find references to other pages. The pages are linked together like a spider web, hence the name World Wide Web. While reading the pages of certain interest, you may see a link to a page of another interest and decide to read it also, thus you wander around the Web from home. This activity is called "surfing the net".

Search Engine

One problem with the Internet is the difficulty in finding the needed information. Millions of Web pages are out there, but where and how to find them? Search can be started from the home page of Internet Service Provider (ISP). We have listed some of the popular search engines here. They have a database of Web pages and let you search for pages containing certain keywords. Good search engines have large frequently updated databases, fast results and a wide range of topics of interest for anyone.

People search some of the most popular resources. Most of the pages have anchors to other search engines, so if you can't find the pages you want, you can go to other engines from there. When going to the search engine web site, type in what you are looking for and click 'Find', the 'button' next to the search box. If you find thousands of results, you may want to narrow your search.

Most Popular Search Engines

* **Google**
* **Yahoo! (Nasdaq:YHOO)** - provider of comprehensive online products and services to consumers and businesses worldwide.
* **AltaVista** - featuring web and newsgroup search engine as well as paid submission services.
* **Lycos** - online destination site combining elements of navigation, community, and commerce.
* **Excite** - provides search, news, email, personals, portfolio tracking, and other services.
* **HotBot** - search engine that offers custom filters, skins, and access various other engines.
* **AllTheWeb** - search engine which indexes web pages, as well as multimedia, audio, FTP, PDF, and MS Word files from around the world.

* **Open Directory Project (DMOZ) (6)**
* **Northern Light** - customize search folders for integrated web and article searching.

Apart from it, there are numerous search engines which operate to locate the relevant information to the users. In addition, Meta Search Engines are used to submit questions to several search engines at one time. Many metasearch engines are now including paid placement sites in their results lists.

Meta Search

By using General Search, one may choose to use search engines, directories, or listings of reviewed sites for your search. You may specify which search sites are used and the amount of time spent on the search. Specific Search offers the option to do metasearches by topic such as health, MP3, sports or science. This site has a privacy policy and offers no cookies.

Search.Com

Search.Com provides general metasearching using search engines and directories. You must use the advanced search option to specify which engines and directories are searched. There is specialized topic metasearching in categories such as news, people, reference, business, computing, and gaming. From C|Net.

ProFusion

You can choose to submit your search to from one to nine search engines, or let Profusion pick the best search engines to fit your terms. Results are combined and duplicates are eliminated. Searches may also be done in topics such as news, business, health, investing, and others.

HotBot

You can choose to search Google, Teoma, Fast or Inktomi. There are a number of different filtering and search options available through Advanced Search.

Kartoo

Kartoo graphically presents relationships between the web sites located for a topic. Kartoo will give you a new perspective on your search results, but it is a good idea to read the Help and FAQ before doing a search.

Vivisimo

Vivisimo uses 8 search engines and directories. Results are combined, and also organized into folders by topic on the left side of the screen. There is no specialized topic searching.

Ask Jeeves

Ask Jeeves a question in plain English and you will receive a reply from either Jeeves' list of human selected sites or from a metasearch of several of the major search engines. There is also Ask Jeeves for Kids. Jeeves is a fun place to visit, but lacks the relevance and precision needed by the serious searcher. Ask Jeeves also includes advertisments in its search results so your search results may include a site that paid to be there.

Highway 61 MetaCrawler

Submit your search to 9 search engines and directories. References are listed on the search results page in order of relevance, and the search engine from which the reference was retrieved is indicated. There are Boolean AND and OR search options. The amount of time spent on the search can be specified, and there are two options for the number of references retrieved. These folks have a sense of humor too which is nice to see in a search site.

Ixquick Metasearch

Sites in the results list are given star ratings according to the their placement in the top 10 of each of the engines and directories searched. It is possible to choose which search engines are used after you have done your initial search. This option is presented in the results list. There are individual searches for the Web, news, MP3, and pictures. This site offers many cookies.

Mama : The Mother of All Search Engines

The basic metasearch uses 6 search engines and directories to search web sites, news, usenet, stock quotes, MP3 files, images, and sounds. The results are combined and duplicates eliminated. If you go to Power Search, you will find that Mama is searching a rather unimpressive group of sites. If you want a wider search range, try another metasearch site.

MetaCrawler

MetaCrawler uses 10 search engines and directories and the results are combined. Use the power search option to specify which engines are used and the amount of time spent on the search.

Datavor

Datavor is not really a metasearch site but it is quite useful. You may enter your search term and get results from Datavor's collection. Then you can run the same search term on a large number of other search engines and compare the results.

Dogpile

Search the web, usenet newsgroups, FTP sites, business news, stock quotes, weather and newswires. The Web Metasearch uses both search engines and subject directories. Results are returned rapidly, but are not combined. This might be the place to go to locate shopping sites but the serious researcher might be wasting time here.

Chubba

Chubba submits searches to Alta Vista, WhatUSeek, Ah-Ha, Infoseek, and Lycos. You may not specify which search engines are to be used. Chubba searches the web, newsgroups, an encyclopedia, a dictionary, auctions, and the weather. Chubba is operated by WhatUSeek.

Debriefing

Debriefing seems to be another manifestation of the Ixquick search site.

WebCrawler

You may not specify which search engines and directories to use, and you do not know which have been used.

The information on the web is growing and being updated every day. There are millions of web pages and there is a lot of information. However, one of the most noticeable problems with the web today is the difficulty in finding a specific piece of information. Unlike a library, there is no central card catalog for the web and it follows no organizational standard. Instead, search tools are used to locate information on the web. For the most part, they are fast, easy to use and open 24 hours a day. A search tool performs searches of the Internet based upon input by the user. This input might include topics, keywords or phrases, or any other type of search criteria. Some of the difficulty in finding information is going away because the tools for locating information are maturing, becoming more powerful and sophisticated every day. Because of the enormous amount of information out there, search tools are indispensable.

There are numerous tools available for finding information on the web, and each of these operates somewhat differently. Some of the tools use a comprehensive approach and try to include all of the information on the web. Other tools only cover a narrow subject matter, for example, there is a tool specific for finding conferences sponsored by the Microsoft Corporation. The results of your search will depend on the type of search tool you are using.

Google and Yahoo are very good at finding general information, because it organizes web sites into popular categories. If you wanted to find the Walt Disney home page, Yahoo would be a good tool to use. In comparison, AltaVista is much more comprehensive. If you wanted to find the name of the producer for Walt Disney's movie "The Lion King", AltaVista would be a good tool to use. These two tools demonstrate many of the features found in other search tools and you should be able to apply this knowledge to other tools.

One gets confused when learning about search tools because there are so many terms. This includes terms like "search engines", "meta indexes", "web guides", "directories", etc. The value of spending a lot of time on these terms is questionable as they are often vaguely defined and misused one should not be overly concerned about all of the terms, but rather how to perform a search.

Therefore, rather then dwelling on specific terms, let's look at two general approaches to finding information on the web. These approaches can be used to find the same information, however, each one has its advantages and disadvantages. Many search tools now support both approaches. For the duration of this module we will refer to these approaches as "browsing" and "keyword searching", however, as you spend more time on the Internet, you will see many other names for these same approaches and their variations.

Searching by Browsing: Searching by browsing is like surfing the web. One start out looking at a very wide range of topics and after following six or seven links you have narrowed your attention to a specific web site. If the specific site does not contain the information you are look for a different page. The search tools that support the browsing approach organize the web sites into categories and sub-categories. You start out with the most general categories and work your way through a series of categories until you get to the information you are looking for. Normally this approach implies that you have some background information related to your search and can identify which categories it will belong to. This approach works well for this simple search because the categories are easy to identify and there is a small number of sub-categories.

Subject Directories: Subject Directories are good for this type of searching because they are good at identifying general information. They group web sites together under similar categories, such as Internet Tutorials, English Universities and Paris Museums. The results of the search will be a list of web sites related to the subject you are searching for.

Keyword Searching

In comparison, keyword searching provides a more direct approach. Most search tools employ a search engine which is a web accessible program that searches a database (index) of words and phrases from web documents, attempting to match key words that you supply. They provide a search entry box where you can enter a word (or, a few words). The tool will then produce a list of resources that contain that word. Occasionally, all of these resources are relevant to the information you were looking for, however, most often only a portion of the list will be relevant. At this point you will have to sort through the list to find the results that contain the information you are looking for. This approach can be much faster than browsing, however, depending on the keywords you select, and the number of "hits" returned, it can be much slower. In addition to sometimes being faster, this approach does not require as much background information.

The WWW will almost certainly become a major part of the infrastructure of the increasingly interconnected world economy. In the near future, using the Web to conduct business will become as commonplace as using a bank card is today. The Web will allow customers to search catalogues, place orders, submit requests, send "digital cash", and more. Companies large and small can do business in their own neighbourhood, or with customers in other countries.

USE IN REFERENCE

Internet is also used to answer the questions of the users in the library. In research establishment it plays a very vital role now a days. The main activities relating to the reference service in the library are;

- Awareness about the available print and electronic sources
- Identification of the proper source of information to answer a query
- Knowledge of the current sources of information

- Identification of reference tools
- Access to electronic databases available on CD ROMs and Internet
- Providing selective dissemination of information

Internet can be help in the above activities by the following means;

- Identification of reference sources according to the needs of the users
- Search of subject directories on Internet and answering the queries
- Guiding users to the reference sources to enable them to search the desired information on their own
- Identification of the available sources and listing them for future use
- Identification of the full-text journals available freely on the Web.

Internet is a very effective tool to provide reference service. About all popular and specialized databases are available to Internet to satisfy the queries of the library users. While it takes more time to answer a query manually, Internet searches the pinpointed information and presents it before the users within a very short time. Some popular reference sources available on Internet are given below:

Citing Electronic and Printed Sources

Dictionaries

Encyclopaedias

Directories

Maps and the World

Citing Electronic and Printed Sources

A collection of references on how to cite both electronic and printed resources. Includes APA & MLA citation styles,

Harvard Systems of Referencing, How to organize Reference Resources and many others.

You can also use the guide on How to wirte a Bibliography that is available both, electronic and printed copies, at the Library For further information ask at the Library Issue Desk.

Citing Electronic Sources

APA Style

A complete guide on how to cite information from the Internet and other electronic resources from APA.

Citing Electronic Sources

Examples for citing resources from materials such as: films; legal; maps; recorded sound; photographs and drawings; special presentations; and texts.

Citing Online Resources

Gives information on citing the most common types of online material.

Cyber Bee Advice

Includes examples for citing electronic information according to the APA and MLA styles, as well as additional links for consultancy.

Dictionaries

Acronyms and abbreviations dictionaries

The World Wide Web Acronym and Abbreviation Server

A list of acronyms and abbreviations. You can search to find out what an acronym means, search for a word to see what acronyms are used, or you can submit a new acronym in the database.

Journal Abbreviations Sources

Journal Abbreviation Sources is a registry of Web resources that list or provide access to the full title of journal abbreviations.

Biographical dictionaries

Biographical dictionary

This dictionary covers more than 28,000 notable men and women who have shaped our world from ancient times to the present day. The dictionary can be searched by birth years, death years, positions held, professions, literary and artistic works, achievements, and other keywords.

Who is and who was

Search over 25,000 of the greatest lives, past and present.

The Nobel Prize Internet Archive

This site maintains information on all winners in all categories. Click on any Nobel category (literature, physics, chemistry, peace, economics, or physiology & medicine) to see an annotated, hyperlinked list of all Nobel laureates in that category.

English Language & Foreign dictionaries

Dictionary.com

The dictionary includes definitions, related words, grammar and usage, finding books or related Web sites, etc.

Dictionaries Index

Lists of 230 on-line dictionaries of all types and for most languages.

Merriam-Webster Online

Online dictionary and thesaurus.

Oxford English Dictionary

The Oxford English Dictionary is the accepted authority on the evolution of the English language over the last millennium. It is an unsurpassed guide to the meaning, history, and pronunciation of over half a million words, both present and past. It traces the usage of words through 2.5 million quotations from a wide range of international English language sources, from classic literature and specialist periodicals to film scripts and cookery books.

Roget's Thesaurus

On-line version from the ARTFL Project at the University of Chicago. 1911 version - supplemented 1991.

Webster's English Dictionary

ARTFL Project: Webster's Revised Unabridged Dictionary, 1913 Edition.

Language resources on the Internet

Internet Resources for Language Teachers and Learners

This is a collection of annotated links to websites of use to both teachers and learners of languages. The collection is broken up into six broad categories, each of which contains various sub-categories. The 'top level' categories are : general (eg linguistics, translation), Language Specific (eg national newspapers), Multilingual (eg literature in multiple languages), Search Engines (Internet sites in a specific country or geographical area), Internet (sites related to the use of the Internet as a medium for language teaching and learning), Commercial (companies selling language products and services)

Subject dictionaries

Grove Dictionary of Art

The most comprehensive online reference resource for all aspects of the visual arts worldwide, from prehistory to the present day. With the exception of film, all the visual arts are examined: from Greek architecture to Nazca ceramics, Giotto to David Hockney, Chinese snuff bottles to Louis XV wallpaper, 14th century painting treatises to feminist art history. All of the 41,000 articles of the Dictionary have been published and are fully searchable. Free trial is available.

Free Online Dictionary of Computing

FOLDOC is a searchable dictionary of acronyms, jargon,

programming languages, tools, architecture, operating systems, networking, theory, conventions, standards, mathematics, telecoms, electronics, institutions, companies, projects, products, history, in fact anything to do with computing.

Harcourt Academic Press Dictionary of Science and Technology

The largest scientific dictionary ever compiled in the English language to the Web. Fields covered: Engineering Sciences, Life Sciences, Medicine, Physical Sciences, Mathematics and Computer Science, Social Sciences, General and Miscellaneous

ODLIS: Library and Information Science

Online Dictionary of Library and Information Science (ODLIS) is designed to be a hypertext reference resource for library and information science professionals, university students and faculty, as well as for users of all types of libraries.

Yahoo's Collection of Dictionaries

Includes commercial, English, language, slang and subject dictionaries.

Encyclopaedias

Britannica.com

The worlds best web sites plus magazines, books and the complete Encyclopaedia Britannica.

Encarta.com

Encarta.com features a reference library (including a dictionary and atlas), a homework help section, pre-college and graduate-school departments, a section especially for parents, a centre filled with online course offerings, and a shop stocked with great deals on educational products.

Encyclpedia.com

Encyclopedia.com is the Internet's premiere free encyclopaedia. Newly updated and expanded with more than

50,000 articles plus links giving you access to millions of articles and pictures in Electric Library, Encyclopedia.com puts tons of information right at your fingertips. It is free, quick and useful.

Infoplease.com

Online encyclopaedia, dictionary, almanac, atlas.

World Fact book 2001

Information for each country of the world including area, boundaries, climate, disputes, population, political system and economy.

Xrefer

Xrefer's free reference site contains encyclopaedias, dictionaries, thesauri & books of quotations from the world's leading publishers. All cross-referenced, all in one place - providing you with a single source for reliable factual information.

Directories

Company directories & reports

Corporate Reports

Online summary pages for Company Reports, Accounts and Financial Information from UK companies.

CAROL World

Carol is a free corporate online service offering one point access to Company Annual Reports Online from major European, Asian and US companies as well as a range of other investor information.

EDGAR Database

Online Annual Reports from US companies.

European Interactive Directories

The interactive European Internet directory for, business, banking, shopping, etc.

Directories of organisations

Union of International Associations

Telephone directories

Find Phone Books

The World's Phone Books on the web, is one of most complete indexes of online phone books, with over 400 links to Yellow Pages, White Pages, Business Directories, Email Addresses and Fax Listings from over 170 countries all around the world.

University and College directories

American Universities

Alphabetical list of universities and colleges in the United States.

UK Universities and Higher Education Colleges

Alphabetical list of universities and colleges in the United Kingdom.

UK Universities – Admissions

The main link for each site is to general admissions information, or to the site's home page. There are also links to specific information for prospective Undergraduate (U/G), Postgraduate (P/G) and International (INT) students where this exists.

International Universities

General Education Online v2 is a free database of links to higher education facilities worldwide for researchers, students, and others, hosted and sponsored by Simple End User Linux.

World Wide University Index

Search for any university and college throughout the world. electronic_reference.htmelectronic_reference.htm

Maps and the World

Expedia

Street maps of the United Kingdom, United States, Canada, France and Germany and topographic maps of places around the globe.

Mapblast

Street maps, driving directions, yellow pages from many European and other countries.

MapQuest

Maps, driving directions, road trip planner, yellow pages from worldwide.

National Geographic Maps and Geography

Maps and geographical information, photography, adventure & expedition, from all over the world.

LIBRARY AND INFORMATION NETWORKS

Network has become a very wide term now a days. It refers to the cooperative activity of man. There are as many networks in the society as are the fields of social activities. But the network we refer to here is about the coordination of the various information-providing agencies. Since the area we are dealing herewith relates to the education and research, we restrict to the networks in higher education only.

Specialized library networks have come up for individual cities like DELNET, CALIBNET, MALIBNET, PUNENET, BALNET, ADINET, BONET, MYLIBNET, etc. These networks are meant essentially for providing a centralized database of library information to be accessed by its user libraries, mostly in a particular city for the purpose of resource sharing.

In the present day of limited resources, it is imperative that an integrated view of these networks and National Information Systems and Centres on the possibility of sharing resources among them should be taken to explore avoiding duplication of efforts, materials and resources and maximizing the utilization as they form the base for successful networking. Access through any network in the globe can be obtained virtually through INTERNET which is widely used international network.

INTERNATIONAL NETWORKS

Online Computer Library Center (OCLC)

Founded in 1967, OCLC is a nonprofit, membership, computer library service and research organization dedicated to the public purposes of furthering access to the world's information and reducing information costs. More than 45,000 libraries in 84 countries and territories around the world use OCLC services to locate, acquire, catalog, lend and preserve library materials.

Researchers, students, faculty, scholars, professional librarians and other information seekers use OCLC services to obtain bibliographic, abstract and full-text information when and where they need it. OCLC and its member libraries cooperatively produce and maintain WorldCat—the OCLC Online Union Catalog.

Consortium of University Research Libraries (CURL)

CURL was established in 1983 to promote co-operation between academic research libraries in Great Britain and Ireland. The rich holdings of the CURL libraries are represented by catalogue records of varying types and quality, and there is a need to take the manual records, which are limited to local use, and make them universally available through electronic databases. This process is known in the library world as retrospective conversion.

The CURL database consists of approximately 18 million machine-readable catalogue records, of which 12 million have been contributed by its member libraries. In 1996 this database became accessible to members of the public through the CURL OPAC (Online Public Access Catalogue) which is available on the World Wide Web. However, the records of many collections within these great academic libraries, particularly those relating to older, scarcer material, remain hidden from view because they are still in manual form, and electronic access to these resources can only be achieved through the provision of machine-readable catalogue records.

Research Library Information Networks (RLG)

The RLG Resources gives access to records of books, journal titles, manuscripts and archival material, music scores, maps, government publications, audiovisual material, art, and rare book auction catalogues and computer files. The material is contributed by over 200 research libraries, archives and museums, public and corporate libraries and learned societies. The RLG Resources include: - the RLG union catalogue for books (RLIN), artifacts and electronic material: Citation Resources (CitaDel), which includes a number of databasesand covers mostly journal articles, but includes sales catalogues (SCIPIO) as well as the English Short Title Catalogue.

INDIAN NETWORKS

Education and Research Network) (ERNET)

Learning and dissemination of information is becoming more important. Internet based education and e-learning are the trends of the day. In what it is described, as the first effort of its kind in the country, the then Department of Electronics had initiated a project "ERNET" with the funding from UNDP. The objective was to create expertise R&D and education in the country in the area of networking and Internet in the country. ERNET is dedicated to the above objective for the last 15 years.

Today ERNET is largest nationwide terrestrial and satellite network of India with point of presence located at the premiere educational and research institutions in major cities in the country. Focus of ERNET is not limited to just providing connectivity, but to meet the entire needs of the educational and research institutions by hosting and providing relevant information to their users. Research and Development and Training are integral parts of ERNET activities.

INFLIBNET

Information and Library Network (INFLIBNET) is regarded as a landmark in the information scenario of higher education. It is the brainchild of Prof. Yashpal, an eminent scientist and the former Chairman of the University Grants Commission. Incepted in the year 1988, INFLIBNET became operational in 1991 and got the status of an autonomous body in 1996.

INFLIBNET is now an Inter-University Centre of the University Grants Commission (UGC) of India. It is a major National Program initiated by the UGC with its Head Quarters at Gujarat University Campus, Ahmedabad. Initially started as a project under the IUCAA, INFLIBNET is involved in modernizing university libraries in India and connecting them as well as information centres in the country through a nation-wide high speed data network using the state-of-art technologies for the optimum utilization of information. INFLIBNET is set out to be a major player in promoting scholarly communication among academicians and researchers in India.

INFONET

ERNET India, scientific society under the Ministry of Communications and Information Technology, in partnership with the University Grants Commission is setting up UGC-Infonet. Under this program it is proposed to use information and communication Technology (ICT) and Internet to transform learning environment from a mono-dimensional one to a multi-dimensional one. UGC-Infonet will be a boon to the higher education systems in several ways.

ERNET India, and autonomous scientific society under Ministry of Communications and Information Technology, is providing Internet access to Education and Research community in the country for over 10 years. ERNET is a nation-wide terrestrial and satellite network with points of presence located at leading education and research institutions in major cities. ERNET infrastructure is a judicious mix of satellite and terrestrial networks ideally suited for the Education and Research community in the country.

Developing Library Network (DELNET)

Delnet started as a network of libraries in Delhi in 1988 and was named as Delhi Library Network. It is the first operational library network in India. It was initiated as a project of the India International Centre with the financial and technical assistance by National Information System for Science and Technology (NISSAT), Department of Scientific and Industrial Research, Govt. of India. It was registered as a society in June 1992 under the Societies Registration Act of 1860 and is currently being promoted by the National Informatics Centre (NIC), Planning Commission, Govt. of India and India International Centre, New Delhi.

Delhi is growing as a major centre of information resources in India. These resources cater both to the specialized and the general users. They are located in activities, information and documentation centres, institutional libraries, research libraries, government libraries, public libraries, department libraries besides the libraries of the universities, colleges and schools. During the recent years, increase in information has led to increase in the demands of the users. It has been noticed that in this area of information explosion, libraries in India are generally ill-equipped to handle and retrieve information effectively, the financial resources and the space requirement for housing library collection are limited in almost all of the libraries. No a single library can afford to house every necessary document even in the area of its interest. Resource sharing, thus assumes great importance at this juncture the option left with the forward looking librarians has been to promote the sharing of resources by automation and networking. With this objective, in January

1988, the India International Centre initiated efforts for the establishment of Delhi Library Network (Now Developing Library Network).

Calcutta Library Network (CALIBNET)

It was the first library network visualized and started by NISSAT. At a meeting in 1986 in Calcutta, DSIR initiated action for preparation of a feasibility study for networking about 40 libraries in Calcutta. CALIBNET now is a society under West Bengal Societies Registration Act 1961 and responsible for Calcutta Library Network, a project sponsored and supported by NISSAT. NISSAT also contributed to the development of MAITRAYEE software package based on INGRESS 5.2 for CALIBNET. This package was developed through CMC Ltd. And given to CALIBNET. So far, no data has been created in machine readable from using MAITRAYEE. At present, CALIBNET has become a centre for CD-ROM databases.

9

Intranet for Rural India

An Intranet is a private system that uses computer hardware and software specially developed to provide communication, information management and information publishing services within an organization An organization, which has many computers usually owns and operates a private network that connects all the computers. Such a network is called Intranet. It is independent of any external support but to provide Internet services, an Intranet is connected with Internet Unlike public access networks, Intranet is restricted to provide security. Only authorized computers at the organization can be connected to it. The restrictions allow computers inside the organization to exchange information but keep the information confidential and protected from outsiders.

As Intranet is a connecting device for many computers within an organization it can solve many problems related to input, storage and dissemination of information without much inconvenience. The other services expected from Intranet are the following:

1. World Wide Web publishing
2. File Transfer Protocol
3. Indexing and Searching Services
4. Facility to run scripts

FEATURES OF THE INTRANET

What is the Intranet and why is it so important? There are several distinguishing features of Internet:

* Uses TCP/IP (transmission control protocol/Internet

protocol) for both wide-area and local-area transport of information,

* Uses HTML (hypertext markup language), SMTP (Simple mail transport protocol) and other open Internet-based standards as the means of moving information from clients to servers,
* Is completely owned by the corporation and not accessible from the Internet-at-large by the general public, and
* Is managed by IS with a similar set of tools, attitudes and procedures as they currently manage their legacy VTAM networks.

The chief distinction between the Intranet and the Internet is more one of semantics than actual technology: both use the same tools and techniques, protocols and products; drawing heavily on the standards of the TCP/IP world. In some cases, Intranet projects began as pilots or skunk-works efforts and have since been exposed for public view on the Internet as a major strategic computing effort. However, there are some differences between the two.

First, much corporate data is not for public consumption. Payroll, sales projections, internal discounts and client memos are all examples of information that corporations don't want broadcast over the Internet, and need to protect carefully, just as they have in the past with their IMS databases and ACF security programs. DEC's Intranet, for example, is accessible by its employees with the proper series of encryption and authentication routines.

Second, many Intranets begin with pilot projects to test out the technologies and understand the skill levels required. They quickly grew into full-time, production-quality information systems that have taken on a particularly corporation's culture and methods. Finally, many corporations want their private Intranets to have the same level of service as their existing SNA networks, and this is only possible when the networks are under complete corporate control from end to end.

One method for developing a corporate Intranet is to combine groupware applications with Internet technology. One such product is Attachmate's Open Mind, which makes use of Internet technologies such as HTML, TCP/IP, and Web browsing to augment the publishing, discussion, document management and general information sharing functions often wanted in a robust corporate Intranet. Version 2.0 of the product offers an integrated Web browser which allows users to permanently attach to and share information on external Web sites. Another example of this is Lotus' InterNotes products, which allow departments to track discussions and record conferences and other group collaborative efforts.

Just because the Intranet uses the same protocols and languages of the Internet doesn't mean it has to follow the same rules of operation and chaotic anything-goes environment: indeed, what many corporations are beginning to realize is that out of this chaos comes some important design considerations for building very reliable Intranets.

One example would be the ability to assign maintenance chores for particular pieces of content to different corporate departments who develop and maintain the information. Other management issues include being able to provide a local cache of popular or u seful Web sites for better performance or to ease network congestion. Other issues include providing a very granular user-based access control and reporting of usage statistics help corporate Intranet developers to fine-tune their applications.

Forthcoming products from Attachmate, such as the Internet Access server and Internet Conferencing and Publishing systems, will include some of these management tools built-in as part of the product. Other vendors are working on additional enhancements to manage changes to content and automating scripting of frequently-used routines.

Intranet if employed in a larger set up will bring efficiency in work and help improve the standard of education and research.

Advantages

* It will connect all organs/departments
* It will be a private network
* It will provide connectivity round the clock
* It will permit decentralization of work
* It will allow resources sharing within the campus
* It is cost effective since only one software package can be used for the entire organization.
* It will provide connectivity from and to the residence of the authorized users
* Recording and dissemination of information/meetings/ lectures from any location
* Data is secured from external risks

Besides the above advantages, the facility may be used for other purposes like vigilance and security of the campus.

The basic requirements for installation of an Intranet are computer hardware, software and a connecting device.

Intranet is based on a client server system where the server is a computer that has the following functions:

* Running the Intranet service software
* Storing some or all of the content that is available to the users

Requirements of Intranet

The requirements of the server computer depend upon the number of connections expected to be provided per hour. For a few hundred connections, a Pentium 4 with 1.6 Gh speed, 64 MB RAM and 40 GB memory is more than sufficient. In case the load increases on the sever, users will find them waiting for retrieval of information. The capacity of a computer system may be enhanced by adding more memory and processors and splitting the contents among them.

Software for the Intranet is available in two categories, the server software and the client software.

Server Software

Intranet needs a server software that runs a computer and provides services such as World Wide Web publishing and File Transfer besides indexing and searching facilities. Server software is available on the Internet free of cost and the commercial packages such as Microsoft's Internet Information Server and Netscape Navigator are available for a variety of operating systems including UNIX and Windows NT server.

Client Software

The software that runs a client is called a browser, which is used to access and browse Web pages. It may also be acquired free of cost or at a reasonably low cost. The most popular server is Netscape Navigator Some other browsers are also available at the Web addresses in Table 1.

Internet is a gold mine of free software One can find any type of software to ran a fall featured Intranet service but the software downloaded from Internet should be used with great care. It is always better to take precautions and invest some money for a well designed, listed and supported software.

Table 1. Web Address of Browsers

S. No.	*Name*	*Web Address*
1.	Midas	WWW
2.	Mosaic	ftp://ftp.ncsa.uiuc.edu/mosaic
3.	Netscape	htt://home.netscape.com
4.	Emacs	ftp://mouse.cs.indiana.edu/pub/elips/w3
5.	Lynx	ftp://ftp2.cc.ukans.edu/pub/lynx/
6.	Internet Explorer	

A connecting device provides links between the server and the client. It is mainly based on the following two devices

* Networking Device capable of running on radio frequencies
* RF Links comprising of Mast and Antennas

There are many devices, which can be used to connect a server with browser but their usage depends upon the convenience and the financial resources of an organization to install and support the device The geographical location of the various departments of an organization is to be taken into consideration because sometimes it is hard to manage the connections besides being in the position of installation of the costlier systems.

INTRANET SERVICES

Intranet services may include some or more of the following:

File Server

A file server is used to store the user files in a common server. With OTM the network is made transparent, that is, any user can login from any machine and he gets all his files, desktop setting etc..

Print Server

A Print Server allows the users to share a common printer at no extra cost. We study the print usage and then determine the number and type of printers required.

Application Server

An application server is used to execute applications from a common server. This reduces the hardware requirement at the client machines but increases the network load. But in some cases such as the X-windows environment, it is a good idea.

Web Server

A Web-Server is used to store the web pages for local usage. Using the company wide web server, the following range of applications can be developed to meet industry specific or general needs

Order processing application

Upon receipt of any order there is tedious process of order approval. Such approval involves movement of paper through various departments and is very lengthy and complex process. A web enabled intranet application would allow you to route any order for approval & easily track the same.

Sales & marketing applications

The biggest challenge for a marketing team is delivering up-to-date information to an often geographically distributed group of people. An intranet can give immediate access to the following types of information:

* Information on company product
* List of company wins/losses.
* On line training materials, sales presentations and sales leads.
* Key Customer and referances can be accessed online

HUMAN RESOURCE APPLICATIONS

The HR department is the nerve center of any organization. It is particularly important for people oriented organizations such as software companies. Using an intranet enables the organization to effectively handle skill set matching for different postings, resumes, leave applications, internal job transfers, benefits information and lots more. Some of the specific applications that can be created are

* Employee handbook
* Employee Telephone directory
* Benefits information
* Newsletters
* Company calendar
* Electronic pay stubs
* Employee classified

* Online entering of employe expense reports
* Leave applications
* Job openings
* Employee feedback

Mail Server

In any organization, communication is a must. We provide a perfect solution which caters to all of the organizations internal and external mailing requirements. We feel that every user must be given an individual account for himself. With such a facility he/she can communicate with anyone inside as well as outside the organization. A mailing system reduces paper cost and makes communication faster than any other medium.

Fax Server

A fax server enables users to share a common modem to send and receive fax messages. Sending a fax to a modem is made as simple as sending a file for printing.

News Server

A News server is used to transmit company news to all the users in the organization. It could be used instead of bulletin boards. Users could also start new news groups where topics of their interests could be discussed. This increases the creativity of the users.

Dialup Server

A dialup server is used to connect offices at different locations. The connection procedure is similar to that provided by ISPs such as VSNL and Satyam Online.

Proxy Server and Caching Server

A proxy server is used to give internet access to all users in the network with a single connection.

FireWall and Intranet security mechanisms

A firewall is a security mechanism implemented to provide

security for a local area network from intruders both from the Internet and from inside the network.

In addition to the above consulting on network management can also be provided Identify the possible businesses

GYANDOOT: A RURAL INTRANET IN INDIA

On January 1, 2000, Dhar district began the new millennium with installation of low cost, self-sustainable and community owned rural Intranet project. Dhar district is located on the south western corner of the central India and has a population of 1.7 million, with 54% population being tribal *(Bhils, Bhilalas, patleiyas)* and 60% population living below poverty line. Computers in 20 village centres in five Blocks of the district were wired through an Intranet network (presently there are 31 such wired village centres). Local rural youth act as entrepreneurs for running cybercafes-cum-cyberoffices on commercial lines without salary or stipend. The computers in the network have been established in *Gram Panchayats* (Village Committee). They have been called *Soochanalayas* (Information Kiosks). The *Soochanalayas* provide user-charge-based services to the rural people. This Intranet system has been named Gyandoot (Messenger of Informat

SOOCHAK (Manager/owner of the kiosk)

The person operating the *Soochanalaya* is a local matriculate operator and is called *Soochak.* A *soochak* is not an employee but an entrepreneur. *Soochak* only needs maintenance and numeric data entry skills. He needs very limited typing skills since most of the Intranet software is menu-driven.

The *Soochaks* for originally started 20 centres were selected interactively by village committees and the local community. Three member panels were selected by the community who received training at their own cost at the District Council. At the end of the training, the best trainees were selected out of a panel of three as *Soochaks*. He / she runs the *Soochanalaya* on commercial lines. He has an initial one year agreement with the village committee. He does not receive any salary. He bears the cost of stationery, maintenance and electric and telephone bills. He pays 10% of income as commission to the *Zila Panchayat* (District Council) for maintaining the net.

The 11 centres started as private enterprise, the *Soochak* is the owner of the establishment who pays Rs. 5,000 as a license fee for one year to district council. Each *Soochak* is expected to earn a net income of at least Rs. 36,000 per annum at conservative projections.

SERVICES AND FACILITIES

During the formation of the project proposal a detailed RRA/PRA exercise was taken up involving the villagers and the community. The selection of the services was a result of this interactive exercise and was based upon the advice and the felt needs of the villagers. In these meetings, it was learnt that due to lack of information regarding the current and prevailing *mandi* (agriculture produce auction centres) rates, the farmers were unable to get the best price for their agricultural produce. Villagers also informed that copies of land records were difficult to obtain. The villager who requires a copy of the land record had to go out in search of the *patwari* (village functionary who maintains all land records) who may or may not be available on that particular day at his headquarters. For small complaints or for giving applications, people had to go to district headquarter which resulted in waste of time, money and potential livelihood earnings. The services offered on the Gyandoot network are:

Agriculture Produce Auction Centres Rates:

The variety-wise current and prevailing rates of prominent cereal crops of the district like wheat, gram, soybean, etc. at local and other prominent auction centres of the country are available on-line. Other statistics of the auction centres e.g. the volume of incoming agricultural produce, previous rates etc. are also provided on demand. The facility is available at a nominal charge of Rs. 5. Horticulture crops like tomato, potato, peas, green chillies, guava etc. are also produced in substantial quantity in the district. The rates of these commodities are also available.

On-line Registration of Applications:

So far, the villagers had to go to the local revenue court to file applications for obtaining income / caste / domicile certificates or for getting demarcation done or for obtaining landholder's loan passbook (*rin pustika*) etc. For this, they would again made repeated visits to the court to enquire about the progress of the application as well as to finally collect the prepared document. Now, through *Soochanalayas* they may send the application at a cost of only Rs. 10 and thereafter, in a maximum period of 10 days, preferably less, an intimation of the readiness of the certificate is sent back to them through e-mail at the concerned *Soochanalaya*. Thereafter, they may go to the concerned court to collect the certificate.

On-line Public Grievance Redressal:

Wherever there is some problem in the delivery of services, the villagers travel at the cost of time, money and livelihood to Block, *tahsil* or district headquarters without any certainty that they would even be able to meet the officer concerned. Now through the *Soochanalaya*, a villager may send his / her complaint with assurance of reply within a maximum period of seven days, preferably lesser, at a charge of Rs. 10. The reply to his complaint after redressal is sent back at the *Soochanalaya* through e-mail. Complaints available on the intranet include complaints regarding drinking water, scholarship sanction / disbursement, quality of seed / fertilizer, employee establishment matters (like leave or provident fund sanction) queries, functioning of school, public distribution system, beneficiary oriented schemes, functioning of village committee etc.

Rural e-mail facility:

A fee based e-mailing facility, which is provided in the intranet, and it has all the features and facilities of a state-of-the-art web based e-mail.

Village auction site:

This facility is started since July 2000 where auction facilities are available to farmers and villagers for land, agricultural machinery, bullocks or equipment or other durable commodities. It opens a new horizon of e-transactions in the rural areas. The middlemen involved in the rural commodity transaction market are sought to be eliminated through this facility. One can put one's commodity on sale for charges of Rs. 25/- for three months. One can browse the list of salable commodities for Rs. 10/-.

On line matrimonial site:

A fee based on-line matrimonial service for the villagers to choose the right match for a prospective bride/groom. Every entry from a *Soochanalaya* by a villager gets added on to a centralized database with search facility on various criteria. The user charges for service rendered is Rs. 25/- for three months. The program has been designed to suit the requirements of the villagers.

Information regarding government programmes :

Detailed Information regarding over a hundred government programmes is now available on the Gyandoot Intranet. The villagers have an access to the information regarding all government programmes related to rural development.

Sawaliram se puchiye:

This site provides opportunity to schoolchildren to ask inquisitive questions regarding career counseling or any other field from *Sawaliram* at no cost. A team of experts at the district headquarter provide the answers within three days. The facility is created to promote inquisitiveness, ability to inquire and scrutinize among the school children.

Ask the expert:

This facility is aimed at farmers and villagers who can inquire about latest techniques, advice for their problems, new technologies etc. from a group of experts pertaining to fields of agriculture, animal husbandry, health, or related to legal opinion. The service is provided at Rs 5/- user charge.

Free E-mail facility on social issues:

Free of cost option are available to the villagers to inform regarding child labour, child marriage, illegal possession of land belonging to Scheduled Tribes etc. Besides they can send e-mails to others connected through the net with the help of this facility in Hindi.

Avedan Patra:

This facility provides on-line application formats required by local administration and departments of the state government. Thus, application forms are available at the doorsteps of the villagers and avoid their running from pillar to post for these application forms.

Transparency in government working:

Updated and latest information regarding public distribution system, list of below poverty line families, beneficiaries of social security pension, beneficiaries of rural development schemes, information regarding government grants given to village committees, etc. are available on the intranet which makes the government functioning transparent.

Gaon ka Akhabar (Village Newspaper):

A local web-based newspaper is available to cater to the rural people. The newspaper delivers micro-news about the happening around the villages where *Soochaks* act as correspondents.

E-education (*shiksha gyandoot*):

This site contains reading material to supplement and help the students in understanding and learning their subjects in a better way. It contains things like syllabuses of various subjects taught in class X and XII, question banks developed by a team of experts to help in preparation of exams, chithi to help them keep in touch with other schools connected to the intranet etc.

Employment News:

This site contains employment news for semi skilled employees.

Below Poverty line list:

The site contains the whole list of below the poverty line families and anyone can check his her name in the list.

STRENGTHENING OF PROJECT:

In order to make *Soochanalayas* economically viable entities and to improve the functioning of the project following steps are being taken:

Additional facilities at *Soochanalayas* :

To make *Soochanalayas* economically viable *soochaks* are given licenses to vendor government judicial stamps and powers of petition writer are also delegated to them. Due to the delegation of above mentioned powers additional incomes are possible and the *Soochanalaya*s are becoming virtual cyber offices. .

On-line linking of all departments with gyandoot server :

A local Area Network (LAN) linking all the major district offices has been installed. As a result, the district heads of various government departments like health, education, tribal development, revenue, food, agriculture, public health engineering, District Council and District Magistrate etc. are connected directly to gyandoot network. This provides backup support and logistics to gyandoot network.

Wireless in Local Loop:

The Gyandoot Samiti is introducing low cost TDMA based Wireless in Local Loop (WiLL) technology in collaboration with Indian Institute of Technology, Chennai. This technology will facilitate large scale multiplication of *Soochanlayas* in the hinterland where traditional plain old telephone system has not reached. The technology has power to increase access speed and provide reliable connectivity. The technology will also help the kiosk operator to run two connections at a time, e.g. STD PCO (voice connectivity) and Internet/Intranet (data communication).

E-education initiatives:

The Gyandoot Samiti, with the help from Member of Parliament, has established 34 kiosks at the high schools and higher secondary schools. We are providing them local educational contents through the server. They are also accessing internet for other educational contents. Each school is having Computer Club to promote activities related to IT among rural students.

EXPANSION OF THE PROJECT:

Some fundamental guidelines were framed for future expansion. They were:

1). Centers to be opened only in the villages where local telephone exchange is having OFC and fair connectivity,

2). New centers to be created through private investment.

3). New services and facilities to be introduced in phased manner.

THE NEW FACILITIES PLANNED OVER NEXT TWO YEARS :

1. E-News for the district
2. Distance education
3. Registration of property transaction
4. Feedback system on the development programmes
5. "Bare foot doctor"

ACTION PLAN FOR INCREASING USAGE OF THE NETWORK

A comprehensive and integrated multi-media mass campaign concentrating on IEC activities has been launched in the district. The campaign focuses on penetration and propagation of the project in the hinterland of the district. Indian Institute of Management, Indore is collaborating to provide structured inputs for the IEC activities. The steps taken include:

Gyandoot *medhavi chhatra* (talented students) scholarship:

From the funds available with gyandoot, two scholarships each of Rs. 1,000/- per month for 5 years have been announced. For the scholarship, only those students of the district would be eligible who motivate 10 or more villagers to use gyandoot facilities between the period 1st September to 31st December 2000. The scholarships will be finalised through an on-line test of the eligible students and the result of the test would be declared on 26th January 2001. This scheme uses the services of the students to propagate new technology and its power among the rural masses.

Visit of school children to nearest Soochnalaya :

Students of class IX, X, XI, XII are taken to the nearest *Soochanalaya* on study tour. These students are given elaborate demonstration on the gyandoot Intranet system and the facilities available at the centre.

***ramsabha* in the villages in the project area :**

Special *gramsabhas* (Meeting of all villagers) in each village in the project area have been started which will be completed by January, 2001. These specially convened village meetings will deliberate on gyandoot and its services, which are available there at nominal cost.

Audio-Visual campaign

Posters and pamphlets have been distributed to all the concerned village committees. TV cable network and cinema halls are being used to popularise gyandoot services. Audiocassettes carrying gyandoot messages are being used in weekly *haat* bazaars (market places).

Use of ISRO-DECU communication project

A communication project has been established by ISRO (Indian Space Research Organisation) which is already functional in 200 villages of the district. The said project carries message on the gyandoot project.

Gyandoot Computer Clubs

Gyandoot Computer Clubs are being established in major high schools and higher secondary schools of the district.

Incentives

Incentive in the form of cash awards (Rs.5,000/-, Rs.3,000/-, Rs. 2,000/-) along with certificate of excellence were given to three best performing S*oochaks* and certificate of appreciation were given to the village head of the concerned village committee on 15th August,2000. These incentives are being offered twice a year.

Sir Ratan Tata Trust Healthy Child Competition

Sir Ratan Tata Trust has granted Rs. three lakhs to organise healthy child competition based on *Soochnalayas*. The scheme has dual objective of promoting good practices of child rearing among rural masses and at the same time let them know about IT and its usages. The competition is organised with *Soochanalayas* as nodal points. It will motivate villagers to come to the kiosks. This competition was recently organised (between 9th to 19th April 2001) and was a huge success with 29140 children (12113 boys and 16027 girls) participating in it. All the people coming to the *soochanalaya* for this purpose were explained the utility of the Gyandoot network. It is expected that this will popularise the use of the network for various purposes.

PROJECT PARTNERS

No	*Organisation name*	*Role in the project*
1	District Council (*Zila panchayat)*	Conceptualisation of the project, bringing together the

		financial resources, management of the server room
2	District Administration	Conceptualisation of the project, co-ordination, Commanding the back-end human system, Liasing with the State Government
3	State Government of Madhya Pradesh	Providing vision to use IT for rural masses
4	District planning Committee	Monitoring and evaluation
5	National Informatics Center	Software Maintenance & all required Technical Support.
6	Gyandoot Society	Enrichment and expansion of the project, IEC, software development, induction of new technology, capacity building

STOCKHOLM CHALLENGE AWARD 2000

Gyandoot project of Dhar District has been awarded Stockholm Challenge IT Award 2000 at a glittering function in Town Hall, Stockholm on 6th June 2000. In the words of the organisers, Stockholm City Economic Development Agency in partnership with the European Commission:

The Stockholm Challenge Award is a challenge between pioneering IT projects world wide ... The Stockholm Challenge award focuses on the benefit that information technology can bring people and society. The technology itself is not the issue. ... The single most important criterion is the benefit the project can bring to individuals, society and the environment by using inspirational approaches within the local context."

Gyandoot was declared winner in "Public Service and

Democracy" category out of 109 IT projects from all over the world. The gyandoot project is the only Indian project to receive the award in any category in last four years.

The 29 member international Jury has stated its motivation in identifying Gyandoot Project as a winner as follows:

Project "Gyandoot" is a unique government to citizen Intranet project implemented in a tribal district (Dhar) in Central India, with numerous benefits to the region, including a people-based self-reliant sustainable strategy. "Gyandoot" is recognised as a breakthrough in e-government, demonstrating a paradigm shift which gives marginalized tribal citizens their first ever chance to access knowledge, with minimum investment."

CSI-TCS NATIONAL IT AWARD

The project is awarded CSI-TCS National IT Award for best IT usage, instituted by the Computer Society of India, for the year 2000. The final contestants for the award were ICICI Bank, Global Trust Bank, SAIL and National Crime Record Bureau, along with the Gyandoot project.

10
Multimedia in Education

Multimedia can be defined as the digital integration of text, graphics, animation, audio, still images and motion video in a way that provides individual users with high levels of control and interaction. The evolution of Multimedia is a story of the emergence and convergence of these technologies. As these technologies developed along separate paths for disparate purposes, visionaries saw the possibilities for the sum of the parts as well potential personal application in the broader societal context. Technological developments from thee printing press to the emergence of the WWW tell the history of multimedia.

Multimedia is a method of instruction that uses the computer to present information with text, graphics, audio and/ or video. It is also referred to as *computer-based training* (CBT) or *Web-based training* (WBT). It can take the form of training, presentations, software simulation, job simulation, testing, reference or online help. Since multimedia instruction is often delivered over the Internet, it can look just like a set of Web pages, but it also can be delivered on CD-ROM, on diskette or over a local area network (LAN) or company intranet.

A huge demand of multimedia by customers for varied purpose is a common sight at every computer shops and book stores. In the time to come it might be recognized as a powerful rival to the broadcast television and books. The applications of multimedia cab be visualized by considering activities that resemble the process of communication information. The common examples include education and training, reference, pointt of information, business presentation, manuals, databases, geographic information system, advertizing, documentaries and so on.

Multimedia has a great potential in education. It is able to assist both the pupil and teacher in many ways. For the teacher it provides a means of putting across information and ideas whereas for the student it can represent one to one teaching environment which moves at the required pace. Multimedia is harnesses as a presentation tool with which only the teacher interacts. Material might represent a pictorial or textual way used to enhance a lesson or lecture. In some instances it might be intended as a complete lesson or a dialogue between teacher/student and system, but shortage of system or terminal restrict this mode of operation.

Interaction with multimedia is a key aspect of its role in education. An Intel paper or Digital Video Interactive (DVI) states that the interactive multimedia can yield as much as 70% recall, or opposed to 45% of audiovisual aids, and just 25% of audio.

Distribution of multimedia lessons, lectures and courseware on CD ROM or CD-1 disc adds another dimension of multimedia in education providing a vehicle for learning materials. For scattered rural community where schools are inaccessible, and for institutes running distance learning courses of any kind, the potential is enormous. Indeed a portion of courses run by institutions that depend upon home learning will certainly be distributed through multimedia in future.

It is also a fact that multimedia is not poised to replace teachers overnight. In addition to the current technical constraints, technology is expansive and therefore inaccessible for many educational establishments. However, with adequate support it will certainly alter the generally accepted study methods in future while transforming traditional teaching methods along the way.

Education and training are the fastest growing markets for multimedia products and training has recently become more technology oriented. Computer based training is now a major activity. Training requirements often differ from one organization to the other. The development of in-house training material is therefore common. This is quite different from the education sector, where a higher level of standardisation exists.

Employees of an organization can interact with video under computer control using computers and multimedia many commercially available authoring systems lend themselves particularly well to the development of courseware. Programming is easier when the package includes commonly used library routines. Such systems must be capable of controlling a video disk player and offer a variety of library routines. Popular authoring system that fit this profile include TenCORE, TopClass, Authorware Professional, Quest and IBM's Audio Visual Connection (AVC).

Like education, the advantages of multimedia also apply in training for corporate and industry professionals. It can offer the additional advantage of constant availability because the multimedia can be made available 24 hours a day.

Consumer education generally consists of publishing product brochures, advertising, allowing the potential customers to pursue in a shop or showroom, and product demonstrations. These generally accepted ways in which the consumer chooses an appropriate product can be aided or replaced being multimedia in a point of information (POI) guise. POI terminals present the with the ability of browsing through product ranges.

POI can be a powerful marketing and advertising tool providing the means to display products. The benefits are clear. It gives an opportunity to promote products in a medium that cannot be rivaled by television advertising. It also allows small and medium sized companies to promote products on terms that only large companies and corporations could previously afford.

There are a few factors which allow POI facility for the common man free of cost or involving lower cost. It is because of the growing number of multimedia systems and the lowering cost of computers. There is also a possibility of distributing short advertisements or demonstrations containing video sequences on floppy disks Transmitting such multimedia directly into the home is also a distinct possibility and is one that is being researched and developed by several US companies.

POI terminals have been installed in museums all over the world in order to give visitors the opportunity to follow user-defined guided tours. Such an approach can allow visitors to experience interesting items which might otherwise be catalogued and hidden away from public view. Many other areas such as career advice geographic information systems, surrogate travel are also possible through POI.

Multimedia instruction works well for all kinds of content. Both very complex material and very simple information can be delivered this way. For companies whose products or services are dangerous or sensitive, multimedia instruction can safely allow trainees to "practice" on the computer. When the trainee makes an error, he or she gets immediate feedback and an opportunity to correct the error.

Audiences for multimedia training may have a wide range of skills, educational levels and computer experience. It has been used to deliver training to such disparate groups as pilots using sophisticated flight simulators with detailed graphics and tightly controlled user responses and teenagers using touchscreen kiosks to learn the dangers of alcohol and tobacco. In the touchscreen application, a user doesn't need any computer skills at all, and information can be entirely graphic, with little or no text.

Advantages

The advantages of multimedia are as under:

* **It's interactive.** Learners are actively engaged. Interactive tools may include multiple-choice questions, fill-in-the-blanks, selecting all right answers or matching by dragging and dropping graphics. Feedback engages the learner even

more. For example, an incorrect answer could provide a hint along with a "Sorry, that's incorrect" response.

* **It's tailored to learner needs.** Learners can take the training when they want, as often as they want, and at a pace that's right for them.
* **It's cost-effective.** Companies don't need to pay for trainers, travel or classrooms. It's especially useful in situations where users are spread over a wide area.
* **It's efficient and effective.** Learners typically learn more in a shorter period of time with multimedia instruction.
* **It's easy to revise and update.** Especially with Internet delivery, changes made to one copy are immediately available to all learners. For example, a company that manufactures car utility racks can easily alter installation instructions for consumers as car manufacturers introduce new models every year.

Suitability

* **Cost.** The expense can vary widely. You can find off-the-shelf or off-the-Web training at very reasonable cost, and sometimes even for free. Custom development of computer-based training can be expensive, but may be worth it if employee or customer training is crucial.
* **Number of learners.** A very large audience, such as a large customer base, may reduce costs greatly and possibly allow you to deliver instruction more effectively and economically than with paper-based instruction.
* **Location of learners.** If your learners are spread over broad geographical areas, such as with sales reps or traveling technicians, CBT or WBT may be the only way to provide accurate and effective training to everyone.
* **Availability of computers.** Equipment doesn't have to be sophisticated—all you may need is an Internet connection.

More Information

Name a topic. You can probably find training on it, either online or on CD-ROM. It is also available for generic computer-based training, such as tutorials and other instruction on software packages. look in your local computer store. On the Web, one can search by subject area or use of keywords like online learning, CBT, WBT, online training, courseware, or e-learning. The following Web sites are just a few that provide online courses on a vast range of topics:

* ElementK—www.zdu.com
* DigitalThink—www.digitalthink.com
* Blackboard—www.blackboard.net

In case of a customized, company-specific instruction, look for consultants with experience in both instructional design and multimedia development. One may be tempted to use a Web design company, keeping in mind that the goal of multimedia instruction is different from the goal of a Web site. A Web design firm can develop effective marketing tools and information delivery, but only an instructional design firm follows instructional principles to help people learn.

MULTIMEDIA FORMATS

* Presentation Tool
* Public Information Kiosks (Point of Sale)
* CD Encyclopaedias
* Commercial CD 'Titles'
* Games ('edutainment' or otherwise)
* Communication Systems
* Computer Based Training (CBT)
* Computer Based Learning (CBL)
* Interactive Multimedia.

MULTIMEDIA PUBLISHING

Publishing has evolved to the point where word processors

are ubiquitous and desktop publishing is used by students for their studies. Once complex technology becomes widespread, commonplace, and a part of daily life.

Multimedia publishing is the next frontier. In a few years we will all be including video and audio in multimedia publications, the same way we now include images, photos and text in print publications today. And these new multimedia publications will be "printed" on DVD.

Low Cost DVD

The laser printer triggered the desktop publishing revolution. What is required to trigger this next step change for multimedia publishing are the low cost DVD "burners".

Multimedia Publishing Requirements

As with every new technology, new uses emerge that the designers don't anticipate. This is now happening with DVD. Designed as an entertainment media, the many powerful DVD features are now being exploited for multimedia uses that go far beyond entertainment and movie distribution.

These new uses put new demands on DVD "authoring" applications, including:

* Support for different types of media
* Improved tools for integrating multimedia
* Ability to publish on all the variations of CD and DVD
* Control over movie and menu timing and actions

Multimedia Publishing

Preparing audio and video for the web is not a difficult process. However, it does require specialized computer equipment, software, and several sequential processes. Different software packages are available for many of the steps, but the software chosen at each step impacts both the quality of the final product and the software that can be used for subsequent steps.

The Four Basic Steps

The four basic steps in preparing media for the web are listed below. In addition to these four steps, completed media files will need to be posted to a web or media server that is compatible with the file type (format) created. Web pages will also need to be written that will allow access to the media files on the server.

1. Digitizing and editing the media
2. Self-containing the media to make it independent of the software that created it
3. Compressing the file to make it a usable size for web transmission
4. Adding the 'hint' track

File format will dictate which software will be used in the final three steps, but the first step is independent of the file format. The first step (digitizing and editing the media) requires specialized equipment. To digitize audio, you will need an audio suite (source such as a cassette deck and amplifier or a boom box that combines the tape player and amplifier in one unit) and a computer with a sound input jack. The machine should have at least 128 Mb of RAM. To digitize analog video, a vcr and a media converter box (such as Dazzle or the Sony DVMC-DA2) and a specialized computer is needed. The converter box actually changes the signal from analog to digital (DV) format that the computer can process and store. Not all computers can handle DV, but most Macintoshes and some high-end PCs can. Any computer destined to process and edit digital video should have a minimum of 256 Mb of RAM.

Considerations When Choosing File Formats

As mentioned above, file format (.wav, .rm/.rp, .wmp or .mov) will dictate which software must be purchased for the processes and server. The table below lists some of the pros and cons for each format

* .wav pro can be played as background to web page
* con limited to PC users
* .mov pro plug-in is free, server software is inexpensive, no licensing required, works well on both platforms
* con not as popular as RealPlayer or Windows Media
* .mp3 pro very popular with students, excellent compression ratio & quality sound
* con audio only
* .rm/.rp pro very popular with students, first 50 streams are free
* con Expensive: Licensing fees for >50 streams from server(an aggregate for all files, not per media clip)
* .wmp pro very popular with students, easy to use
* con Not truly cross-platform

REPURPOSING VIDEO FOR THE WEB

Web pages are quickly becoming the 21st century equivalent of photocopying. They require little storage space on a server, transfer quickly, and give immediate access to everyone. But, more often than not, the information is distributed widely without clear cut purpose.

Conversely, video and audio files for the web require more storage space, can require long downloads and larger files are difficult for users with slow modems. This creates an opportunity for stringent content analysis. If media files should be as small as possible (and right now that means short), then any video clips must be succinct and to the point. I recommend a three-minute rule for video—if the clip is longer than three minutes, it is going to be too large for most users. (With the great audio compressions available, I use a 5 minute rule —because after 5 minutes, who is still listening?)

To supplement the three minute clip, the web page should become a complex media experience. The page can offer text and activities supporting the media so that the user has something to do during the download. In language learning contexts, the page can provide vocabulary/idiom support or provide background information on the cultural aspects of the video. Thus, video on the web becomes a more enriching experience than a photocopied handout.

A terrific example of just such an enriching experience can be seen at SUNY Cortland, on a web site developed by French professor, Marie Ponteiro in a lesson on Europe for her French Civilization course. My apologies if you don't read French.

Getting Started

You will need a specialized computer and software. I use and recommend Macintosh computers. They are designed to process media and there are many software programs already available for this platform. The following recommendations are for Macintosh platform only. Faculty, staff and students have access to these programs in the Instructional Technology Center (ITC- 217 Chafee) and the Fine Arts lab (Fine Arts - F102).

Audio: Macromedia SoundEdit 16 (if you can find it) or Bias Peak. Peak reduces the number of steps in the process by self-containing the file when saving to QuickTime format. (One less step is good.) I use Cleaner for Compression—using either the Qualcomm Pure Voice codec or .mp3. Lyrical or slurred voices (such as Russian or Portuguese) sound better using teh .mp3 codec. English and other languages I have tried work well with Qualcomm. Cleaner can hint the tracks automatically (this saving another step).

Video: I use Final Cut Pro to log and capture video. Apple's iMovie would work just as well if you have minimal editing needs. You can also trim the beginning and end with QuickTime Pro, but this is like using a saber instead of a scalpel. I self-contain the files in QuickTime Pro and then compress them in Cleaner. The codec varies depending on high/low motion and desired file size. Again, let Cleaner hint your tracks for you.

STORAGE ISSUES

Media just devours drive space. Anyone working with media needs an external firewire drive with lots of empty space. If you can't afford an external drive, I recommend partitioning your hard drive. Once you start capturing video, you'll need to defrag the drive on a recurring basis. You won't have to reinstall programs, if you have a separate media storage space that can be defragged independently from the system and programs drive.

Why defrag? Because video clips should be stored (even on the scratch [capture] disk) without dropping frames. If the drive is clean, the media file can be written in one continuous loop, without skips, jumps or breaks. If the drive is fairly full, the computer will have to write the file in sections, 8 MB here, 8 MB there, oops dropped a frame... You get the picture. Norton Utilities can defrag your media drive while you sleep.

Another reason to have an external portable firewire drive is just that, portability.

GETTING IT ON THE WEB

I haven't mentioned authoring web pages yet (that could be a treatise by itself), but if you intend to embed audio or video directly into the web page, I RECOMMEND YOU DON'T USE MS FRONTPAGE. Take my advice and write the code yourself or invest in DreamWeaver, it is just too difficult to get the code right in FrontPage.

PUBLISHING APPLICATIONS FOR EVERYONE

Just as there is a range of desktop publishing solutions, a number of applications are being provided to publish on DVD. The focus is to go beyond traditional "entertainment" applications, and to provide capabilities for true Multimedia Publishing with products like Sonic DVDit! and MyDVD.

BIBLIOGRAPHY

Aggarwal, A. (2000). (Ed.) Web-based learning and teaching technologies: Opportunities and challenges. Hershey, PA: Idea Group Publishing.

Agnew, P. W., Kellerman, A. S. & Meyer, J, M. (1996). Multimedia in the classroom. Boston: Allyn and Bacon.

Alden, J. (1998). A trainer's guide to Web-based instruction. Alexandria, VA: Amer Society Training & Dev.

Alessi, S. M. & Trollip, S. R. (1985). Computer-based instruction methods and development. Englewood Cliffs, NJ: Prentice-Hall.

Alesso, H. P. & Smith, C. F. (2001). The Intelligent Wireless Web. Addison Wesley Professional.

Ambron, S. & Hooper, K. (1988). Interactive multimedia. Redmond, WA: Microsoft Press.

Ambron, S. & Hooper, K. (1990). Learning with interactive multimedia: developing and using multimedia tools in education. Redmond, WA: Microsoft Press.

Ambron, S. & Hooper, K. (1988). Interactive multimedia; visions of multimedia for developers, educators, and information providers. Redmond, WA: Microsoft Press.

American Association of School Librarians. (1999). Information literacy standards for student learning. Chicago: American Library Association Editions.

American Association of School Librarians. (1998). Information power: Building partnerships for learning. Chicago: American Library Association Editions.

Angelo, T. A. & Cross, P. (1994). Classroom assessment techniques: A handbook for college teachers. San Francisco: Jossey-Bass Publishers.

Anglin, Gary J. (1999). Critical Issues in Instructional Technology (Instructional Technology Series). Englewood, CO: Teacher Ideas Press.

Anderson, R. H. (1976). Selecting and developing media for instruction. New York: Van Nostrand Reinhold.

Anderson, C.J. & Veljkov, M.D. (1990). Creating interactive multimedia. Glenview, IL: Scott, Foresman.

Anglin, G. J. (Ed.). (1995). Instructional Technology: Past, Present, and Future (2nd ed.). Englewood, CO: Libraries Unlimited.

Armstrong, S. (1995). Telecommunications in the classroom. (2nd ed.). Eugene, OR: International Society for Technology in Education.

Armstrong, T. (1996). Multiple intelligences in the classroom. Alexandria, VA: Association for Supervision and Curriculum Development.

American Society for Training & Development (1999). ASTD Trainers toolkit job descriptions in workplace learning and performance. Alexandria, VA: American Society for Training & Development.

Ashby, W.R. (1956). An introduction to cybernetics. London, UK: Chapman and Hall.

Atieh, S. (1998). How to get a college degree via the Internet: The complete guide to getting your undergraduate or graduate degree from the comfort of your home. Prima Publishing. -

Azarsma, R. (1991). Educational computing: Principles and applications. New Jersey: Educational Technology Publications.

Baecker, R. M., Buxton, W. & Grudin, J. (1995). Readings in human-computer interaction: Toward the year 2,000. Los Altos, CA: Morgan-Kaufmann Publishers.

Baecker, R. M., Buxton, W. (Eds.). (1995). Readings in human-computer interaction: A multidisciplinary approach. Los Altos, CA: Morgan-Kaufmann Publishers.

Bailey, G. D. (Ed.). (1993). Computer-based integrated learning systems. Englewoood Cliffs, N J: Educational Technology Publications.

Baker, E. & O'Neil, H.F. (1994). Technological assessment in education and training. Hillsdale, NJ: Erlbaum.

Banathy, B. (1992). A systems view of education. Englewood Cliffs, NJ: Educational Technology Publications.

Banathy, B. (1991). Systems design of education: A journey to create the future . Englewood Cliffs, NJ: Educational Technology Publications.

Banathy, B. (1973). Developing a systems view of education . Belmont, CA: Lear Siegler, Inc/Fearon Publishers.

Banathy, B. (1968). Instructional systems . Belmont, CA: Lear Siegler, Inc/Fearon Publishers.

Bartram, S. & Gibson, B. (1997). Training needs analysis. Hampshire, UK: Gower Pub Co.

Barrett, E. (Ed.). (1992). Sociomedia: Multimedia, hypermedia, and the social construction of knowledge. Cambridge, Mass.: MIT Press

Barron, A. E. & Orwig, G. W. (1995). Multimedia technologies for training: An introduction. Englewood, CO: Libraries Unlimited.

Barron, A. E. & Orwig, G. W. (1995). New technologies for education: A beginner's guide. Englewood, CO: Libraries Unlimited.

Barrows, H. S. (1985). How to design a problem-based curriculum for the preclinical years. New York: Springer.

Bates, T. (1995). Technology, open learning, and distance education. London, New York: Routledge.

Bauer, D. G. (1998). The teacher's guide to winning grants. San Francisco, CA: Jossey-Bass.

Bear, J. & Bear, M. (2000). Bears guide to earning degrees by distance learning. Ten Speed Press. -

Bear, J. & Bear, M. (2000). College degrees by mail & Internet. Ten Speed Press. -

Bearchamp, D.G., Braden, R. A. & J. C. Baca, J. C. (Eds.). (1994). Visual literacy in the digital age. Blacksburg, VA: The International Visual Literacy Association.

Belanger, F. & Jordan, D. (1999). Evaluation and Implementation of Distance Learning: Technologies, Tools and Techniques. Hershey, PA: Idea Group Publishing.

Berge, Z. L. (Ed.). (2000). Sustaining distance training: Integrating learning technologies into the fabric of the enterprise. Jossey-Bass.

Berge, Z. L., & Collins, M. P. (Eds.). (1997). Wired together: The online classroom in k-12: Case studies (vol. 2). Cresskill, NJ: Hampton Press.

Berge, Z. L., & Collins, M. P. (Eds.). (1997). Wired together: The online classroom in k-12: Perspectives and instructional design (vol. 1). Cresskill, NJ: Hampton Press.

Berge, Z. L., & Collins, M. P. (Eds.). (1995). Computer-mediated communication and the online classroom (Vol. 3). Cresskill, NJ: Hampton Press.

Berge, Z. L., & Collins, M. P. (Eds.). (1994). Computer-mediated communication and the online classroom (Vol. 2). Cresskill, NJ: Hampton Press.

Berge, Z. L., & Collins, M. P. (Eds.). (1994). Computer-mediated communication and the online classroom (Vol. 1). Cresskill, NJ: Hampton Press.

Berge, Z. L. (1994). Computer-Mediated Communications & the Online Classroom (Communication Series Communication Pedagogy & Practice Subseries). Cresskill, NJ: Hampton Press.

Berger, M. (1996). Cross Cultural Team Building : Guidelines for More Effective Communication and Negotiation. New York: McGraw-Hill.

Berk, E. & Devlin, J. (1991). Hypertext/Hypermedia Handbook. New York: McGraw-Hill.

Beyer, B. K. (1995). How to conduct a formative evaluation. Alexandria, VA: Association for Supervision and Curriculum Development.

Beyer, H. & Holtzblatt, K. (1997). Contextual design: A customer-centered approach to systems designs. Boston: Academic Press.

Bias, R. G. & Mayhew, D. J. (Eds.). (1994). Cost-justifying usability. Boston: Academic Press.

Bitter, G. & Pierson, M. E. (1999). Using technology in the classroom.

Bitter, G. & Skintik, C. (1998). Working with computers. Computer Literacy Press Inc. -

Blanchard, P. N. & Thacker, J. W. (1998). Effective training: Systems, strategies, and practices. Englewood Cliffs, NJ: Prentice Hall.

Blattner, M. M. & Dannenberg, R. B. (1992). Interactive multimedia computing. Reading, MA: Addison- Wesley.

Bloom, B. & Krathwohl, D. R. (1984). Taxonomy of educational objectives, handbook 1: The cognitive domain. New York: Addison-Wesley Pub Co.

Bloom, B. (1984). Taxonomy of educational objectives: The affective domain. New York: Addison-Wesley Pub Co.

Bonk, C. J., & King, K. S. (Eds.). (1998). Electronic collaborators: Learner-centered technologies for literacy, apprenticeship, and discourse. Mahwah, NJ: Erlbaum.

Boyle, T. & Boyle, T. (1996). Design for multimedia learning. Englewood Cliffs, NJ: Prentice Hall.

Braden, R. A. & Griffin, R. E. (Eds.). (1995). Imagery and visual literacy. The International Visual Literacy Association.

Bradley, P. (1999). Internet power searching: The advanced manual. New York: Neal Schuman Pub.

Branch, R. M. & Fitzgerald, M. A. (Eds.). (1999). Educational media and technology yearbook 1999 (Serial). Englewood, CO: Teacher Ideas Press.

Branch, R. M. & Minor, B. B. (Eds.). (1997). The educational media and technology yearbook 1997. Englewood, CO: Libraries Unlimited.

Bransford, J. D., Brown, A. L. & Cocking, R. R. (1999). How people learn: Brain, mind, experience, and school. Washington, DC: National Academy Press.

Brethower, D. M., Smalley, K. A. & Alexander, L. (1998). Performance-based instruction: Linking training to business results. San Francisco, CA: Jossey-Bass.

Briggs, L., Gustafson, K. L. & Tillman, M. H. (1991). Instructional design: Principles and applications (2nd ed.). Englewood Cliffs, NJ: Educational Technology Publications.

Briggs, L. J. (1960). Sequencing instruction in relation to hierarchies of competence. Pittsburgh: AIR.

Brien, R. & Eastman, N. (1994). Cognitive science and instruction. Englewood Cliffs, NJ: Educational Technology Publications.

Brookfield, S. D. (1991). Understanding and facilitating adult learning: A comprehensive analysis of principles and effective practices. San Francisco, CA: Jossey-Bass.

Brooks, D. W. (1997). Web-teaching: A guide to designing interactive teaching for the world wide web. New York: Plenum.

Brown, C. M. (1988). Human-Computer Interface Design Guidelines. Norwood, NJ: Ablex Publishing Corp.

Brown, L. A. (1996). Designing and developing electronic performance support systems. Digital Press.

Brown, S. M., & Seidner, C. J. (1997). Evaluating corporate training: Models and issues. Norwell, MA: Kluwer Academic Publications.

Bruer, J. T. (1993). Schools for thought: A science of learning in the classroom. Cambridge, MA: The MIT Press.

Bruner, J. (1974). Toward a theory of instruction. Cambridge, MA: Harvard University Press.

Bruning, R. H., Schraw, G. J. & Ronning, R. R. (1999). Cognitive psychology and instruction. Merrill Pub Co.

Bucher, K. T. (1994). Computers & technology in school library media centers (professional growth).Linworth Publishing, Inc.

Burger, J. (1992). The desktop multimedia Bible. Reading, MA: Addison- Wesley Pub. Co.

Burgess, W. E. (ed). (2000). The Oryx Guide to Distance Learning : A Comprehensive Listing of Electronic and Other Media-Assisted Courses. Natl Conference of State.

Caffarella, R.S. (1994). Planning programs for adult learners: A practical guide for educators, trainers, and staff developers. San Francisco, CA: Jossey-Bass.

California Instructional Technology Clearinghouse. (Ed.). (1998). Guidelines for the evaluation of instructional technology resources. Eugene, OR: International Society for Technology in Education.

Campbell, D., & Campbell, M. (1995). The student's guide to doing research on the Internet. Reading, MA: Addison-Wesley.

Cannings, T. & Finkel, L. (1993). The technology age classroom. Wilsonville, OR: Franklin, Beedle & Assoc.

Cantor (1992). Delivering instruction to adult learners. Toronto: Wall & Emerson.

Capin, T. K. (Ed.) (1999). Avatars in networked virtual environments. New York: John Wiley & Sons.

Card, S. K., Moran, T. P. & Newell, A. (1983). The psychology of human-computer interaction. Hillsdale, NJ: Lawrence Erlbaum Associates.

Carlisle, KE (1986). Analyzing jobs and tasks. Englewood Cliffs, NJ:Educational Technology Pubs.

Carr, C. (1992). Smart training: The manager's guide to training for improved performance. Highstown, NJ: McGraw Hill.

Carroll, J. (1990). The nurnberg funnel: Designing minimalist instruction for practical computer skill. Cambridge, MA: MIT Press.

Carter, M. E. (1996). Electronic highway robbery: An artist's guide to copyrights in the digital era. Berkeley, CA: Peachpit Press.

Castro, C. M. (Ed.). (1998). Education in the information age: What works & what Doesn't. Washington, DC: Inter-American Development Bank.

Cavazos, E. A., & Morin, G. (1994). Cyberspace and the law: Your rights and duties in the on-line world. Cambridge, MA: The MIT Press.

Chaiklin, S. & Lave, J. (Eds.). (1995). Understanding practice: Perspectives on activity and context. Boston, MA: Cambridge University Press.

Charney, C. & Conway, K. (1997). The Trainer's Tool Kit. New York: AMACOM.

Chute, A. G., Thompson, M. & Hancock, B. (1998). Handbook of distance learning. New York: McGraw-Hill.

Cipolla, R. & Pentland, A. (1999). Computer vision for human-computer interaction. Cambridge Univ Press. -

Clark, C. L. (1996). The student's guide to the Internet. Indianapolis: Alpha Books.

Clark, R. C. (19..). Developing technical training: A structured approach for the development of classroom and computer-based instructional materials. —

Cocking R. R. & Renninger, K. A. (Eds.). (1993). The development and meaning of psychological distance. Hillsdale, NJ: Lawrence Erlbaum Associates.

Collis, B. & Knezek G. (1997). Teaching and learning in the digital age-research into practice with telecommunications in educational settings Eugene, OR: International Society for Technology in Education.

Collis, B. (1996). Tele-learning in a digital world. London: International Thomas Computer Press.

Collis, B. (Ed.). (1996). Children and computers in school. Hillsdale, NJ: Lawrence Erlbaum Associates.

Collis, B. & Carleer, G. (19..). Technology enriched schools: Nine case studies with reflections. Amsterdam: North-Holland.

Collis, B. & Davies, G. (Ed.). (1995). Innovative adult learning with innovative technologies. Amsterdam: North-Holland.

Collison, G., Elbaum, B., Haavind, S. & Tinker, R. (2000). Facilitating Online Learning: Effective strategies for moderators. Madison, WI: Atwood Pub.

Connick, G. P. (Ed.). (1998). The distance learner's guide. Englewood Cliffs, NJ: Prentice Hall.

Considine, D. M. & Haley, G. E. (1999). Visual messages: Integrating imagery into instruction. Englewood, CO: Teacher Ideas Press.

Cooper, A. (1995). About face: The essentials of user interface design. Foster City, CA: IDG Books.

Cornell, R.A. & Murphy. K. (Eds.). (1995). An international survey of distance education and teacher training: From smoke signals to satellite II. Orlando, FL: University of Central Florida, and Paris: International Council for Educational Media.

Cotton, E. G. (1998). The online classroom: Teaching with the internet (2nd ed.). Bloomington, IN: EDINFO Press.

Craig, M. (199?). Analysing learning needs. Hampshire, UK: Ashgate Publishing Company.

Craig, R. L. (Ed.) (1996). The ASTD training and development handbook: A guide to human resource development (4th ed.). New York: McGraw-Hill.

Creswell, J. W. (1997). Qualitative inquiry and design: Choosing among five traditions. Thousand Oaks, CA: Sage Publications.

Criscito, P. (1999) Barron's guide to distance learning: Degrees, certificates, courses. Barrons Educational Series. -

Cronin, M.J. (1996). The Internet strategy handbook. New York: McGraw-Hill.

Cross, K. P. (1992). Adults as learners: Increasing participation and facilitating learning. San Francisco, CA: Jossey-Bass.

Cuban, L. (1986). Teachers and machines: The classroom use of technology since 1970. NY: Teachers College Press.

Cummins, J., & Sayers, D. (1995). Brave new schools: Challenging cultural literacy through global learning networks. New York: St. Martin's Press.

Cunningham, S., & Hubbold, R. J. (Eds.). (1992). Interactive learning through visualization. New York: Springer-Verlag.

Cyrs, T. E. (1997). Teaching and learning at a distance: What it takes to effectively design, deliver, and evaluate programs. San Francisco, CA: Jossey-Bass.

Cyrs, T. E. (1997). Teaching at a distance with the merging technologies: An instructional systems approach. New Mexico State University: Center for Educational Development.

Daniel, J. (1998) Mega-universities and knowledge media: Technology strategies for higher education. Stylus Pub Llc. -

Darden, E., et al. (1999). Legal issues & education technology: A school leader's guide. Alexandria, VA: National School Boards Association.

Davies, I.(1973). Competency based learning: Technology, management, and design. New York: McGraw-Hill.

Davenport, T. H. (1993). Process innovation: Reengineering work through information technology. Boston, MA: Harvard Business School Press

Davidson, N. & Worsham, T. (Eds.). (1992). Enhancing thinking through cooperative learning. New York: Teachers College Press.

Deal, T. E. & Kennedy, A. A. (1999). The new corporate cultures. Perseus Books. -

Dean, G. J. (1994). Designing instruction for adult learners. Florida: Krieger Publishing Co.

Dean, P. (1994). Performance engineering at work. Batavia, IL: International Board of Standards for Training, Performance & Instruction.

Dick, W. & Carey, L. (1996). The systematic design of instruction (3rd ed). Glenview, IL: Scott Foresman.

Dick W. & Reiser, R. (1989). Planning effective instruction. Englewood Cliffs, NJ: Prentice Hall.

Dijkstra, S., Seel, N. M. & Schott, F. (Eds). (1997). Instructional design: International perspectives: Solving instructional design problems. Hillsdale, NJ: Lawrence Erlbaum Associates.

Dix, A. (Ed.). (1998). Human-computer interaction. Hillsdale, NJ: Prentice Hall.

Dictionary of computing and multimedia (NTC Pocket References) (1996). Lincolnwood, IL: NTC Publishing Group.

Dills, C., & Romiszowski, A.J. (Eds.). (1997). Instructional development: The paradigms of the field. Englewood Cliffs, NJ: Educational Technology Publications.

Dixon, P. (1996). Virtual College : A Quick Guide to How You Can Get the Degree You Want With Computer, Tv, Video, Audio, and Other Distance-Learning Tools. Petersons Guides.

Dolence, M. & Norris, D. (1995). Transforming higher education: A vision for learning in the 21st century. Ann Arbor, Michigan: Society for College and University Planning.

Dreyfus, H. L. & Dreyfus, S. E. (1986). Mind over machine: The power of human intuition and expertise in the era of the computer. New York: Macmillan.

Driscoll, M. M. & Alexander, L. (1998). Web-based training: Using technology to design adult learning experiences. San Francisco, CA: Jossey-Bass.

Druin, A. & Solomon, C. (1996). Designing multimedia environments for children: Computers, creativity & kids. New York: John Wiley & Sons.

Driscoll, M. P. & Driscoll, M. P. (1994). Psychology of learning for instruction. Boston: Allyn & Bacon.

Dubois, D. D. (1998). The competency case book. Amherst, MA: Human Resource Development Press.

Duffy, J. P. (1997). College online: How to take college courses without leaving home. New York: John Wiley & Sons.

Duffy, T. & Jonassen, D. (Eds.). (1992). Constructivism and the Technology of Instruction. Hillsdale, NJ: Erlbaum.

Dumas, J. S., & Reddish, J. C. (1993). A practical guide to usability testing. Norwood, NJ: Ablex Publishing Corporation.

Duning, B., Van Kekerix, M., & Zaborowski, L. M. (1993). Reaching learners through telecommunications. San Francisco, CA: Jossey-Bass.

Dwyer, F.M. (1987). Enhancing visualized instruction. State College, PA: Learning Services.

Earnshaw, R. & Vince, J. (Eds.). (1997). The Internet in 3D: Information, images, and interaction. San Diego: Academic Press.

Eastmond D. V. (1995). Alone but together: Adult distance study through computer conferencing. New York: Hampton Press.

Eby, J.W. (1997). Reflective planning, teaching, and evaluation: K-12. Prentice Hall College Div.

Egan, K. (1998). The educated mind: How cognitive tools shape our understanding. Chicago and London: University of Chicago Press.

Ellis, A. L., Longmire, W. R. & Wagner, E. D. (1999). Managing Web-based training. Alexandria, VA: American Society for Training & Development.

Ellsworth, J. H. (1994). Education on the Internet: A hands-on book of ideas, resources, projects, and advice. Indianapolis: Sams Publishing.

Ely, D. P. (1996). Trends in educational technology. Syracuse University: Informational Resources Publications.

Ely, D. P. & Plomp, T. (Eds.). (..). Classic writings on instructional technology. Englewood, CO: Libraries Unlimited.

Eraut, M. (Ed.). (1989). International encyclopedia of educational technology (Advances in Education). New York: Pergamon Press.

Ertmer, P. A. & Quinn, J. (1999). The ID casebook: Case studies in instructional design. Merril Press. -

Evans, T., & Nation, D. (Eds.). (1996). Opening education: Policies and practices from open and distance Education. New York: Routledge

Eurich, N. (1985). Corporate classrooms: The learning business. N.J.: Princeton University Press.

Faith, K. (Ed.). (1988). Toward new horizons for women in distance education: International perspectives. London: Routledge.

Falk, D. R. & Carlson, H. L. (1995). Multimedia in higher education: A practical guide to new tools for interactive teaching and learning. Medford, NJ: Learned Information, Inc.

Farnham-Diggory, S. (1993). Cognitive processes in education (2nd ed.). New York: HarperCollins.

Faulkner, C. (1998). The essence of human-computer interaction. Prentice Hall Computer Books.

Fenrich, P. (1997). Practical guidelines for creating instructural multimedia applications. Hbj College & School Div.

Fields, D. K. & Kolb, M. A. (2000). Web development with JavaServer pages. Manning Publications Company.

Filho, W. L. & Tahir, T. (Eds.). (1998). Distance education and environmental education. New York: Peter Lang Publishing.

Finkelstein, M. J., Frances, C., Jewett, F. I. & Scholz, B. W. (Eds.) (2000). Dollars, distance and online education. Oryx Press.

Flagg, B. (1990). Formative evaluation for educational technologies. Hillsdale, NJ: Lawrence Erlbaum.

Fleming, M. & Levie, W.H. (1993). Instructional message design. (2nd ed.). Englewood Cliffs, NJ: Educational Technology Publications.

Fleming, M. & Levie, W.H. (1993). Principles from the behavioral and cognitive sciences. Englewood Cliffs, NJ: Educational Technology Publications.

Forcier, R. C. (1999). The computer as an educational tool: Productivity and problem solving. Englewood Cliffs, NJ: Prentice Hall.

Forsyth, F., Provenzo, Jr, Provenzo, E. F. & Forsyth (1999). The Internet and the World Wide Web for preservice. Boston: Allyn & Bacon.

Frank, D. (1996). Terrific training materials: High impact graphic designs for workbooks, Handouts, Instructor Guides, and Job AIDS. Amherst, MA: Human Resource Development Press.

Frazier, D., with Kurshan, B, & Armstrong, S. (1998). Internet for kids. Alameda, CA: SYBEX.

Frazier, G., & Frazier, D. (1994). Telecommunications and education: Surfing and the art of change. Alexandra, VA: National School Boards Association.

Freeman, H., Routen, T., Patel, D., Ryan, S. & Scott, B. (1999). The Virtual University: The Internet and Resource Based Learning (The Open and Distance Learning Series). London: Kogan Page.

French, D., Hale, C., Johnson, C. & Farr, G. (Eds.). (1999). Internet based learning: An introduction and framework for higher education and business. Sterling, VA: Stylus Pub Llc.

Frey, J. (1994). College Degrees You Can Earn from Home : How to Earn a First-Class Degree Without Attending Class. Live Oak Pubns.

Fripp, J. (1993). Learning through simulations: A guide to the design and the use of simulations in business and education. New York: McGraw-Hill.

Fullan, M. (1982). The meaning of educational change. Toronto: OISE.

Fuller, J., Farrington, J. & Fuller, J. (1999). From training to performance improvement. San Francisco: Pfeiffer.

Fuller, J. (1997). Managing performance improvement projects. San Francisco: Pfeiffer.

Gardner, H. E. (1993). Multiple intelligences: The theory in practice. New York: Basic Books.

Gardner, H. E. (1993). Frames of mind: The theory of multiple intelligences/tenth anniversary edition. New York: Basic Books.

Gagne, E. D., Yekovich C. W. & Yekovich, F. R. (1993). The cognitive psychology of school learning. New York: Addison-Wesley Pub Co.

Gagne, R. (1997). The conditions of learning and theory of instruction. New York: Holt, Rinehart and Winston.

Gagne, R. (1989). Studies of learning 50 years of research. Florida State University.

Gagne, R. (1987). Instructional technology: Foundations. Hillsdale, NJ: Erlbaum Assoc.

Gagne, R. M. & Medsker, K.L. (1996). The conditions of learning: Training applications. Ft. Worth: Harcourt Brace & Company.

Gagne, R. & Driscoll, M. P. (..). Essentials of Learning for Instruction (2nd ed.). Englewood Cliffs, NJ: Prentice-Hall.

Gagne, R., Twitchell, D. & Merrill, M. D. (1991). Robert M. Gagne and M. David Merrill—in conversation. Englewood Cliffs, NJ: Educational Technology Publications.

Gagne, R., Briggs, L. & Wager, W. (1992). Principles of instructional design (4th ed.). Englewood Cliffs, NJ: Prentice-Hall.

Gagne, R.M., Tennyson, R.D. and Gettman, D.J. (1991). Designing an advanced instructional design advisor: Conceptual frameworks. AL-TP-1991-0017-Vol-5. Brooks Air Force Base, TX.

Galdo, D. E. & Nielson, J. (1996). International user interfaces. New York: John Wiley & Sons.

Gascoyne, R.J. and Ozcubucku, K. (1996). The corporate Internet planning guide. NY: Van Nostrand Reinhold.

Gates, B. (1996). The road ahead. New York: Penguin.

Galbraith, M. W. (Ed.). (1998). Adult learning methods: A guide for effective instruction. Malabar, FL: Krieger Publishing Company.

Galegher, J. R., Kraut, R. E. & Egido, C. (Eds.). Intellectual teamwork: Social and technological foundations of cooperative work. Hillsdale, NJ: Lawrence Erlbaum Associates.

Garrison, D. R., & Shale, D. (Eds.). (1990). Education at a distance: From issues to practice. Malabar, FL: Robert E. Krieger Publishing Company.

Gayeski, D. (1998). Designing and managing computer mediated instruction: An interactive toolkit . Ithaca, New York: OmniCom Associates.

Gayeski, D. (1993). Multimedia for learning. Englewood Cliffs, NJ: Educational Technology Publications.

Gehris, D. O. (1997). Using multimedia tools and applications on the Internet. Belmont, CA: Wadsworth.

Gentry, C. (1994). Introduction to instructional development. Belmont, CA: Wadsworth.

Gery, G. (1991). Electronic performance support systems. Boston, MA: Weingarten.

Gery, G. (1987). Making CBT happen: Prescriptions for successful implementation of computer-based training in your organization. Gery Assoc.

Giagnocavo, G., McLain, T., & DiStefano, V. (1996). Educator's Internet companion-classroom connect's complete guide to educational resources on the Internet. Lancaster, PA: Wentworth Worldwide Media.

Gibbons, A. S. & Fairweather, P. G. (1998). Computer-based instruction: design and development. Englewood Cliffs, NJ: Educational Technology Publications

Gibson, C. C. (Ed.). (1998). Distance learners in higher education. Overland Park, KS: Atwood Publishing.

Giardina, M. (Ed). (1992). Interactive multimedia environments. Heidelberg: Springer-Verlag.

Gillis, L. (2000). Quality standards for evaluating multimedia and online training. McGraw-Hill.

Gilbert, T. F. (1996). Human competence: Engineering worthy performance (2nd ed.). New York: McGraw-Hill.

Glavac, M. (1998). The busy educator's guide to the World Wide Web. NIMA Systems. -

Glennan, T.K. and Melmed, A. (1996). Fostering the use of educational technology: Elements of a national strategy. Santa Monica CA: RAND.

Gilster, P. (1998). Digital literacy. New York: John Wiley & Sons.

Goodson, B. (1991). Teachers and Technology Staff Development for Tomorrows Schools. Alexandria, VA: National School Boards Association.

Gordon, S. E. (1994). Systematic training program design: Maximizing effectiveness and minimizing liability. Englewood Cliffs, NJ: Prentice Hall.

Grabinger, R. S., Wilson, B. W. & Jonassen, D. H. (1990). Building expert systems in training and education. New York: Praeger Publishers.

Greenblat, C. S. (1987). Designing games and simulations: An illustrated handbook. Newbury Park, CA: Sage Publications.

Greer, M. (1992). ID project management: Tools and techniques for instructional designers and developers. Englewood Cliffs, NJ: Educational Technology Publications.

Greer, M. (1996). Project manager's partner: A step-by-step guide to project management. Englewood Cliffs, NJ: Educational Technology Publications.

Greer, M. (1997). Project management for workgroups; facilitator's suide for the project manager's partner. Englewood Cliffs, NJ: Educational Technology Publications.

Gustafson, K. & Branch, R. M. (1997). Survey of instructional development models. Syracuse: ERIC Clearing-house on Information Resources, Syracuse University.

Gunter, M., Estes, T., & Schwab, J. (1995). Instruction: A models approach. Boston: Allyn & Bacon.

Gupta, K. (1998). A practical guide to needs assessment. San Francisco: Pfeiffer.

Hackbarth, S. (1996b). The educational technology handbook: A comprehensive guide: process and products for learning. Englewood Cliffs, NJ: Educational Technology Publications.

Hackos, J. T. & Redish, J. C. (1998). User and task analysis for interface design. New York: John Wiley & Sons.

Hale, J. A. (1998). The performance consultant's fieldbook: Tools and techniques for improving organizations and people. San Francisco, CA: Jossey-Bass.

Hall, B. (1997). Web-based training cookbook. New York: Wiley.

Hammer, M. & Champy, J. (1994). Reengineering the corporation - a manifesto for business revolution. London: Nicholas Brealey.

Handler, M. G. & Dana, A. S. (1998). Hypermedia as a student tool: A guide for teachers. Englewood, CO: Libraries Unlimited.

Hanna, D. E., Glowacki-Dudka, M. & Conceicao-Runlee, C. (2000). 147 Practical tips for teaching online groups: Essentials of Web-based education. Madison, WI: Atwood Publishing.

Hannafin, M. J. & Peck, K. L. (1988). The design, development, and evaluation of instructional software. Hew York: Macmillan Publishing.

Hannum, W. & Hansen, C. (1989). Instructional systems development in large organizations. Englewood Cliffs, NJ: Educational Technology Press.

Hanson, D., Maushak, N., Schlosser, C., Anderson, M., Sorenson, C., & Simonson, M. (1997). Distance education: Review of the literature (2nd ed.) Washington, DC: Association for Educational Communications and Technology.

Hansen, D. E. (1991). The educational technology telecommunications dictionary with acronyms. Englewood Cliffs, NJ: Educational Technology Press.

Harasim, L., Hiltz, S.R., Teles, L. & Turoff, M. (1995). Learning networks: A field guide to teaching and learning online. Cambridge, MA: MIT Press.

Harasim, L. (1993). Global networks: Computers and international communication. Cambridge, MA: MIT Press.

Harasim, L. (Ed.). (1990). Online education: Perspectives on a new environment. New York: Praeger.

Harless, J. H. (1975). An ounce of analysis is worth a pound of objectives. GA: Newman.

Harmon, C. (1996). Using the Internet, online services, & CD-ROMs for writing research and term papers. New York: Neal-Schuman.

Harper, D., Hardy, J. & Murray, R. (1999). Generation www.Y curriculum guide. Eugene, OR: International Society for Technology in Education.

Harris, J. (1998). Virtual architecture: Designing & directing curriculum based telecomputing.Eugene, OR: International Society for Technology in Education.

Harrison, N. (1998). How to Design Self-Directed and Distance Learning: A Guide for Creators of Web-Based Training, Computer-Based Training, and Self-Study Materials. New York: McGraw-Hill.

Harrison, N. (1996). Practical instructional design for open learning materials: A modular course covering open learning, computer-based training, multimedia. New York: McGraw-Hill.

Harry, K. (1999). Higher Education Through Open and Distance Learning. London: Routledge.

Harry, K., John, M., & Keegan, D. (Eds.). (1993). Distances education: New perspectives. London: Routledge.

Hartley, J. (1985). Designing instructional text (3rd ed.). New York: Nichols Publishing Co.

Haughey, M. & Anderson, T. (1998). Networked learning: The pedagogy of the Internet. Toronto: McGraw-Hill.

Havelock, R.G. & Zlotolow, S. (1995). The change agent's guide. Englewood Cliffs, NJ: Educational Technology Publications.

Havelock, R.G. (1973). Change Agents Guide to Innovation in Education. Englewood Cliffs, NJ: Educational Technology Publications.

Hawkins, B. (Ed.). (1998). The mirage of continuity: Reconfiguring academic information resources for the 21st century. Washington, DC: Council on Library and Information Resources.

Head, A. J. (1999). Design wise: A guide to evaluating the interface design of information resources. Information Today Inc. -

Hegarty, M., Phelan, A. & Kilbride, L. (Eds.). (1998), Classrooms for distance teaching and learning: A blueprint. Leuven, Belgium: Leuven University Press.

Heide, A., & Stilborne, L. (1999). The teacher's complete & easy guide to the Internet. Buffalo, NY: Trifolium Books.

Heinich, R., Molenda, M., Russell, J., & Smaldino, S. (1996). Instructional media and technologies for learning. Upper Saddle River, NJ: Prentice-Hall, Inc.

Heines, J. (1984). Screen design strategies for computer-assisted instruction. Bedford, MA: Digital Press.

Helander, M., Landauer, T. K. & Prabhu, P. V. (1997). Handbook of human-computer interaction. Amsterdam: North-Holland.

Heldman, R. (1993). Future telecommunications information applications, services, & infrastructure. Washington, DC: McGraw-Hill.

Henry, J. (1994). Teaching through projects. (Open and Distance Learning Series). Kogan Page Ltd., London.

Hiltz, S. R. (1994). The virtual classroom: Learning without limits via computer networks. Norwood, NJ: Ablex Publishing.

Hiltz, S. R. (1993). The virtual classroom: A new option for learning via computer networking. Norwood, NJ: Ablex.

Hiltz, S. R. & Turoff, M. (1993). The network nation: Human communication via computer. Cambridge, MA: MIT Press.

Hix, D., & Hartson, H. R. (1993). Developing user interfaces: Ensuring usability through product & process. New York: John Wiley & Sons.

Hixson, S.& Schrock, K. (1998). Developing web pages for school and classroom authors: beginner's handbook.

Hollands, W. D. (1999). Teaching the Internet to library staff and users: 10 ready-to-go workshops that work. New York: Neal Schuman Pub.

Holmberg, B. (1995). Theory and practice of distance education. London: Routledge.

Horn, R.E. (1990). Mapping hypertext: The analysis, organization, and display of knowledge for the next generation of on-line text and graphics. Lexington, MA: The Lexington Institute.

Horton, S. (2000). Web teaching guide: A practical approach to creating course Web sites. Yale Univ Press.

Horton, W. K. (2000). Designing Web-based training: How to teach anyone anything anywhere anytime. John Wiley & Sons.

House, W. (1974). The politics of educational innovation. Berkeley, CA: McCutchan.

Hofstetter, F. T. (1997). Multimedia Literacy. New York: McGraw-Hill.

Hudspeth, D. (1985). Instructional telecommunications. New York: Praeger Publishers.

Hupp, T., Polak, C. & Westgaard, O. (1995). Designing work groups, jobs, and work flow (from training to performance in the twenty-first century, set 2: redesigning work processes). San Francisco, CA: Jossey-Bass.

Hyerle, D. (1996). Visual tools for constructing knowledge. Alexandria, VA: Association for Supervision and Curriculum Development.

Idol, L. & Jones, B. F. (Eds.). (1990). Educational values and cognitive instruction: Implications for reform. Hillsdale, NJ: Lawrence Erlbaum Associates.

Insinnia, E. (Ed.). (1999). Educators take charge: Teaching in the Internet revolution. Eugene, OR: International Society for Technology in Education.

ISTE Accreditation and Standards Committee. (1998). Educational computing and technology programs: A folio preparation manual (3rd ed.). Eugene, OR: International Society for Technology in Education.

Ivers, K. S. & Barron, A. E. (1997). Multimedia projects in education: Designing, producing, and assessing. Englewood, CO: Libraries Unlimited.

Jacobs, H. H. (Ed.). (1989). Interdisciplinary curriculum: Design and implementation. Alexandria, VA: Association for Supervision and Curriculum Development.

Jacobson, R. E. (Ed.). (1999). Information design. Cambridge, MA: MIT Press.

Jager, R., & Ortiz, R. (1998). In the company of giants: Candid conversations with visionaries of the digital world. Washington, DC: McGraw-Hill.

Jenlink, P. M. (Ed.) (1995). Systemic Change: Touchstones for the Future School. Andover, MA: Skylight Publishing.

Johansen, R., Martin, A., Mittman, R., Saffo, P., Sibbet, D., & Benson, S. (1991). Leading business teams: How teams can use technology and group process tools to enhance performance. New York: Addison-Wesley.

Johnson, D. W., Johnson, R.T., & Holubec, E. J. (1994). The new circles of learning: Cooperation in the classroom and school. Alexandria, VA: Association of Supervision and Curriculum Development.

Johnson, J. K. (1995). Degree curricula in educational communications and technology: A descriptive directory 1995/with disk. (5th Ed). Washington, DC: Association for Educational Communications and Technology.

Jonassen, D.H. (Ed.). (1996). Handbook of research on educational communications and technology: A project of the association for educational communications and technology. New York, NY: MacMillan.

Jonassen, D.H. (1996). Computers in the classroom: Mindtools for critical thinking. Englewood Cliffs, NJ: Prentice-Hall.

Jonassen, D.H. (1985). The technology of text. Englewood Cliffs, NJ: Educational Technology Publications.

Jonassen, D. & Land, S (Eds.) (2000). Theoretical foundations of learning environments. Mahwah, NJ: Erlbaum.

Jonassen, D.H., Peck, K.L. & Wilson, B. G. (1999). Learning with technology: A constructivist perspective. New York, NY: MacMillan.

Jonassen, D.H. & Grabowski (1993). Handbook of individual differences, learning, and instruction. Hillsdale, NJ: Erlbaum Assoc.

Jonassen, D.H. & Mandl, H. (1990). Designing hypermedia for learning. New York: Springer-Verlag.

Jonassen, D.H.., Hannum, W. H. & Tessmer , M. (1989). Handbook of task analysis procedures. Greenwood Publishing Group.

Jones, S (2000). The Internet for educators and homeschoolers. Etc Publications. -

Junion-Metz, G. (1996). K-12 resources on the Internet: An instructional guide. Berkeley: Library Solutions Press.

Kafai, Y. & Resnick, M. (Eds.). (1996). Constructionism in practice: Designing, thinking, and learning in a digital world. Hillsdale, NJ: Lawrence Erlbaum Assoc.

Kagan, S. (1997). Cooperative learning. San Juan Capistrano, CA: Kagan Cooperative Learning.

Katz, R. (Editor). (1999) Dancing with the devil: Information technology and the new competition in higher education. San Francisco, CA: Jossey-Bass.

Kaplan Guide to Distance Learning.

Kaye, A. (Ed.). (1992). Collaborative learning through computer conferencing: The Najaden papers. Berlin, Germany: Springer-Verlag.

Kaufman, R., Rojas, A.M., & Mayer, H. (1993). Needs assessment: A user's guide. Englewood Cliffs, NJ: Educational Technology Publications.

Kaufman, R., Thiagarajan, S. & MacGillis, H. (Eds.). (1996). The guidebook for performance improvement - working with individuals and organizations. San Francisco, CA: Jossey-Bass.

Kavelaar, E. K. (1997). Conducting training workshops: A crash course for beginners. San Francisco, CA: Jossey-Bass.

Kearsley, G. (2000). Online Education: Learning and Teaching in Cyberspace. Belmont, CA: Wadsworth.

Kearsley, G. (1984). Training and technology. Reading, MA: Addison-Wesley.

Kearsley, G. (Ed.). (1987). Artificial intelligence and instruction: Applications and methods. Reading, MA: Addison-Wesley.

Kearsley, G., Hunter, B., & Furlong, M. (1992). We teach with technology. Wilsonville, OR: Franklin, Beedle & Assoc.

Kearsley, G. & Lynch, W. (1994). Educational technology: Leadership perspectives. Englewood Cliffs, NJ: Educational Technology Publications.

Keegan, D. (1996). Foundations of distance education. London: Routledge.

Keegan, D. (Ed.). (1993). Theoretical principles of distance education. London: Routledge.

Kegan, M. (1995). Scenario educational software: design and development of discovery learning. Englewood Cliffs, NJ: Educational Technology Publications.

Kelleher, K. & Cross, T. B. (1985). Teleconferencing: Linking people together electronically. Englewood Cliffs, NJ: Prentice-Hall.

Kelly, L. (Ed.). (1995). The ASTD technical and skills training handbook (American Society for Training and Development). New York: McGraw-Hill.

Kember, D. (1995). Open learning courses for adults: A model of student progress. Englewood Cliffs, NJ: Educational Technology Publications.

Kemp, J. E. (1985). The instructional design process. NY: Harper & Row.

Keith, H. (Ed.) (1999). Higher education through open and distance learning. London: Routledge.

Kemp, J. E., Morrison, G. R., & Ross, S. M. (1997). Designing effective instruction. New York: Merrill.

Khan, B. H. (Ed.). (1997). Web-based instruction. Englewood Cliffs, NJ: Educational Technology Publications.

*Khan, B. H. (Ed.). (in press). Web-based training. Englewood Cliffs, NJ: Educational Technology Publications.

Kinlaw, D. C. (1999). Handbook of leadership training activities. New York: McGraw-Hill.

Kinlaw, D. C. (1996). Facilitation skills: The ASTD trainer's sourcebook. New York: McGraw-Hill.

King, L. A. (1995). Directory of electronics journals newsletters and academic discussion lists. Washington, DC: Association of Research Libraries.

Kirkpatrick, D. L. (1994). Evaluating training programs: The four levels. San Francisco, CA: Berrett-Koehler Publishers.

Kirkup, G., Jones, A. & Kirkwood, A. (1993). Personal computers for distance education: The study of an educational innovation. New York: St. Martin's Press.

Kirshner, D. & Whitson, J. A. (1997). Situated cognition: Social, semiotic, and psychological perspectives. Mahwah, NJ: Erlbaum.

Klopfenstein, B. C. (1996). The whole Internet user's guide and catalog. Sebastopol, California: O'Reilly & Associates, Inc.

Knowles, M. S. (1988). Self-directed learning: A guide for learners and teachers.Cambridge Book Co.

Knowles, M. S. (1984). The adult learner: A neglected species (building blocks of human potential). Houston, TX: Gulf Publishing.

Knowles, M. S., Holton, E. F. & Swanson , R. A. (1998). The adult learner: The definitive classic in adult education and human resource development. Houston, TX: Gulf Publishing.

Kommers, P.A.M., Grabinger, S., & Dunlap, J.C. (1996). Hypermedia learning environments: Instructional design and integration. Mahwah, NJ: Lawrence Erlbaum.

Knott, T. (1994). Planning & evaluating distance education: A guide to collaboration. Memphis: Diphara Publications.

Kristof, R. & Satran, A. (1995). Interactivity by design. Indianapolis, IN: Hayden Books.

Krol, E., & Loukides, M. (1996). The whole Internet and users guide and Catalog. Sebastopol, CA: O'Reilly & Associates.

Kurz, R. A., Newland. B. G., Lieberman, S. & Jimenez, C. M. (1996). Internet and the law: Legal fundamentals for the Internet user. Rockville, MD: Government Institutes.

Landow, G. P. (Ed.). (1994). Hyper / text / theory. Baltimore, MD: The Johns Hopkins University Press.

Langdon, D. G., Whiteside, K. S. & McKenna, M. M. (1999). Intervention resource guide: 50 performance improvement tools. San Francisco, CA: Jossey-Bass.

Lajoie, S. P. & Derry, S. J. (1993). Computers as cognitive tools. Hillsdale, NJ: Lawrence Erlbaum Associates.

Lamb, A.C. (1998). Building treehouses for learning: Technology in today's classroom. Evansville, IN: Vision To Action.

Lamb, A.C. (1998). The magic carpet ride: Integrating technology into the k-12 classroom. Evansville, IN: Vision To Action.

Lamb, A.C. (1997). Spinnin' the Web: Designing & developing Web projects. Evansville, IN: Vision To Action

Lamb, A.C., & Johnson, L. (1995). Cruisin' the information highway: Internet and the k-12 classroom. Evansville, IN: Vision To Action.

Lamb, A. (1991). Emerging technologies & instruction: Hypertext, hypermedia, & interactive multimedia. Selected Bibliography Series, v.4. Englewood Cliffs, NJ: Educational Technology.

Lambert, S. & Sallis, J. (Ed.). (1987). CD-I and interactive videodisc technology. Indianapolis: Howard W. Sams.

Latchem, C., Lockwood, C. (Eds.). (1998). Staff development in open and flexible learning. London: Routledge.

Latchem, C., Williamson, J. & Henderson-Lancett, L. (Eds.). (1993). Interactive multimedia: Practice and promise. London: Kogan Page.

Laurel, B. (Ed.). (1990). The art of human-computer interface design. Reading, MA: Addison-Wesley.

Laurel, B. (1991). Computers as theater. Reading, MA: Addison-Wesley.

Laurillard, D. (1993). Rethinking university teaching: A framework for the effective use of educational technology. London: Routledge.

Lave, J. & Wenger, E. (1991). Situated learning: Legitimate peripheral participation. Cambridge, MA: Cambridge University Press.

Lawlor, P. & Handley, P. (1997). The creative trainer: Holistic facilitation skills for accelerated learning. New York: McGraw-Hill.

Lawson, K. (1998). The trainer's handbook. San Francisco, CA: Jossey-Bass.

Lennon, J. A. (1997). Hypermedia systems and applications: World wide web and beyond. New York: Springer Verlag.

Leshin, C. B., Pollock, J. & Reigeluth, C.M. (1992). Instructional design strategies and tactics. Englewood Cliffs, NJ: Educational Technology Publications.

Leshin, C.B. (1998). Focus on curriculum integration through: Internet adventures. Englewood Cliffs, NJ: Prentice Hall.

Lesser, G. (1978). Children and television: Lessons from sesame street. New York: McGraw-Hill.

Liao, T. T. (Ed.). (1996). Advanced educational technology: Research issues and future potential (NATO ASI series. series F, computer and systems sciences, no 145). New York: Springer Verlag.

Lifter, M. (1997). Make and take technology. Westminster, CA: Teacher Created Materials.

Lifter, M. (1996). Integrating technology into the curriculum: Grade levels 1st - 3rd. Westminster, CA: Teacher Created Materials.

Lifter, M. (1996). Writing & desktop publishing on the computer. Westminster, CA: Teacher Created Materials.

Lopuck, L. (1996). Designing multimedia: A visual guide to multimedia and online graphic design. Berkeley, CA: Peachpit Press.

Lochte, R. (1994). Interactive television and instruction: A guide to technology, technique, facilities design, and classroom management. Englewood Cliffs, NJ: Educational Technology Publications.

Lockwood, F. (Ed.). (1995). Open and distance learning today. London: Routledge.

Lynch, P. J. Horton, S. (1999). Web style guide: Basic design principles for creating web sites. New Haven, CT: Yale Univ Press.

McAleese, R. (1998). Hypertext: Theory into practice. Intellect. -

McArdle, G. (1999). Training design & delivery. Alexandria, VA: American Society for Training & Development.

McCormack, C. & Jones, D. (1997). Building a web-based education system. New York: John Wiley & Sons.

McKenzie, J. A. (1993). Administrators at risk : Tools and technologies for securing your future. Natl Educational Service. -

McKnight, C., Dillon, A., & Richardson, J. (Eds.). (1993). Hypertext: A psychological perspective. New York: Ellis Harwood.

McLellan, H. (Ed.). (1996). Situated learning perspectives. Englewood Cliffs, NJ: Educational Technology Publications.

Madaus, G. F. & Scriven, M. S. (Eds.) (1983). Evaluation models: Viewpoints on educational and human services evaluation/student edition. Norwell, MA: Kluwer Academic Publications.

Maddux, C. D. & Milheim, W. D. (Eds.). (1992). Distance education: A selected bibliography. Englewood Cliffs, NJ: Educational Technology Publications.

Mager, R. (1999). What every manager should know about training. Atlanta, GA: Center for Effective Performance.

Mager, R. (1997). Preparing instructional objectives: A critical tool in the development of effective instruction. Belmont, CA: Lake Publishers.

Mager, R. (1997). How to turn learners on... without turning them off : ways to ignite interest in learning. Atlanta, GA: Center for Effective Performance.

Mager, R. (1997). Making instruction work. Atlanta, GA: Center for Effective Performance.

Mager, R. (1992). What every manager should know about training: Or i've got a training problem and other odd ideas. Atlanta, GA: Center for Effective Performance.

Mager, R. F. & Pipe, P. (1997). Analyzing performance problems. Or "you really oughta wanna."Belmont, CA: Fearon.

Malone, S. A. (1997). How to set up and manage a corporate learning centre. Hampshire, UK: Gower Pub Co.

Mandl, H. & Levin, J. R. (Eds.). (1989). Knowledge acquisition from text and pictures. Amsterdam: North-Holland.

Mantyla, K. & Gividen, J. R. (1997). Distance learning: A step-by-step guide for trainers. Washington, DC: CRC Press.

Marcus, A. (1992). Graphic design for electronic documents and user interfaces. New York: Addison-Wesley Pub Co.

Margolis, P.E. (1999). Random House personal computer dictionary (3nd ed.). New York: Random House.

Mark, M. M., & Shotland, R. L. (Eds.). (1987). Multiple methods in program evaluation. San Francisco, CA: Jossey-Bass.

*Marks-Tarlow, T. (1995). Creativity inside out: Learning through multiple intelligences. Reading, MA: Addison-Wesley

Marquardt, M. J. & Kearsley, G. (1998). Technology-based learning: Maximizing human performance and corporate success. Washington, D.C: CRC Press.

Marsh, J. P., Gorayska, B. & Mey, J. L. (Eds.). (1999). Humane interfaces: Questions of method and practice in cognitive technology (human factors in information technology, 13). Oxford, UK: Elsevier Science Ltd.

Martin, B.M, & Briggs, L.J. (1986). The affective and cognitive domains: Integration for instruction and research. Englewood Cliffs, NJ: Educational Technology.

Martin, L. E. (1997). The challenge of internet literacy: The instruction-web convergence.Haworth Press. -

Mason, R. (1998). Globalising education: Trends and applications. London: Routledge.

Mason, R., & Kaye, A. (Eds.). (1989). Mindweave: Communication, computers, and distance Education. New York: Pergamon Press.

Maurer, M. M. & Davidson, G. (1997). Leadership in instructional technology. Prentice Hall College Div.

Maybury, M. T. & Wahlster, W. (1998). Readings in intelligent user interfaces. Academic Press/Morgan Kaufmann. -

Mayhew, D. J. (1991). Principles and Guidelines in Software User Interface Design. Englewood Cliffs, NJ: Prentice Hall.

Mayhew, D. J. (1999). The usability engineering lifecycle: A practitioner's handbook for user interface design. San Francisco: Morgan Kaufmann Publshers.

Means, B., Blando, J. & Olson, K. (1993). Using technology to support education reform.U.S. Department of Education, Office of Education Research and Improvement.

Mehlinger, H. (1995). School reform in the information age. Bloomington: IN: Center for Excellence in Education.

Medsker, K. L., & Roberts, D. G. (Eds.). (1992). ASTD trainer's toolkit: Evaluating the results of training. American Society for Training and Development.

Meister, J. C. (1998). Corporate universities: Lessons in building a world-class work force. Irwin Professional Pub. -

Merriam, S. B. (Ed.). (1993). An update on adult learning theory. San Francisco, CA: Jossey-Bass.

Merrill, M. D. (1994). Instructional design theory. Englewood Cliffs, NJ: Educational Technology Publications.

Merrill, M. D., Tennyson, R. D., & Posey, L. O. (1992). Teaching concepts: An insturctional design guide. Englewoood Cliffs, NJ: Educational Technology Publications.

Milano, M. & Ullius, D. (1998). Designing powerful training: The sequential-iterative model. San Francisco, CA: Jossey-Bass.

Miller, S. (1998). Searching the World Wide Web: An introductory curriculum for using search engines. Eugene, OR: International Society for Technology in Education.

Miller, E.B. (1996). The Internet resource directory for k-12 teachers and librarians 98/99 (Serial). Englewood, CO: Libraries Unlimited.

Minoli, D. (1996). Distance learning technology and applications. Cambridge, MA: Artech House.

Misanchuk, E. R, Schwier, R. A. & Boling, E. (2000). Visual design for instructional multimedia. University of Saskatchewan, Canada: U-Learn Extension Division.

Mitchell, G. (1998). The trainer's handbook: The ama guide to effective training. New York: AMACOM.

Moll, L. C. (Ed.). (1990). Vygotsky in education: Instructional implications of sociohistorical psychology. NY: Cambridge.

Mood, T.A. (1995). Distance education: An annotated bibliography. Englewood, Colorado: Libraries Unlimited, Inc.

Moore, M. & Kearsley, G. (1996). Distance education: A systems view. Belmont, CA: Wadsworth.

Moore, M. (Ed.). (1996). Distance education for corporate and military training. University Park, PA: American Center for the Study of Distance Education.

Moore, M. (Ed.). (1996). Distance education for corporate and military training. University Park, PA: American Center for the Study of Distance Education.

Moore, M. (Ed.). (1995). Video-based telecommunications in distance education. University Park, PA: American Center for the Study of Distance Education.

Moore, D. M. & Dwyer, M. (Eds.). (1994). Visual literacy: A spectrum of visual learning. Englewood Cliffs, NJ: Educational Technology.

Moore, M. G., & Thompson, M. M. (1990). The effects of distance learning: A summary of literature. University Park, PA: American Center for the Study of Distance Education.

Moore, M. G., & Thompson, M. M. (1997). The effects of distance learning (ACSDE research monograph series vol 15). University Park, PA: American Center for the Study of Distance Education.

Moore, M. G., Cookson, P., & Donaldson, J. (Eds.) (1990). Contemporary issues in American distance education. New York: Pergamon Press.

Moore, M. G. & Clark, G. C. (Eds.). (1989). Readings in distance learning and instruction. University Park, PA: ACSDE.

Morgan, C. & O'Reilly, M. (1999). Assessing open and distance learners. UK: Kogan Page Publishers.

Morrison, G. R., Lowther, D. L. & Demeulle, L. (1999). Integrating computer technology into the classroom. Prentice Hall College Div.

Morrison, J. (1991). Training for performance: Principles of applied human learning. NY: Wiley.

Moses, J. (1999). The survey of distance learning programs in higher education 1999. Primary Research Group.

Moursund, D. (1997). The future of information technology in education. Eugene, OR: International Society for Technology in Education.

Mowe, R. (1993). Evaluating technology integration in the elementary school: A step by step guide (Rev. ed.). Eugene, OR: International Society for Technology in Education.

Mulder, M., Nijhof, W. J., & Brinkerhoff, R. O. (Eds.). (1995). Corporate training for effective performance (evaluation in education and human services). Norwell, MA: Kluwer Academic Publications.

Mullet, K. & Sano, D. (1995). Designing visual interfaces: communication oriented techniques. Hillsdale, NJ: Prentice Hall.

Munson, L. S. (1992). How to conduct training seminars: A complete reference guide for training managers and professionals (2nd ed.). New York: McGraw-Hill.

Nardi, B. (Ed.). (1996). Context and consciousness: Activity theory and human-computer interaction. Cambridge, MA: MIT Press.

Nardi, B. A. & O'Day, V. L. (1999). Information ecologies: Using technology with heart. Cambridge, MA: MIT Press.

Negroponte, N. (1996). Being digital. Vintage Books.

Newby, T. J., Russel, J. D., Stepich, D. A. & Lehman, J. D. (1996). Instructional technology for teaching and learning: Designing instruction, integrating computers, and using media. Hillsdale, NJ: Prentice Hall.

Newby, A. C. (1992). Training evaluation handbook. San Diego: Pfeiffer & Company.

Nickerson, R. S. & Zodhiates, P. P. (Eds.). (1988). Technology in education: Looking toward 2020. Hillsdale, NJ: Erlbaum.

Nielsen, J. (1999). Designing websites with authority: Secrets of an information architect. New Riders Publishing.

Nielsen, J. (1996). Multimedia and hypertext: The Internet and beyond. San Diego: Academic Press.

Nielsen, J. (1994). Usability engineering. San Diego: Academic Press.

Nielsen, J. & MacK, R. L. (1994). Usability inspection methods. New York: John Wiley & Sons.

Nielsen, J. (1993). Usability engineering. Boston: Academic Press, Inc.

Nielsen, J. (1990). Hypertext and hypermedia. San Diego: Academic Press, Inc.

Nielsen, J. (Ed.). (1990). Designing user interfaces for international use. Amsterdam: Elsevier.

Nielsen, J. (1985). Advances in Human-Computer Interaction, Vol. 5. Norwood, NJ: Ablex Publishing Corp.

Nilson, C. (1999). Training & development yearbook 1999 (annual). Prentice Hall Trade.

Nix, D. & Spiro, R. (1990). Cognition, education, and multimedia. Hillsdale, NJ: Erlbaum Assoc.

Norman, D. A. (1998). The invisible computer: Why good products can fail, the personal computer is so complex, and information appliances are the solution. Cambridge, MA: MIT Press.

Norman, D. A., & Draper, S. W. (1986). User centered system design: New perspectives on human-computer interaction. Hillsdale, NJ: Lawrence Erlbaum Associates.

O'Donnell, James. (1998). Avatars of the word: From papyrus to cyberspace. Cambridge, MA: Harvard Univ Press.

Oblinger, D. G. (Ed.). (1997). The learning revolution: The challenge of information technology in the academy. Boston, MA: Anker Pub Co.

O'Malley, C. (Ed.). (1995). Computer supported collaborative learning. New York: Springer-Verlag.

O'Reilly Associates. (Ed.). (1997). The Harvard conference on the Internet and society. Cambridge, MA: Harvard Univ Press.

Olsen, D. R., Jr. (1998). Developing user interfaces. Boston: Academic Press/Morgan Kaufmann.

Olsen, G. J. (1997). Getting started in multimedia design. Cincinnati: North Light Books.

Olson, J. R., Ryan, D. F. & Reigeluth, C. M. (1996). Public school restructuring: A selected bibliography. Englewood Cliffs, NJ: Educational Technology Publications.

Overfield, K. (1998). Developing and managing organizational learning. Alexandria, VA: American Society for Training & Development.

Owen, T. & Ownston, R. (1998). The learning highway: Smart students and the net. Toronto: Key Porter Books.

Petit, A. (1994). Secrets to enliven learning: How to develop extraordinary self-directed training materials. San Francisco: Pfeiffer.

Palloff, R. M. & Pratt, K. (1999). Building learning communities in cyberspace: Effective strategies for the online classroom. San Francisco, CA: Jossey-Bass.

Papert, S. (1994). The children's machine: rethinking school in the age of the computer. New York: Basic Books.

Papert, S. (1999). Mindstorms: Children, computers, and powerful ideas. New York: Basic Books.

Papert, S. & Negroponte, N. (1996). The connected family: Bridging the digital generation gap. Longstreet Press. -

Pappo, Harry A. (1998). Simulations for skills training. Educational Technology Publications: Englewood Cliffs.

Paton, R. & Neilson, I. (1999). Visual Representations and Interpretations. New York: Springer Verlag.

Parry, T. & Gregory, G. (1998). Designing brain-compatible learning. Andover, MA: Skylight Publishing.

Perkins, D. (1995). Smart schools: Better thinking and learning for every child. New York, NY: Free Press.

Perkins, D. N. (1986). Knowledge as design. Hillsdale, NJ: Lawrence Erlbaum Associates.

Perlman, G., Green, G. K. & Wogalter, M. S. (Eds.) Human factors perspectives on human-computer interaction: Selections from proceedings of human factors and ergonomics society annual meetings 1983-1994. Santa Monica, CA: Human Factors & Ergonomics Soc.

Perelman, L. J. (1993). School's out. Avon.

Peterson, B. L. (1996). Using design basics to get creative results. Cincinnati: North Light Books.

Peterson, P. L., Wilkinson, L. C. & Hallinan, M. (Eds.). (1983).The social context of instruction. New York: Academic Press.

Peterson, R. (1997). Training needs assessment: Meeting the training needs for quality performance. Stylus Pub Llc.-

Pettersson, R. (1990). Visuals for information. Englewood Cliffs, NJ: Educational Technology Publications.

Phillips, J. (1997). Measuring the return on investment: Volume 2. Alexandria, VA: American Society for Training and Development.

Philips, J. J. (1995). In Action conducting needs assessment (conducting needs assessment series). Alexandria, VA: American Society for Training and Development.

Phillips, J.J. (1991). Handbook of training evaluation and measurement methods (2nd ed.). Houston, TX: Gulf Publishing Co.

Phillips, V. & Yager, C. (1999). The best distance learning graduate schools 1999: Earning your degree without leaving home (serial). Burlington, MA: Princeton Review.

Pike, R. W. (1994). Creative training techniques handbook. Lakewoods Publications.

Piskurich, G. M. (Ed.). (1993). The ASTD handbook of instructional technology. New York: McGraw-Hill.

Place, R., Dimmler, K., & Powell, T. (1996). Educator's Internet yellow pages. Englewood Cliffs, NJ: PTR Prentice Hall.

Plomp, T. & Ely, D. P. (Eds.). (1996). International encyclopedia of educational technology (2nd ed.). New York: Pergamon Press.

Polanyi, M. (1967). The tacit dimension. New York: Doubleday Anchor.

Polson, M. C. & Richardson, J. J. (Eds.). (1988). Foundations of intelligent tutoring systems. Hillsdale, NJ: Lawrence Erlbaum Associates.

Porter, L. R. (1997). Creating the virtual classroom: Distance learning with the Internet. New York: John Wiley & Sons.

Portway, P. & Lane, C. (..)Guide to teleconferencing and distance learning. Cleveland, OH: Advanstar Communications.

Postman, N. (1995). The end of education: Redefining the value of school. New York: Knopf.

Provenzo, E. F., Brett, A. & McCloskey, G. N. (1998). Computers, Curriculum, and Cultural Change: An Introduction for Teachers. Hillsdale, NJ: Lawrence Erlbaum Associates.

Preece, J., Rogers, Y., Sharp, H. & Benyon, D. (1994). Human-computer interaction. Wokingham, UK: Addison Wesley.

Queeney, D. S. (1995). Assessing needs in continuing education: An essential tool for quality improvement. San Francisco, CA: Jossey-Bass.

Quarterman, J. S. (1990). The matrix: Computer networks and conferencing systems worldwide. Bedford, Mass.: Digital Press.

Reed, W. M., Burton, J.K, & Liu, M. (1994). Multimedia and megachange: New roles for educational computing. Haworth Press. -

Reese, J. (1999). Internet books for educators, parents and children. Englewood, CO: Libraries Unlimited.

Reigeluth, C. (1999). Instructional design: Theories and models. (Vol. 2). Hillsdale, NJ: Erlbaum Assoc.

Reigeluth, C. & Garfinkle, R. (Eds.). (1994). Systemic change in education. Englewood Cliffs, NJ: Educational Technology Publications.

Reigeluth, C. (1983). Instructional design: Theories and models. Hillsdale, NJ: Erlbaum Assoc.

Reigeluth, C. & Merrill, D. M. (19..). Extended task analysis procedure: User's manual. - -

Reiser, R.A., & Dick, W. (1996). Instructional planning: A guide for teachers. Boston: Allyn & Bacon.

Reiser, R.A. & Gagne, R.M. (1983). Selecting media for instruction. Englewood Cliffs, NJ: Educational Technology Publications.

Resnick, L. B. (Ed.). (1989). Knowing, learning, and instruction: Essays in honor of Robert Glaser. Hillsdale, NJ: Lawrence Erlbaum Associates.

Resnick (Ed.). (1989). Cognition and instruction: Issues and agendas. Hillsdale, NJ: Lawrence Erlbaum Associates.

Reynolds, A. & Thomas, I. (1996). Multimedia training: Developing technology-based systems. New York: McGraw-Hill.

Rheingold, H. (1993). The virtual community. Reading, MA: Addison Wesley.

Richie, M. L. (1994). Quality management for educational technology services: A guide to application of the deming management method for district, univeristy and regional. Washington, DC: Association for Educational Communications and Technology.

Richey, R. (1992). Designing instruction for the adult learner: Systematic training theory and practice. London JN: Kogan Page.

Richey, R. (1986). The theoretical and conceptual basis of instructional theory. London: Kogan Page.

Rieber, L. (1994). Computers, graphics and learning. Madison, WI: WCB Brown & Benchmark.

Roberts, N., Blakeslee, G, Brown, M., & Lenk, C. (1990). Integrating telecommunications into education. Englewood Cliffs: Prentice Hall.

Robinson, D. G. & Robinson, J. C. (1989). Training for impact: How to link training to business needs and measure the results. San Francisco, CA: Jossey-Bass.

Rogoff, B. (1990). Apprenticeship in thinking: cognitive development in social context. New York: Oxford University Press.

Rogers, E. M. (1983).Rogers, E. M. (1995). Diffusion of innovations. New York: The Free Press.

Romiszowski, A.J. (1993). New technologies in education and training. East Brunswick, NJ: Nichols.

Romiszowski, A.J. (1992). The selection and use of instructional media (2nd ed.). Chicago, IL: Nichols Publishing Co.

Romiszowski, A.J.(1986). Developing auto-instructional materials. Chicago, IL: Nichols Publishing Co.

Romiszowski, A.J. (1984). Producing instructional systems. London, UK: Kogan Page.

Romiszowski, A. J. (1981). Designing instructional systems. London: Kogan Page.

Rosch, W. L. (1995). Multimedia Bible. Indianapolis, IN: Sams Pub.

Rose, C. P. & Nicholl, M. J. (1998). Accelerated learning for the 21st century: The six-step plan to unlock your master-mind. New YorK: Dell Pub Co.

Rosenberg, M. J. (2001). E-Learning: Strategies for delivering knowledge in the digital age. New YorK: McGraw-Hill.

Rosenfeld, L. and Morville, P. (1998). Information architecture for the world wide web. Cambridge: O'Reilly & Associates.

Rossett, A. (1998). First things fast: A handbook for performance analysis. San Francisco: Pfeiffer.

Rossett, A. (1987). Training needs assessment (techniques in training and performance development series). Englewood Cliffs, NJ: Educational Technology Publications.

Rossett, A. (1991). A handbook of job aids. San Francisco: Pfeiffer & Co.

Rossman, M. H., & Rossman, M. E. (Eds.). (1995). Facilitating distance education. San Francisco, CA: Jossey-Bass.

Rothwell, W.J. & Cookson, P.S. (1997). Beyond instruction: Comprehensive program planning for business and education. San Francisco, CA: Jossey-Bass.

Rothwell, W. & Kazanas, H.C. (1994). Improving on-the-job training: How to establish and operate a oomprehensive OJT program. San Francisco, CA: Jossey-Bass.

Rothwell, W. & Kazanas, H.C. (1992). Mastering the instructional design process. San Francisco, CA: Jossey-Bass.

Rouet, J., Levonen, J. J., Dillon, A., and Spiro, R. (Eds.). (1996). Hypertext and cognition. Mawhaw, NJ: LEA.

Rowntree, D. (1990). Teaching through Self-Instruction: How to Develop Open Learning Materials. New York: Nichols Publishing Co.

Rubin, J. (1994). Handbook of usability testing: How to plan, design, and conduct effective tests. New York: John Wiley and Sons, Inc.

Rubinstein, R. & Hersh, H. (1984). The human factor: Designing computer systems for people. Maynard, MA: Digital Press.

Rudisill, M., Lewis, C., Polson, P. G. & McKay, T. (Eds.). (1995). Human-computer interface design: Success stories, emerging methods, and real-world context. Academic Press/Morgan Kaufmann.

Ryder, R.J., & Hughes, T. (1998). Internet for Educators. Upper Saddle River, New Jersey: Prentice Hall.

Saettler, P. (1990). The evolution of american educational technology. Littleton, CO: Libraries Unlimited.

Salisbury, D.F. (1996). Five technologies for educational change: Systems thinking, systems design, quality science, change management, instructional technology. Englewood Cliffs, NJ: Educational Technology Publications.

Salomon, G. (Ed.). (1996). Distributed cognitions: Psychological and educational considerations (learning in doing - social, cognitive, and computational perspectives). Cambridge, UK; New York; Melbourne: Cambridge University Press.

Salomon, G. (1979). Interaction of media, cognition, & learning. San Francisco, CA: Jossey-Bass.

Salvendy, G. (Ed.). Handbook of human factors and ergonomics. New York: John Wiley & Sons.

Sanders, M. S. & McCormick, E. J. (1992). Human factors in engineering and design (7th Ed.). New York, NY: McGraw-Hill Book Company.

Sandholtz, J. H., Ringstaff, C. & Dwyer, D. C. (1997). Teaching with technology: Creating student-centered classrooms. Teachers College Press.

Scannell, E. E. & Newstrom, J. W. (1995). The complete games trainers play: Experiential learning exercises. New York: McGraw-Hill.

Schank, R. C. (1997). Virtual Learning: A Revolutionary Approach to Building a Highly Skilled Workforce. New York: McGraw-Hill.

Scholtes, P. R., Joiner, B. L. & Streibel, B. J. (1996). The team handbook (2nd ed). Madison, WI: Oriel Inc.

Schramm, W. (1977). Big media, little media: Tools and technologies for Instruction Beverly Hills, CA: Sage.

Schreiber, D. A. & Berge, Z. L. (1998). Distance training: How innovative organizations are using technology to maximize learning and meet business objectives. San Francisco, CA: Jossey-Bass.

Schrum, L. & Berenfeld, B. (1997). Teaching and learning in the information age: A guide to educational telecommunications. Boston: Allyn & Bacon.

Schwier, R. & Masanchuk, E.(1987). Interactive multimedia instruction. Englewood Cliffs, NJ: Educational Technology

Seels, B. & Glasgow, Z. (1997). Making instructional design decisions. Englewood Cliffs, NJ: Prentice Hall.

Seels, B. & Richey. (1994). Instructional technology: The definition and domains of the field. Washington, DC: Association for Educational Communications and Technology (AECT),

Senge, P. (1994). The fifth discipline: The art and practice of the learning organization. New York: Doubleday.

Serim, F. & Koch, M. (1996). Netlearning: Why teachers use the Internet (Songline guides). Cambridge: O'Reilly & Associates.

Shackel, B. & Richardson, S. (Eds.). (1991). Human factors for informatics usability. Cambridge, MA: Cambridge.

Shadish, W. R., Cook, T. D., & Leviton, L. C. (1991). Foundations of program evaluation: Theories of practice. Newbury Park, CA: Sage Publications.

Shambaugh, R. N. & Magliaro, S. G. (1997). Mastering the Possibilities: A Process Approach to Instructional Design. Boston: Allyn & Bacon.

Shandler, D. (1996). Reengineering the training function: How to align training with the new corporate agenda. Saint Lucie Press. -

Sharp, V., Levine, M. & Sharp, R. (1998). The best Web sites for teachers (2nd ed.). Eugene, OR: International Society for Technology in Education.

Shneiderman, B. (1978). Designing the user interface: Strategies for effective human-computer interaction. Reading, MA: Addison-Wesley Publishing Company.

Shneiderman, B. & Kearsley, G. (1989). Hypertext hands-on!: An introduction to a new way of organizing and accessing information. Reading, MA: Addison-Wesley Publishing Co.

Shoemake, C. J. (1998). Leadership in continuing and distance education in higher education. Boston: Allyn & Bacon.

Shrock, S. A. & Coscarelli, W. C. (19..). Criterion-referenced test development: Technical and legal guidelines for corporate training. - -

Shuman, J. E. (1997). Multimedia in action. Belmont, CA: Wadsworth.

Siegel, D. (1997). Creating killer Web sites (2nd ed.). Indianapolis, IN: Hayden Books.

Siegel, D. (1997). Secrets of successful Web sites: Project management on the world wide web. Indianapolis, IN: Hayden Books.

Sims, R. R. (1999). Reinventing training and development. Quorum Books. -

Silberman, M. (1996). Active learning: 101 strategies to teach any subject. Boston: Allyn & Bacon.

Silberman, M. (1995). 101 ways to make training active. San Francisco: Pfeiffer & Co.

Skinner, B. F. (1976). About Behaviorism. New York: Random House.

Skinner, B. F. (1970). Science and Human Behavior. New York, NY: Free Press.

Slavin, R. (1995). Co-operative learning: Theory, research and practice. Boston: Allyn & Bacon.

Slavin, R. (Ed.) (1985). Learning to cooperate, cooperating to learn. New York: Plenum Press.

Soriano, F. I. (1995). Conducting needs assessments: A multidisciplinary approach. Sage Publication.

Smith, I. (1998). On the Web or off: Hypermedia design basics. Eugene, OR: International Society for Technology in Education.

Smith, I. (..). Hypermedia review of the literature. - -

Smith, M. (1986). Introduction to performance technology. Washington, DC: Intl Society for Performance Improvement.

Smith, M. C. & Pourchot, T. (Eds.). (1998). Adult learning and development: Perspectives from educational psychology. Mahwah, NJ: Lawrence Erlbaum Associates.

Smith, P. & Kearny, L. (1994). Creating workplaces where people can think. San Francisco, CA: Jossey-Bass.

Smith, W. L. & Lamb, A.C. (1998). Virtual sandcastles. Evansville, IN: Vision To Action.

Smith, P. L., & Ragan, T. J. (1999). Instructional design. New York: John Wiley & Sons.

Smedinghoff, T. J. (Ed.). (1996). Online law: The SPA's legal guide to doing business on the Internet. Reading, MA: Addison-Wesley Developers Press.

Snow, R. E. & Farr, M. J. (Eds.). (1987). Aptitude, learning and instruction: Cognitive and affective process analysis. Hillsdale, NJ: Erlbaum.

Snowman, J. & Biehler, R. F. with Bonk, C. J. Technology Contributor (2000). Psychology Applied to Teaching (9th Ed.). Boston, MA: Houghton Mifflin.

Snyder, T. & Palmer, J. (1986). In Search of the most amazing thing: Children, education, and computers Reading, MA: Addison-Wesley.

Spector, J., Polson, M.C., & Muraida, D.J. (1993). Automating instructional design: Concepts and issues. Englewood Cliffs, NJ: Educational Technology Publications.

Spencer, K. (1991). The psychology of educational technology and instructional media (2nd ed.). Liverpool:United Writers Press.

Spille, H. A., Stewart, D. W. & Sullivan, E. (1997). External Degrees in the Information Age: Legitimate Choices. American Council on Education/Oryx Press Series on Higher Education.

Spiro, R.J., Coulson, R.L., Feltovich, P.J., & Anderson, D.K. (1988). Cognitive flexibility theory: Advanced knowledge acquisition in ill-structured domains. (Tech Report No. 441). Champaign, IL: University of Illinois, Center for the Study of Reading.

Spiro, R.J. & Nix, D. (1990). Cognition, education, and multimedia: Exploring ideas in high technology. Hillsdale, NJ: Lawrence Erlbaum Associates.

Sproull, L. & Kiesler, S. (1991). Connections: New ways of working in the networked organization. Cambridge, MA: MIT Press.

Stammen, R. M. (1996). Using Multimedia for distance learning in adult, career, and vocational education. DIANE Publishing Company. -

Steinaker, N.W. & Bell, M.R. (1979). The experiential taxonomy: A new approach to teaching and learning. New York: Academic Press.

Sternberg, R. (Ed.). (1994). Thinking and problem solving. New York: Academic.

Stevens, G. H. & Stevens, E. F. (1995). Designing electronic performance support tools: Improving workplace performance with hypertext, hypermedia, and multimedia. Englewood Cliffs, NJ: Educational Technology Publications.

Stolovitch, H. & Keeps, E. (Eds.). (1999). Handbook of performance technology: Improving individual and organizational performance worldwide. San Francisco, CA: Jossey-Bass.

Sweller, John (1999). Instructional Design in Technical Areas. Australia: Stylus Publications.

Tapscott, D. (1997). Digital economy, promise and peril in the age of network intelligence. New York: McGraw-Hill.

Tait, A. & Mills, R. (1999). The convergence of distance and conventional education: Patterns of flexibility for the individual learner. London: Routledge.

Tauber, M. J. & Ackermann, D. (Eds.). (1991). Mental models and human-computer interaction 2 (human factors in information technology, vol 7). Amsterdam: Elsevier.

Teare, Richard, Davies, D. & Sandelands, E. (1999) The Virtual University: An Action Paradigm and Process for Workplace Learning. London: Cassell Academic.

Teeters, J. R. (1997). Teach with style! An instructor's guide to better adult teaching. Adults Teaching Adults. -

Tennyson, R. D., Schott, F. & Seel, N. M. (1997). Instructional design: International perspectives: theory, research, and models. Hillsdale, NJ: Lawrence Erlbaum Associates.

Thiagarajan, S. & Parker, G. M. (1999). Teamwork and teamplay: Games and activities for building and training teams. San Francisco, CA: Jossey-Bass.

Thiagarajan, S. (1995). Diversity simulation games (games by Thiagi series). Amherst, MA: Human Resource Development Press.

Thiagarajan, S. (1997). Framegames by Thiagi (8th ed.). Bloomington, IN: Workshops by Thiagi.

Thiagarajan, S. (1997). More Framegames: Interactive Learning Designs (7th ed.). Bloomington, IN: Workshops by Thiagi.

Thiagarajan, S. (1997). Simulation Games by Thiagi (6th ed.). Bloomington, IN: Workshops by Thiagi.

Thiagarajan, S. (1997). Interactive Experiential Training: 10 Breakthrough Strategies. Bloomington, IN: Workshops by Thiagi.

Thiagarajan, S. (1989). Barnga: A simulation game on cultural clashes. Yarmouth, ME: Intercultural Press.

Thompson, M. M. (1996). Internationalism in distance education: A vision for higher education. University Park, PA: American Center for the Study of Distance Education.

Thompson, A. D., Simonson, M. R. & Hargrave, C. P. (1992). Educational technology: A review of the research. Washington, DC: Association for Educational Communications and Technology.

Thornburg, D. D. (1998). Brainstorms and lightning bolts: Thinking skills for the 21st century. San Carlos, CA: David D. Thornburg and Starsong Publications.

Thornburg, D. D. (1996). Putting the web to work. San Carlos, CA: Starsong Publications.

Thornburg, D. D. (1994). Education in the communication age. San Carlos, CA: Starsong Publications.

Thornburg, D. D. (1992). Edutrends 2010: Restructuring, technology, and the future of education. San Carlos, CA: Starsong Publications.

Tiffin, J. & Rajasingham, L. (1995). In search of the virtual class: Education in an information society. London: Routledge.

Tobin, D. R. (1996). Transformational learning: Renewing your company through knowledge and skills. New York: John Wiley & Sons.

Toffler, A. (1991). The third wave. Bantam Books. -

Tognazzini, B. (1992). Tog on interface. Reading, MA: Addison-Wesley.

Torres, C. & Fairbanks, D. M. (1996). Teambuilding: The ASTD trainer's sourcebook. New York: McGraw-Hill.

Towne, D.M. (1995). Learning and instruction in simulation environments. Englewood Cliffs, NJ: Educational Technology Publications.

Tracey, W. (1984). Designing training and development systems. New York: AMACOM.

Truelove, S. (1997). Training in practice. Blackwell Pub. -

Tufte, E. R. (1997). Visual explanations: Images and quantities, evidence and narrative. Norcross, GA: Graphics Press.

Tufte, E. R. (1992). The visual display of quantitative information. Graphics Press. -

Tyner, K. (1998). Literacy in a digital world: Teaching and learning in the age of information. Hillsdale, NJ: Lawrence Erlbaum Associates.

Valauskas, E.J., & Ertel, M. (1996). The Internet for teachers and school library media specialists: Today's applications, tomorrow's prospects. New York: Neal-Schuman.

Van Merrienboer, Jeroen J. G. (1997). Training complex cognitive skills: A four component instructional design model. Englewood Cliffs, NJ: Educational Technology Publications.

Vaughn, T. (1993). Multimedia: Making it work. New York: McGraw-Hill.

Vega, D. (1998). Learning the Internet for kids: A voyage to Internet treasures. DDC Publishing, Inc. -

Verduin, J. R. & Clark, T. A. (1991). Distance education: The foundations of effective practice. San Francisco, CA: Jossey-Bass.

Vygotsky, L. (1978). Mind in society. The development of higher psychological processes. Cambridge, MA: Harvard University Press.

Wagner, E. D. & Koble, M. A. (Eds.). (1997). Distance education symposium 3: Course design. University Park, PA: American Center for the Study of Distance Education.

Waggoner, M.D. (Ed.). (1992). Empowering networks: Computer conferencing in education. Englewood Cliffs, NJ: Educational Technology Publications.

Ward, A. (Ed.). (1998). Technology & school design: Creating spaces for learning. Alexandria, VA: National School Boards Association.

Ward, A. (Ed.). (1993). Multimedia and learning: A school leaders guide. Alexandria, VA: National School Boards Association.

Warda, M. (1997). How to register a U. S. copyright. Clearwater, FL: Sphinx Publishing.

Welling, K. (1998). Internet exploration: Activities and concepts. Computer Literacy Press Inc.

Waterworth, J. A. (Ed.). (1991). Multimedia: Technology & applications. Englewood Cliffs, NJ: Prentice Hall.

Waterworth, J. A. (1992). Multimedia interaction with computers: Human factors issues. New York: Ellis Harwood.

Wenger, Etienne (1987). Artificial intelligence and tutoring systems: Computational and cognitive approaches to the communication of knowledge. Los Altos, CA: Morgan Kaufmann.

Wertsch, J. (Ed.). (1985). Culture, communication, and cognition: Vygotskian perspectives. Cambridge, UK; New York; Melbourne: Cambridge University Press.

West, C.K., Farmer, J.A., & Wolff, P.M. (1991). Instructional design: Implications from cognitive science. Boston: Allyn & Bacon.

Western Cooperative for Educational Telecommunications. (1998). The distance learner's guide. Upper Saddler River, NJ: Prentice Hall.

White, M. A. (Ed.). (1987). What curriculum for the information age? Hillsdale NJ: Erlbaum.

White, K. W. & Weight, B. H. (Eds.). (2000). The Online Teaching Guide. Needham Height, MA: Allyn & Bacon.

Wiklund, M. E. (Ed.). (1994). Usability in practice: How companies develop user-friendly products. Boston: Academic Press.

Wilcox, J. (1993). ASTD trainers toolkit: More needs assessment instruments. San Francisco, CA: Jossey-Bass.

Willis, B. (1994). Distance Education: A Practical Guide. Englewood Cliffs, NJ: Educational Technology Publications.

Willis, B. (Ed.). (1994). Distance education: Strategies and tools. Englewood Cliffs, NJ: Educational Technology Publications.

Williams, B. (1995). The Internet for teachers. Indianapolis: IDG Books.

Williams, R. & Quandt, C. (Eds.). (1994). The non-designer's design book: Design and typographic principles for the visual novice. Berkeley, CA: Peachpit Press.

Williamson, M. (1993). Training needs analysis: Library training guide. Lanham, MD: Unipub.

Wilson, R. A. & Keil, F. C. (Eds.). (1999). The MIT encyclopedia of the cognitive sciences. Cambridge, MA: MIT Press.

Wilson, B.G. (1996). Constructivist learning environments: Case studies in instructional design. Englewood Cliffs, NJ: Educational Technology Publications.

Winograd, T. & Flores, F. (1986). Understanding computers and cognition: A new foundation for design. Norwood, NJ: Ablex.

Wittrock, M.C. & Baker, E.L. (Eds.). (1991). Testing and cognition. Englewood Cliffs, NJ: Prentice Hall.

Wlodkowski, R. (1993) Enhancing adult motivation to learn. San Francisco, CA: Jossey-Bass.

Worthern, B.R. & Sanders, J.R. (1996). Educational evaluation: Alternative approaches and practical guidelines. NY: Longman.

Young M. J. & Reigeluth, C. M. (19..). Improving the textbook selection process (fastback 275 ser.). –

INDEX

[illegible]

[illegible] large number of [illegible] the use of [illegible] [illegible] [illegible]

According to the [illegible] Planning Commission, the [illegible] in the country will grow from [illegible] during the 10th Five-Year Plan [illegible] private agencies [illegible] numbers as well.

A recent study by the [illegible] the country has [illegible] for 2001 [illegible] Manufacturers' Association of Information Technology (MAIT) has revealed that [illegible] in the decade [illegible] compounded annual growth rate (CAGR) [illegible] per cent. The number of active Internet [illegible] by March 2001 [illegible] owning business establishments [illegible] PC owning homes.

IDC India [illegible] grow [illegible] CAGR of [illegible] [illegible] in the Asia Pacific [illegible]